WOUNDED VISIONS

Wounded Visions

*Unity, Justice, and Peace
in the World Church after 1968*

Jonas Jonson

Translated by
Norman A. Hjelm

WILLIAM B. EERDMANS PUBLISHING COMPANY
GRAND RAPIDS, MICHIGAN / CAMBRIDGE, U.K.

Originally published in Sweden under the title *Ekumenik på världens villkor: Kyrkornas världsråd i den ekumeniska rörelsen efter Uppsala 68.*
© 2008 Jonas Jonson. Published by permission of
Verbum publishing, Stockholm, Sweden.

English translation © 2013 Wm. B. Eerdmans Publishing Co.
All rights reserved

Published 2013 by
Wm. B. Eerdmans Publishing Co.
2140 Oak Industrial Drive N.E., Grand Rapids, Michigan 49505 /
P.O. Box 163, Cambridge CB3 9PU U.K.
www.eerdmans.com

I

Library of Congress Cataloging-in-Publication Data

Jonson, Jonas, 1939-
[Ekumenik på världens villkor. English]
Wounded visions: unity, justice, and peace in the World Church after
1968 /Jonas Jonson; translated by Norman A. Hjelm.
pages   cm
Previously published as: Ekumenik på världens villkor: Kyrkornas världsråd
i den ekumeniska rörelsen efter Uppsala 68. Stockholm: Verbum, 2008.
Includes bibliographical references and index.
ISBN 978-0-8028-6778-0 (pbk.: alk. paper)

1. World Council of Churches — History.   2. Christian union — History.
3. Ecumenical movement — History.   4. Christianity — 20th century.
I. Hjelm, Norman A., 1931 — translator.   II. Title.

BX6.W78J6613   2013
270.8′25 — dc23

2012037211

The translation of this book has been made possible in part by the
Nathan Söderblom Memorial Fund of Sweden.

Contents

Abbreviations — vi

Introduction — viii

1. The Road to Uppsala — 1
2. All Things New — 19
3. God Loves the Poor — 36
4. The Decolonization of Mission — 53
5. Unity in Diversity — 67
6. The Ecumenical Landscape — 84
7. The Fourth Church — 104
8. After the Wall — 120
9. The Retreat of Three Traditions — 135
10. A New Road Map — 153

Notes — 171

Selected Reading List — 185

Index of Names — 190

Abbreviations

Dictionary of the Ecumenical Movement
Nicholas Lossky, José Míguez Bonino, John Pobee, Tom F. Stransky, Geoffrey Wainwright, and Pauline Webb, eds. *Dictionary of the Ecumenical Movement*. 2nd ed. Geneva: WCC Publications, 2002.

History of the Ecumenical Movement, 1
Ruth Rouse and Stephen Charles Neill, eds. *A History of the Ecumenical Movement, 1517-1948*. Philadelphia: Westminster Press and London: SPCK, 1954.

History of the Ecumenical Movement, 2
Harold E. Fey, ed. *A History of the Ecumenical Movement*. Vol. 2, *1948-1968*. Philadelphia: Westminster Press and London: SPCK, 1970.

History of the Ecumenical Movement, 3
John Briggs, Mercy Amba Oduyoye, and Georges Tsetsis, eds. *A History of the Ecumenical Movement*. Vol. 3, *1968-2000*. Geneva: WCC Publications, 2004.

WCC, Uppsala, 1968
Norman Goodall, ed. *The Uppsala Report 1968: Official Report of the Fourth Assembly of the World Council of Churches, Uppsala July 4-20, 1968*. Geneva: WCC Publications, 1968.

Abbreviations

WCC, Nairobi, 1975
David M. Paton, ed. *Breaking Barriers, Nairobi 1975: The Official Report of the Fifth Assembly of the World Council of Churches, Nairobi, 23 November–10 December, 1975.* London: SPCK, 1976.

WCC, Vancouver, 1983
David Gill, ed. *Gathered for Life: Official Report, VI Assembly World Council of Churches, Vancouver, Canada, 24 July–10 August, 1983.* Geneva: WCC Publications and Grand Rapids: Eerdmans, 1983.

WCC, Canberra, 1991
Michael Kinnamon, ed. *Signs of the Spirit: Official Report, Seventh Assembly, Canberra, Australia, 7-20 February 1991.* Geneva: WCC Publications and Grand Rapids: Eerdmans, 1991.

WCC, Harare, 1998
Diane Kessler, ed. *Together on the Way: Official Report of the Eighth Assembly of the World Council of Churches.* Geneva: WCC Publications, 1999.

WCC, Porto Alegre, 2006
Luis N. Rivera-Pagán, ed. *God, in Your Grace: Official Report of the Ninth Assembly of the World Council of Churches.* Geneva: WCC Publications, 2007.

Introduction

The Cold War had divided the world into two camps. The Berlin Wall cut straight through Germany. Just as the Second Vatican Council (1962-1965) began, the Cuban Missile Crisis occurred. The whole world held its breath. Just as a catastrophic atomic war seemed about to break out, Pope John XXIII intervened at the last minute. That crisis averted, the Council brought about a thoroughgoing renewal of the Roman Catholic Church. The Church adjusted itself to the modern world and developed new bases for participating in the ecumenical movement, for conversing and cooperating with other churches. A nearly thousand-year-old conflict with the Orthodox Churches came to an end.

A few years later, in 1968, the World Council of Churches gathered for its Fourth General Assembly in Uppsala, Sweden, where Nathan Söderblom, one of the pioneers of the ecumenical movement, had been archbishop. In the United States the civil rights movement was in full force. Martin Luther King Jr., who was to have preached at the opening worship of the Assembly, had been murdered only months earlier. The Vietnam War had escalated, and protests against it were taking place throughout the world. Students were in revolt at American and European universities. In China, Mao Zedong had unleashed the Cultural Revolution, and young people attacked everything related to capitalism, imperialism, and religion. In Latin America, heavy-handed dictators ruled, and in Africa liberation movements struggled for national independence. The apartheid regime still controlled South Africa.

Events in the surrounding world exerted great influence on the ecumenical movement. At Uppsala it was said that the daily agenda was determined by youth, women, and church leaders from Africa, Asia, and Latin America. Just as the Council influenced the Catholic Church, so the Assembly set the tone for the large Protestant churches. Ecumenism felt the wind in its sails, and the World Council of Churches and other ecumenical organizations were strengthened. Relations with the Roman Catholic Church developed at all levels. Emphasis was laid on social justice and peace.

The 1970s and '80s became the ecumenical movement's most dynamic decades. The major churches — Orthodox, Catholic, and Protestant — drew closer to each other, sharing theology, liturgy, and experience. Simultaneously, however, conservative evangelical and charismatic movements, which distanced themselves from the ecumenical movement, became extremely influential in the United States at the cost of the mainline churches, and new tensions appeared in Christendom. Christianity's numerical center of gravity shifted to countries in the Global South. Independent congregations and megachurches after them arose in all parts of the world, and church divisions followed. The most exciting theology was no longer formulated at the famous universities of Europe and the United States but rather in countries like Peru, South Africa, and South Korea. The national confessional churches of Europe were not strong enough to resist secularism, and they lost much of their influence. The whole ecumenical map was redrawn: the Reformation churches ringing the North Atlantic, churches that founded the ecumenical movement, gave way to others as the world was globalized.

It is not a simple task to give an overview of ecumenical developments over the last fifty years. The presuppositions of ecumenism have been altered in basic ways, and visions of its future are contradictory. I have, nevertheless, in this book ventured to summarize the contours of the main developments. The book was originally written in 2008 for a Swedish audience but has now been updated and adjusted for an international circle of readers.

I myself have an academic background as a scholar of mission with an emphasis on China. I have participated in all assemblies of the World Council of Churches since 1968, been a member of the Council's Central Committee, and have been given a long list of assignments in that organization, most recently as co-moderator of the Joint Working Group with the Roman Catholic Church. Before I became a diocesan bishop in the Church of Sweden in 1989, I held the position of Assis-

INTRODUCTION

tant General Secretary for Ecumenical Affairs in the Lutheran World Federation in Geneva. My analysis of ecumenical developments is colored by personal experience — there are many other ways in which to understand the ecumenical movement's complex history, emphasis, and present situation.

Baptism makes it possible for us to be called Christian. Nearly all churches now acknowledge each other's baptism where water is used in the name of the Father, Son, and Holy Spirit. The church grows and is changed, ages, and is renewed. Communities are given birth, and new movements shape Christianity. To make visible the unity in Christ shared by all the baptized and to liberate the church to humble witness and sacrificial service is the task of ecumenism.

When I prepared this book there were many friends from my lifelong ecumenical journey who shared memories, experiences, knowledge, and hopes with me. I will name some of the many who continue to hold the ecumenical vision alive and devote themselves to working for the visible unity of the church: Anna Marie Aagard, Wesley Ariarajah, Huibert van Beek, Tom Best, Gene Brand, Avery Dulles†, Leonardo Emberti, Aruna Gnanadason, Wolfgang Huber, Walter Kasper, Tony Kireopoulos, Leonid Kishkovsky, Yorgo Lemopoulos, Ishmael Noko, James Puglisi, Konrad Raiser, William Rusch, and Mary Tanner. My special thanks go to Norman Hjelm, my former colleague at the Lutheran World Federation, who not only shared his rich insight with me but took it upon himself to translate this book into English.

We all live with past dreams of unity, justice, and peace, with the memory of our visions for a future world. We also live with the memory of Jesus Christ, whose life, death, and resurrection we celebrate in the hope that he will make all things new. On our pilgrimage toward the visible unity of the church the landscape is changing, but the call remains.

JONAS JONSON
Strängnäs, Sweden
October 2012

CHAPTER 1

The Road to Uppsala

... the road to holiness necessarily passes through the world of action.

DAG HAMMARSKJÖLD

Nothing begins when one thinks it does. The World Council of Churches (WCC) began its fourth assembly in Uppsala, Sweden, on 4 July 1968. Many delegates could, even then, remember the atmosphere that had been pervasive in Amsterdam twenty years earlier when the Council was established. The war was just over and it was finally possible to establish the long-planned-for organization for the churches' co-operation and unity. Some delegates were even old enough to have been at Nathan Söderblom's pioneering and visionary conference on "Life and Work," held in Stockholm in 1925. Yet following that conference hope had been diminished and world catastrophes had made some persons uncertain about the progressive but starry-eyed ideology that marked the 1960s. Reality was something quite different than the revolutionary youth of the north and the hopeful nations of the south wanted to believe.

The theme for the assembly was taken from the Revelation of John: "Behold, I make all things new" (21:5). The glorified Christ encountered humanity in a world that wanted to leave the old order behind. The theme admonished church leaders who struggled in their cumbersome institutions to defy both secular and ideological pressures. It resonated in lands that had recently been freed from colonialism. It inspired students who wanted to be there when God scattered the proud, brought down the powerful from their thrones, lifted up the lowly, fed the hungry, and sent the rich away empty (Luke 1:51-52). Nothing was impossible; the people of God were on their way toward the future of God.

More than twenty years had passed since the first assembly. The second was held in Evanston in 1954, the third in New Delhi in 1961. Now 2700 church leaders, theologians, men, women, and youth had come to Uppsala for the fourth assembly. Sweden, the host country, had been marked for many years by high prosperity; it was a rational and modern welfare state without equal. Its union of democratic socialism with a market economy had created the "responsible society" that had been advocated at Amsterdam. The country was a social laboratory and a model for others. The United Nations was popular among the people and there was broad engagement in support of aid to other countries. Sweden was seen as a sensible, forward-looking nation without entangling alliances. It was also questioned, however, for its uniformity of opinions, the monopolization of its public sector, and the free sexual habits of its youth. The WCC could hardly have chosen a more appropriate place for its deliberations.

For a few summer weeks Uppsala was the center of world Christianity. Archbishop Söderblom's dreams were being fulfilled. In his final sermon at the 1925 conference he had spoken with mixed emotions of the encounter of Christian traditions:

> Two men are here gathered together. John, the Apostle of tender love and contemplation, and Paul, the greatest disciple of the Savior . . . [whose] faith worked by love. The third man, Peter, the spokesman of the disciples, still tarries. Christendom stands out as divided, but Christ is one.[1]

The Church of Rome had not been present in Stockholm, but now, in Uppsala, Peter had finally arrived. The Roman Catholic Church, which made up half of Christianity, had taken steps toward the ecumenical movement and there was even a lively discussion as to whether it would take on membership in the World Council of Churches. Expectations were great. It felt as though the ecumenical movement had reached maturity.

The Road to Uppsala

A World in Transformation

The 1960s were an eventful and fateful decade. The balance of power between the United States and the Soviet Union was maintained by the threat of nuclear warfare. Five hundred years of European dominance moved toward its end as, simultaneously, colonialism expired. New nation-states had been born and were in the process of organizing their political life, becoming part of the international community and developing agriculture, economic order, education, legal systems, and health care. All hoped for a better future, but freedom, development, and social welfare were being threatened by the misuse of power, violence, corruption, and massive international debts. The wealthy countries held on to their dominance by means of loans, development with strings attached, and military alliances. When neither capitalism nor socialism, military coups nor revolutions fulfilled expectations, discouragement was widespread and social and moral institutions showed signs of crumbling. Faith communities took on great significance. The churches were an essential and integrating force in many societies.

The developing countries began to be called the "Third World," but they were pawns in the chess games of the great powers. If the nations of the West comprised the "First World," it was the socialist countries of Eastern Europe and the Soviet bloc that formed the "Second World." Second World nations were marked by planned economies and strictly regulated trade, by the abolition of class, and by solidarity. Socialism attracted many lands that had escaped the grip of colonialism but now found themselves hopelessly disadvantaged. The Western nations, on the other hand, offered market economies and deregulation, believing it was trade, fixed exchange rates, and long-term loans that would help the young nations to industrialize, become democratic, and take their places in the global community.

The United Nations and its affiliated organs were a guarantee for the international system of justice. The Universal Declaration of Human Rights provided a new language to a new world and was a new basis for a global ethic. One steadily heard metaphors such as "the global village," "the family of humanity," and "spaceship Earth." The Russian satellite *Sputnik* lifted off in 1957 and American astronauts landed on the moon in 1969. The picture of Earth as a shimmering blue pearl was a symbol both for humanity's greatness and earth's vulnerability. The Cold War, militant nationalism, and extensive violations of human rights did not inhibit a feeling of togetherness and mutual dependence. Cultures came closer to one another. Humanity received a face. With good will and common effort, it was believed that poverty would be overcome. The population explosion, starvation, and conflicts would not hinder progress. Faith in science and technology was unbridled and questions about the environment were still rare. The force called "development" reigned in both East and West, but understandings of the "new" society were not uniform. With China, Cuba, Tanzania, and North Vietnam as inspirational models, even many Christians believed that some sort of socialist order was best for society.

Independence in India and Indonesia marked the beginning of the dismantling of colonialism. The Chinese Revolution of 1949 brought down the most widespread missionary enterprise of modern history and many thousands of foreign missionaries were forced to leave the country. Even so, many Chinese Christians welcomed the revolution, at least at its beginning, and adapted themselves to the new order. Missions were confronted with a difficult test: if God was leading history toward his goal, how could one understand this social and political upheaval which forced a quarter of all humanity to turn their backs on every form of religion? Would the end of colonialism be the end of all Christian mission?

The liberated nations of Africa, in contrast to China and to a certain degree India, did not turn against the Christian mission. It, after all, had given Africans education and the greater portion of their health care. The churches became independent, but could not take complete economic responsibility for the schools, hospitals, and other institutions established by missionaries. If they subordinated themselves to the African church leaders they were welcome to continue their work. With the exception of Ethiopia, the churches of Africa had no long history to fall back on. Church divisions, which were worse in Africa than anywhere else, were caused by doctrinal conflicts that originated on other continents. As Christianity had come to Africa in such a variety of forms, it was scarcely seen as an ecumenical problem when local evangelists and prophets began to gather great movements around themselves and form thousands of new independent churches. Yet the proliferation of such movements lessened the church's possibilities for contributing to national unity.

The Road to Uppsala

The Ecumenical Movement Takes Shape

During these years the World Council of Churches had gained more and more members. Between 1954 and 1968, seventy-four new church bodies had joined, most of them from the Third World. These new members admonished the old churches to leave their obsolete perspective on mission behind and look at reality through the eyes of the young, forward-looking churches. The Bible was their book and it held the gospel. The gospel, in turn, contained the promise of God's future, in heaven but also on earth, and it also contained the stories about Jesus who gathered marginalized and underprivileged people around him and gave them freedom and dignity. If the social and economic situation of the poor is viewed in the light of these stories, the young churches pointed out, then the churches are challenged radically to change their course. This process began in earnest at Uppsala. The same year, in Medellín in Colombia, the Latin American Conference of Catholic Bishops coined an expression that immediately became an ecumenical watchword — "God's preferential option for the poor."

The modern ecumenical movement had come into existence in the early part of the twentieth century, when an international order prevailed that was based on bourgeois, Western, and Christian values. The world was, politically and economically, more united than at any previous time. Europe and its former colonies in North America controlled 84 percent of the earth's landmass, nearly 50 percent of its population, and about 70 percent of its economy. It was nearly possible to describe humanity in terms of a global Christian civilization. The blooming world missionary movement was a sibling to colonialism. The Kingdom of God would be realized. Hundreds of mission societies were busy going about the world's evangelization. Churches were founded at a rapid pace and Christendom reached virtually to the ends of the earth. Yet divisions compromised its credibility; a deeper unity was necessary if the vision of one Christian world was to be realized. Accordingly, a World Missionary Conference was held in Edinburgh in 1910,[2] an event now regarded as the birth of the modern ecumenical movement. For participation it was sufficient to "accept Jesus Christ as God and Savior."

The First World War shattered dreams both of a united world and of faith in Europe as the prime model for human civilization. Orthodox, Catholic, and Protestant countries devastated one another and opened the gates for secularization. The Russia of the czars, the Germany of the kaisers, and the Ottoman Empire of the sultans all collapsed. The identification between churches, states, and the people was broken. Anti-Christian ideologies occupied the space of "Christian" cultures. And just as the old world lay on its deathbed, the ecumenical movement came into being. It bore with it the promise of a renewal of the churches.

The Second World War led to the establishment of a new world order. Ideologies which put humans in the place of God tested the substance of Christian faith. After the Holocaust there was no place for Christian presumption, but thanks to those who had held fast to their confession and died for their faith the church preserved at least a part of its trustworthiness. The ecumenical movement gathered those who inherited the Confessing Church, liberation theologians, church leaders, and those who opposed apartheid — in other words, those who, armed with the gospel, would work to make the world whole again.

The WCC became the most important but far from the only ecumenical instrument for this task. Its constitution's first article was no ordinary confession of faith but was rather a short summary of the faith and commitment which brought the churches together. This article took its present form in 1961 and stands as a crucial key for those who wish to understand what the Council is:

> The World Council of Churches is a fellowship of churches which confess the Lord Jesus Christ as God and Savior according to the scriptures and therefore seek to fulfill together their common calling to the glory of the one God, Father, Son, and Holy Spirit.[3]

Three movements had united to form the Council. They had different directions and views of the unity of the church. They complemented each other and gave ecumenism its breadth, but there remained a tension between them which would persist in the WCC. Indeed, this tension was so great that it could have pulled down the ecumenical house.

The first of these, the Life and Work Movement, had come into existence in the 1920s as an answer to the severe social problems that followed World War I. Archbishop Nathan Söderblom of the Church of Sweden provided the charismatic inspiration that gathered Orthodox and Protestants to work for peace and justice. He believed that "dogma divides, but service unites." Practical cooperation was, accordingly, the best way to unity. The Faith and Order Movement, on the other hand, chose a different way: to attempt first to reach agreement in faith, doctrine, and church order. The Anglican missionary bishop from America Charles H. Brent was at the forefront of this movement. The third organization, the International Missionary Council, which was established after the conference at Edinburgh in 1910 with the legendary American Methodist layman John R. Mott as its leader, was integrated into the World Council of Churches in 1961. The leaders of these three movements were all socially radical academics shaped by nineteenth-century revivals. They were to give Christianity a new role in a new world.

For these leaders world history was a linear movement from creation to fulfillment. In this movement were to be found the development, justice, reconciliation, and peace which every Christian longed for from the God revealed in Christ. For them, history had a direction and sought a goal. Culture and religion were on the way home. All would be fulfilled in Jesus Christ, who is "the image of the invisible God, the firstborn of all creation; for in him all things in heaven and on earth were created, things visible and invisible, whether thrones or dominions or rulers or powers" (Colossians 1:15-16). All history was "salvation history" and in spite of all setbacks the world was on its way toward God.

Unity: God's Gift and Humanity's Responsibility

The church was God's partner on the way toward the fulfillment of time. God wanted to restore the fallen creation, liberate alien humanity and make its relation to God whole again. The Constantinian unity of Christendom and society was over and the churches needed a new description of their task. *Missio Dei,* "mission of God," was the theological proposal that gave direction to the churches and renewed their consciousness that they did not exist for themselves but for the sake of the world. The people of God are to take part in the mission of God and be a sign and a model for humanity.

Yet it seemed that humanity had turned its back on God and built its own Tower of Babel. It had plundered the creation and lived at the expense of others. Thus both judgment and salvation were seen as essential elements in God's acting; sin must die for humanity to live. Division stood against wholeness, indifference against love, oppression against freedom. Poverty deprived humanity of its possibilities and bondage its dignity. An atomic war could destroy the earth and environmental pollution could make it uninhabitable. The ecumenical movement found itself in a struggle against all that threatened life.

Jesus prayed for those who followed him "that they may all be one. As you, Father, are in me and I am in you, may they also be in us, so that the world may believe that you have sent me" (John 17:21-22). This prayer became the word of institution for ecumenism, although the whole New Testament provided its guiding principle and motivation. Theological agreement that the church is one and that the divided churches are united with each other in Christ was the basis for the ecumenical movement. Its task was not to create unity but rather to set unity free by clearing away the causes of division. All that is written in the New Testament about the church presupposes its fundamental unity. Further, the church is described in the Nicene Creed as "one, holy, catholic, and apostolic." The goal of ecumenism is that the church should become what it already — in Christ — is. It is an ecumenical indicative that the church is one, an imperative to make this unity visible. In his typical way, W. A. Visser 't Hooft of the Netherlands, the first General Secretary of the WCC, wrote:

> We do not come together as people who have to begin by finding a common foundation for their relationships. That foundation has been laid; the starting point is given. We seek koinonia [communion], because there is koinonia in our common submission to Christ, not to an inactive Christ but to the living Christ who gathers his scattered children together.[4]

Unity is God's gift and humankind's responsibility, a treasure that the church already possesses yet must find. The Father, Son, and Spirit's interdependence, freedom, and fellowship in the Holy Trinity is to be reflected in the life of believers. The Apostle Paul wrote of one body, one spirit, one hope, one Lord, one baptism, and one faith (Ephesians 4:4-6). The Book of Revelation describes a picture of all people on earth gathered before God's throne (Revelation 7:9-17). It is the glorified Christ, *Pantocrator*, who meets his church with the words, "Behold, I make all things new."

Visser 't Hooft spoke of "christocentric universalism" when he described the theological starting point for ecumenism.[5] Christ and the humanity for which he gave his life were inextricably bound together. The gospel of Christ as God's self-revelation had universal scope. It possessed universal truth and was intended for all. The church was God's chosen instrument for saving the world. Visser 't Hooft grounded his theology in the work of Karl Barth, who was the most influential systematic theologian in the post–World War II world; he was also the author of the Barmen Declaration of 1934, the Confessing Church of Germany's stand against Nazism. The two men corresponded extensively. Barth was somewhat skeptical concerning the ecumenical project but his persistent assertion that the church, bound by God's word, could not negotiate its faith or for tactical reasons renounce its freedom was taken over by the ecumenical movement. This gave it its prophetic character as a critic of society and protected its ideological integrity. All statements about the unity of the church were given a christological basis. Visser 't Hooft consistently claimed both that the ecumenical movement was christocentric or nothing at all, and that unity, evangelization, and social responsibility were three sides of one and the same thing. The future of ecumenism rested on its faithfulness to the Christian confession. Therefore, syncretism was a greater threat than atheism.

Focus on the Identity of the Church

The developing ecumenical movement had close contact with academic theology. After the war, university theologians discarded the dominant liberal theology and oriented themselves toward ecclesially based exegetical and dogmatic studies. A christocentric theology was thus accompanied by a focus on the church's identity. The unity between Christ and the church became the presupposition for the visible unity of the church. Unity was thus a christological postulate; it was not possible to separate ecclesiology from christology. If one started with the incarnation one was led to a sacramental and diaconal view of the church that accentuated the presence of Christ among humans. Or if one started with the glorified Christ the church became primarily a means to realize his universal dominion in anticipation of the kingdom of God. In both cases the church and its basic structure were given by God. This christocentric ecclesiology together with the perspective of salvation history made it possible for Orthodox and Catholic churches to be a part of the ecumenical movement. They could participate in the movement on the basis of their own presuppositions and with their own theological language, thus mediating an objective, sacramental view of the church to the churches of the Reformation. This was of considerable importance since many Protestant communions, regarding themselves basically as unions of invisibly united faithful persons, had difficulty believing that the church was more than the sum of its members who had made human decisions regarding its structure and its ministry.

Initial Roman Catholic Distance from the Ecumenical Movement

After the Enlightenment, the Roman Catholic Church resisted modern academic scholarship, created its own culture, rejected contacts with other churches, and developed a high degree of self-sufficiency. In 1907 Pope Pius X judged "modernism" in extremely aggressive tones. This attitude came to mark the church's life and theology for the first half of the twentieth century. The Roman Catholic Church kept its distance from both liberal democracy and all forms of socialism, was suspicious with respect to human rights, and became a fortress against the present time and environment. In effect, half of Christianity lived in practice as a sect, governed by iron hands, inspired by the past, while claiming to possess all truth.

In his encyclical of 1928, *Mortalium Animos,* Pius XI forbade all Catholics from having anything to do with the burgeoning ecumenical movement, which he charged with theological relativism. Those who had such contacts were forewarned, forbidden to publish, and barred from serving as theological teachers. In the 1950s, before the winds of Vatican II began to blow, some Roman Catholic scholars — notably Karl Rahner, Yves Congar, and Henri de Lubac — were marked as such dissidents.

In 1950 Pope Pius XII, who also rejected every ecumenical invitation, proclaimed *ex cathedra* the dogma of Mary's bodily assumption to heaven. This was received with some reservation even within his own church and surely in the Protestant world. Leaders of the Orthodox churches which had no theological problems with the dogma as such but who for centuries had felt humiliated by the papal claim of supremacy also kept their distance.

The WCC, which desired to gather all Christians under one roof, adopted a wait-and-see policy. Perhaps new possibilities would open up even when things appeared hopeless. There were, after all, some signs of promise: ongoing contacts since 1916 with Roman Catholics in observing the Week of Prayer for Christian Unity, along with a degree of conversation between biblical, patristic, and liturgical scholars. Moreover, high church Lutheran clergy had contacts not only with Anglicans and Orthodox but also with some Roman Catholics. During the 1950s the ecumenical community at Taizé in France, the Orthodox Theological Seminary of Saint-Serge in Paris, and the Benedictine monastery of Chevetogne in Belgium became places of significant encounter for those who sought a wider ecumenical fellowship on the basis of a common conviction that the church's ministry and sacraments were God's gifts to the whole world.

John XXIII and the Second Vatican Council

In 1958 the seventy-seven-year-old Patriarch of Venice, Angelo Roncalli, was chosen pope; he took the name John XXIII. His theology and piety were extremely traditional. He was uncontroversial, unpretentious, from a simple family background, and of a charming good nature. Within three months he announced, to the genuine amazement of the world and to the total surprise of the church, that he intended to call an "ecumenical council." This decision was, by his own admission, a sudden inspiration. Yet this council became an historic event, comparable in scope to the subsequent fall of the Berlin Wall. In it, half of world Christianity took a step into the modern world and acknowledged "a real though incomplete" fellowship with other churches.

John XXIII had no clear understanding of what the council would accomplish, but he was certain how it should work: more pastoral than dogmatic, more inviting than judging. He would himself, he wrote, rather be a gardener who nurtured beautiful flowers than a guard at a museum. He eagerly expected a new Pentecost when the Spirit would flow through the church and inspire her to truth, goodness, and peace.

It was high time for such an updating to present times, an *aggiornamento*. The protectionist mentality which characterized the Roman

Church's curia and also its bishops needed to change. The pope had taken account of the signs of the times. In his encyclical *Pacem in Terris* (1963) he identified three of those signs: the improvement of conditions for workers, changes in the public role of women, and the end of imperialism. He spoke of the church of the poor, human rights, and religious freedom. During the Cuban Missile Crisis of 1962, when the world stood at the brink of atomic war, he helped the leaders of the great powers to retreat without losing face.

The council began on 12 October 1962.[6] John XXIII was filled with joy. With the Spirit's help the common Christian faith would be renewed and deepened. He reminded the council fathers that the substance of the church's tradition and faith was one thing, but ways of expressing it could vary. Thus he made it possible with integrity to carry on a dialogue with other Christians. He was criticized for his optimism and naïve view of the future when he spoke with confidence of how Providence could lead humanity toward an ever greater community. The sluggish Roman curia pushed on the brakes as hard as it could, but when the pope died in 1963 the council had definitely begun to move in his direction. The public support for the humble old man was by that time so overwhelming and expectations were so great that nothing could hinder the council's progress.

A Secretariat for Christian Unity had already been established with the eighty-one-year-old German Cardinal Augustin Bea, S.J.,[7] as its leader and with the ecumenically well known Dutch theologian Johannes Willebrands at his side. Council observers were invited from the Orthodox churches, the World Council of Churches, and several confessional organizations. Roman Catholic observers began to be sent to WCC conferences. Relations between Rome and Geneva were regularized. A "Joint Working Group" was formed to guarantee continuity and a regular exchange of information. Many Protestants had difficulty in believing that the Roman Catholic Church was serious, just as conservative Roman Catholics refused to see how the times were changing. Nevertheless, council decisions began quickly to be translated into practical actions. For ecumenism, three council documents were particularly important.

The first was the Dogmatic Constitution on the Church, *Lumen Gentium* ("Light of Humanity").[8] This document described the church in several biblical images, emphasizing most strongly the church as the people of God on their way through history. This image had a totally different dynamic than the more common canonical and institutional definitions. The church, God's chosen people, must live so that God's intentions become visible to the world. The church, the body of Christ, must have his heart and hands. The church, the temple of the Holy Spirit, must be obedient both to God's whispers and to the cries of humanity.

Vatican II took away claims of identity between the church of Christ and the Roman Catholic Church. God's grace is everywhere present and active in the world. The church is a sign of that grace, a proclamation and a promise of salvation, but one cannot firmly establish the church's boundaries. It is greater than Roman Catholicism even if the Roman Church alone is the communion which, gathered around the pope, in all respects reflects the church of Christ in its fullness:

> This Church, constituted and organized as a society in the present world, subsists in the Catholic Church, which is governed by the successor of Peter and by the bishops in communion with him. Nevertheless, many elements of sanctification and of truth are found outside its visible confines. Since these are gifts belonging to the Church of Christ, they are forces impelling towards Catholic unity.[9]

Although other churches have defects in confession and sacramental life and stand outside direct fellowship with the pope, they possess in different degrees elements of the true church, which means that they cannot be dismissed:

> The Church knows that she is joined in many ways to the baptized who are honored by the name of Christian, but who do not however profess the Catholic faith in its entirety or have not preserved unity or communion under the successor of Peter. For there are many who hold sacred scripture in honor as a rule of faith and life, who have a sincere religious zeal, who lovingly believe in God the Father Almighty and in Christ, the Son of God and the Saviour, who are sealed by baptism which unites them to Christ and who indeed recognize and receive other sacraments in their own Churches or ecclesiastical communities. Many of them possess the episcopate, celebrate the Holy Eucharist, and cultivate devotion of the Virgin Mother of God. There is furthermore a sharing in prayer

and spiritual benefits; these Christians are indeed in some real way joined to us in the Holy Spirit for, by his gifts and graces, his sanctifying power is also active in them and he has strengthened some of them even to the shedding of their blood. And so the Spirit stirs up desires and actions in all of Christ's disciples in order that all may be peaceably united, as Christ ordained, in one flock under one shepherd. Mother Church never ceases to pray, hope, and work that this may be achieved, and she exhorts her children to purification and renewal so that the sign of Christ may shine more brightly over the face of the Church.[10]

Second, the decree *Unitatis Redintegratio* ("Restoration of Unity")[11] laid out the guiding principles for ecumenism. It built on *Lumen Gentium* and asserted that there is "some, though imperfect,"[12] communion between all Christians. Churches and communities separated from the Roman Catholic Church did not lack a role in God's plan of salvation; the Holy Spirit used them as means for human salvation. This pertained especially to the Orthodox churches whose theology, liturgy, and organization were most complementary to the Catholic Church. After a millennium of separation, the conditions now existed for restoring full communion between these two bodies. This became clear both in the meeting between Pope Paul VI and the Patriarch Athenagoras I of Constantinople in Jerusalem, 5-6 January 1964, and in their common declaration of 7 December 1965, at the conclusion of Vatican II.

Unitatis Redintegratio, the Decree on Ecumenism, was at first generally interpreted to mean that the Roman Catholic Church had given up its exclusive claims and opened itself to genuine albeit still incomplete encounter with other ecclesial bodies. Much later, when the initial euphoria had passed, the conservative head of the Vatican's Congregation for the Doctrine of the Faith, Cardinal Joseph Ratzinger (who was to become Pope Benedict XVI), denied that the council in any way altered the Roman view of the church. Yet it could not be doubted that the council had altered the Catholic Church's way of relating to other Christians. No longer was it said that other Christian groups must "return home," but rather it was acknowledged that such groups in spite of defects had positive meaning for the salvation of humans. There was a "hierarchy of truths." Parts of church doctrine carried greater weight than others. Even the Roman Catholic Church in certain respects fell short. Christians who had previously been known as "heretics" were now referred to as "separated brethren," and in official theological dialogues it became apparent that old judgments made by all parties were no longer applicable. The visible unity of the church required renewal, conversion, and a holy life on the part of both Roman Catholics and other Christians. Their unity would grow through prayer, common worship, and dialogue. "Spiritual ecumenism" was what was required.

In the subsequent three decades, the churches drew closer to each other. Today, Rome's Pontifical Council for Promoting Christian Unity, originally the Secretariat for Christian Unity, has created a network for all the churches of the world. Ecclesiological questions are discussed together as never before. The pope is acknowledged by most to be Christianity's chief spokesperson. Suspicion of the Roman Catholic Church has abated. Common efforts have deepened in respect to Bible translation, liturgical renewal, patristic studies, and even Luther research. Nevertheless, when the WCC increased its emphasis on social activism and when many of the churches which had come near to the Catholic Church began to ordain women as priests and bishops, to use gender-neutral liturgical language, and to bless same-sex unions, relations began to be strained. The reality is that divergent views on moral questions have quickly become more divisive than dogmatic differences.

Changes in the surrounding world made the Second Vatican Council necessary. It was no longer adequate merely to speak *to* the world; on the basis of its own commitments the church had to carry on an informed dialogue *with* society. The third document, the Pastoral Constitution on the Church in the Modern World, *Gaudium et Spes* ("Joy and Hope"),[13] after its introduction described the church's role in the transition from an agrarian society to an industrial world. Changes in society were a consequence of human intelligence and creativity and they influenced attitudes toward life and the church. Economic growth, however, did not reach everyone. The abundance of the wealthy contrasted sharply with the misery of many. While some were given increased freedom, others were trapped in dependence, subordination, and pervasive powerlessness. Ideologies clashed with one another. A perplexed church could maintain its integrity and relevance only by adapting itself realistically to complicated social and political realities.

To be sure, the council's words carried weight. Yet its interpretation of the contemporary world perhaps received a more lasting authority than it merited. When the world continued to change, the church found itself bound to texts which Vatican II had solemnly promulgated. *Gaudium et Spes,* however, is to be seen as a far-reaching adaptation to the world, an ongoing introduction to dialogue on moral, philosophical, scientific, and political issues.

The 1966 Geneva Conference on Church and Society

While Vatican II was carrying the Roman Catholic Church into the modern world, preparations were under way for a World Conference on Church and Society to be held in Geneva during the summer of 1966 under the sponsorship of the WCC. This conference was to be the culmination of decades of work in social ethics initiated by the Life and Work Movement. The American Paul Abrecht had chief responsibility for the conference. He possessed remarkably wide contacts with researchers and scientists at many universities and envisioned a forum where theologians, leaders of industry, social scientists, politicians, and church leaders from developing and developed countries could meet and face the churches' role in the "technological and social revolutions" of the times.

After the Second World War, when European civilization was on the verge of collapse, it was necessary to reconstruct society in order to establish democratic structures. "The responsible society" became the frame of reference for ecumenical social ethics. This was defined at the World Council's first Assembly at Amsterdam in 1948 as a society in which freedom belonged to those who took responsibility for law and order, and where persons of political and economic power exercised their stewardship toward God with responsibility toward the persons whose welfare was dependent on their public administration. "The responsible society" was not an alternative order for public life but rather a measuring rod for guidance.[14] This frame of reference functioned well for a few decades, but when revolutionary movements in the third world challenged prevailing orders and when industrialization accelerated, "the responsible society" came to be seen as an all too static model.

Global processes of change had many dimensions, but the critical issue at Geneva centered on the political revolutions which were taking place in many lands. For many conference participants it was unthinkable to stand behind a "normal" revolution even if the need for thorough structural changes was obvious. Others, in contrast, welcomed revolution as a sign of God's participation in human history; they asserted that it was high time for the development of a theology of revolution. These developments received a great deal of attention in the media and among conservative critics of the WCC who, becoming more and more shrill with time, began to voice their concerns. They accused the organization of being altogether too concerned — with excessively radical overtones — with social and political questions.

The conference worked with three questions. The first was how biblical and theological traditions could be applied in modern society in order to contribute to a relevant social ethic. The second asked in what sense the various revolutions and political upheavals were the last resort for attaining national freedom, equality, and justice. The third question was how ecclesial confessional heritages determined the churches' relation to social change and the struggle for justice.

Everyone argued for open and free societies. The tone, as so often in the 1960s, was hopeful. Delegates from the Third World who demanded programs of concrete solidarity and radical action received the most attention. The American professor and missionary Richard Shaull, who was later to lead the Student Christian Movement through a violent political storm which almost ended in shipwreck,[15] admonished the churches explicitly to reject capitalistic market economies since they created new forms of colonialism and oppression. Those who championed "the responsible society" were criticized for seeking stability by holding on to traditional structures. In consequence, a showdown took place between those who were prepared to support political revolution and spokespersons for "the responsible society." This contrast would mark the debate for years to come. Yet the conference, though chaotic at times, was united in the view that the churches must move from words to deeds. It would soon be seen that deeds were far more controversial than even the most radical words.[16]

New Leaders Reconsider Ecumenical Assumptions

Three weeks after the Geneva conference, Mao Zedong initiated the massive "Cultural Revolution" in China. The ravages carried out by the Red Guards demonstrated that revolutionary change in a society came at a very high price. Nevertheless, Western students found themselves infected by these violent protests against the dictatorial nature of the Chinese bureaucracy. Above all these students desired to change an educational system that they perceived was strengthening the oppressive structures of the existing order. The political left appropriated to itself the privilege of formulating the problem according to a Marxist analysis of society, an analytical method that earlier had been abandoned but now was again seen as viable. The first generation of students produced in welfare states, they became spokespersons for the working class and "the wretched of the earth." Even ecumenism, which was permeated by the spirit of postwar liberal democracy and by a quest for common understandings that transcend all boundaries, was marked by internal protest, a *contestation* which the student movement saw as its special calling.

The 1960s were initially the ecumenical movement's most successful and promising years, but they were transformed into its most turbulent decade. In the 1930s ecumenical pioneers had translated their vision into the creation of organizations. The World Council of Churches was developed by legendary Westerners like W. A. Visser 't Hooft, Lesslie Newbigin, Suzanne de Diétrich, Madeleine Barot, Kathleen Bliss, Eugene Carson Blake, and Leslie Cooke. Now it was time for a third generation of leaders to appear. Many were Asians, such as M. M. Thomas, D. T. Niles, Paulus Mar Gregorius, and Masao Takenaka. Some were Orthodox, such as Nikos Nissiotis and Nicolas Lossky. A handful were from Latin America, such as José Míguez Bonino and Emilio Castro. Among Africans Desmond Tutu, Brigalia Bam, and Mercy Amba Oduyoye should be noted. The one who most set the tone was Philip Potter from Jamaica. These persons began by listening to voices from "the underside of history" in order to identify the contextual character of the gospel. Such contextualization quickly came into conflict with the catholicity that had been the bedrock of the ecumenical institutions. The reconsideration that began in 1968 at the Uppsala assembly focused not only on ecumenism's direction and goal but also on its most fundamental assumptions.

CHAPTER 2

All Things New

We have good reason to study "the agenda of the world." But if the Church is the church of Jesus Christ, it knows only one destination: the Kingdom of God.

W. A. VISSER 'T HOOFT

The procession from the university to the cathedral was like an avalanche with four to a row, totaling over seven hundred delegates from two hundred thirty-five churches. There was Metropolitan Alexei from Tallinn, who was destined to become patriarch in Moscow; Martin Niemöller, who had spent seven years in a concentration camp on account of his opposition to Nazism; Michael Ramsey, the archbishop of Canterbury; and Kathleen Bliss, the university lecturer who was one of the first women to have genuine influence in the World Council of Churches. Many noted the physician and provincial governor Francis Akanu Ibiam from Biafra, clad in the flowing white *agbada* characteristic of Yoruba dress. He had chosen to side with his people during the civil war that was then raging within the central Nigerian regime; he had rejected the honor of knighthood, since Britain supported Nigeria. There also went the energetic layman M. M. Thomas, who was one of the founders of the Christian Institute for the Study of Religion and Society in Bangalore and who was to become chairman of the World Council's Central Committee during the crucial years after the Uppsala assembly. Among the delegates there were some sixty women.

Willem Adolf Visser 't Hooft, who had been a part of the movement since 1925, had just retired as general secretary. He was a Reformed Hollander from the educated upper class; his friends were in the academic world, in the houses of finance, and in parliaments. After an interlude of a few years when the American Presbyterian Eugene Carson Blake was general secretary, Philip Potter would assume the position. He came from Jamaica accompanied by the music of slaves, the common touch of Methodism, the impatience of the student world, and the destiny to become the most audacious and colorful of WCC leaders. Visser 't Hooft, Blake, and Potter were all in Uppsala, the first with his long experience, the second with his great energy, the third with his ears toward both the Third World and the youth.

The youth — in everyday clothes and gathered in a group — were united in protest against the ecclesiastical splendor of the procession, and also against the assumption that well-known older men would dominate the proceedings. A young Swiss climbed up a lamppost to show contempt for the power which that day was symbolized by the elderly Swedish King Gustav VI Adolf and also by the youthful president of Zambia, Kenneth Kaunda. The police carried him away, but the event was a portent of what was to come. The youth had prepared themselves during the spring in East Berlin, and even before the assembly was to begin they had formulated critical questions and laid out a strategy. They planned demonstrations, printed signs, made contact with media, and decided when they would march out of the plenary hall or other main events. They held that the World Council of Churches in both its theology and its structure upheld imperialism and paternalism. Seven hundred journalists guaranteed that their views would be spread across the world. In general, however, the youth made little impact on section reports, and, when all was said and done, it was the reports that would guide the future work of the Council.

The archbishop of the Church of Sweden, Ruben Josefson, came last in the procession. He was at home in the world of Lutheran theology, thoughtful and wise, but he was scarcely audacious in respect to ecumenical visions. The opening service of worship was marked by newly composed Swedish music even as the perennial "Now Thank We All Our God" reverberated in many languages under the Gothic arches of the cathedral. D. T. Niles, a Methodist from Sri Lanka, preached. He was the ecumenical movement's dynamic evangelist who proclaimed the promise of God's future and urged the churches to find new ways. "We are always surrounded by signs to be seen now of what God will accomplish hereafter ... the complete transformation of all that already is." Even though God's promise is eschatological it has implications here and now. It must be heard in the midst of the secularized world: "Here the cities of our dwelling are places where God is remembered and forgotten, acknowledged and denied; so that here must be maintained the testimony to God as God which is essential to the health of human living."[1] And in a creaky voice the archbishop then blessed the most representative gathering in the long history of Christianity.

This opening service of worship at the Uppsala assembly provided an overwhelming awareness of the church's universality. Israel's God spoke to every culture so that everyone could hear his message in his or her own heart. The Spirit of God made communication possible across every boundary, inspiring Christians to confess their faith together and to stand up against the world's injustices and all violations of human rights and dignity. This was uplifting especially for those churches in Europe that had been weakened both by pervasive secularism and deep crises of faith. *The Secular City* by the Harvard professor Harvey Cox was current and much debated, showing how marginalized the churches had become in modern urban settings.[2] *Honest to God* by the Anglican bishop John Robinson, which was being read by millions, described how strained traditional interpretations of Christian faith had become.[3] The Uppsala assembly could not change these realities, but it shifted attention toward other parts of the world where the church was vibrant and alive, and where Christ's promise of a new world was anticipated by youth and the young churches. It was not heaven that called, but rather a revolutionary transformation of humankind's social and economic conditions here and now.

The World Sets the Agenda

Key words at Uppsala included *structure, catholicity, development, racism, dialogue, education, mission,* and *lifestyle*. Debates were carried on in heated and provocative tones although the assembly was surrounded by world-class music and art. The Britisher Norman Goodall, who edited the final report, described the meeting in this way:

> The most obvious and widely acknowledged feature of the assembly was its preoccupation — at times, almost, obsession — with the

revolutionary ferment of our time, with questions of social and international responsibility, of war and peace and economic justice, with the pressing, agonizing physical needs of men, with the plight of the underprivileged, the homeless and starving, and with the most radical contemporary rebellions against all "establishments," civil and religious. It was not only recognized that — as it was often expressed — the world was writing the agenda for the meeting; the right of the world to do this was largely taken for granted and Uppsala tried to read the writing, understand it and respond to it in a willingness to accept the necessity for changes as tumultuous for the Church itself as for the rapidly changing world.[4]

The assembly's moorings in ecumenical history, however, were strong. Modern biblical scholarship had encouraged a nonconfessional reading of the Bible that crossed over boundaries; daily Bible studies reminded participants of the church's common tradition of faith. *On That Day*, a liturgical drama based on the prophet Amos by the Swedish theologian and dramatist Olov Hartman, admonished the churches to return to their primary task, to "let justice roll down like waters, and righteousness like an ever-flowing stream" (Amos 5:24).[5] There were echoes of the early church in all the services of worship, even if some of the orders were new and experimental. Although Roman Catholics and Protestants obstinately refused to share the Eucharist and the youth sang their songs accompanied by guitars, most of the worship was rather traditional. The assembly was heavy with a level of experience that militated against simplifications. Politicians, scholars, and bishops allowed no irresponsible analyses. Nevertheless, throughout Uppsala's work-filled days the light summer nights' fresh winds blew in from "the new heaven and the new earth where righteousness dwells."

This was most strongly felt when the youth gathered in the evenings. Nothing was impossible, not even a changed world. The transformation of unjust structures was on its way. No one could then believe that the future would be marked by genocide, pandemics, and fateful climate change. The warnings about the ambiguity of technology and the first signs of the ecological crisis were not really heard or seen. The human environment was vulnerable and wounded, but with correct politics and development everything would be alright.

The one hundred twenty-seven youth and student delegates hardly belonged to the extreme left, but many of them had read Herbert

Marcuse, "the father of the new left," and could not avoid being influenced by the intense ideological debate of the time. Likewise, Marshall McLuhan had taught them something about the conditions for communication in the new media culture where "the medium is the message." They were often more aware of the totalitarian elements of capitalistic democracies than of the abuse of power in China, and they criticized all who used "repressive tolerance" as a means to silence uncomfortable voices.[6]

The folksinger Pete Seeger was forty-nine years old that summer and a gray-haired icon of the American left. He came to Uppsala and sang hits from the 1950s like "If I Had a Hammer" and "Where Have All the Flowers Gone?" Opposition was necessary; change was possible. Debates with internationally known scholars such as the economists Gunnar Myrdal and Samuel Parmer, the cultural anthropologist Margaret Mead, and the Czechoslovakian theologian Josef Hromádka took place late into the night in university student buildings. Before dawn *Hot News,* the youth's saucy paper, was printed, and tactics were laid out for the next day's confrontations.

The Race Question Radicalizes the Ecumenical Movement

James Baldwin had a special role at Uppsala. He was a celebrated American author, black, homosexual, a one-time Pentecostal with close ties to the black power movement. He presented himself to the assembly as one who always stood outside the church, even when he attempted to work within it. "I address you as one of God's creatures whom the Christian church has most betrayed," he began his summary of the long history of racial discrimination. The Christian personality had been split into light and dark and was now lost in conflict with itself. He doubted that there was sufficient moral energy and spiritual courage for Christianity to better itself, to reconcile with its past, and to be born again, but he challenged the entire assembly: the church must unambiguously and concretely take up the struggle against racism, which was so obviously a denial of Christian faith. It was not enough to appeal to humanity's conscience and good will. Racism was coupled with economic and political exploitation and therefore the structures of both society and church which made racism possible must be changed.[7]

The race question triggered the radicalization of the ecumenical movement. Thanks to two centuries of mission work in Asia and Africa, the churches did have a global conscience and racism had been on the ecumenical agenda since the 1920s. By now it was clear that programs of charity and assistance were not sufficient to bring about justice. Thousands of schools, mission hospitals, and development projects were important, but a thorough alteration of the world's social, political, and economic structures was required if justice was to be done for the poor. A certain amount of welfare could possibly be distributed from above, but authentic justice could be accomplished only if the injured could take things into their own hands. Light shone brightly on the white racism which legitimated the dominance of the northern European colonial powers. Racism with its explosive force must be taken as seriously as the threat of nuclear war.

The WCC, born of Western missions and saturated with the good intentions of Protestantism, now must become a forum for Africans, Asians, and Latin Americans who desired to liberate their societies from oppression and misery. Nothing would be as it had been. There must be a renewed trust in the Holy Spirit to lead the churches and the ecumenical movement in new ways.

Differing Attitudes toward the Eastern European Churches

From a very close distance, the Cold War, the East-West conflict, cast its shadow over Uppsala. The WCC had long wished to include all Eastern European churches within its membership, and in 1961, just as the wall which brutally divided Europe in half was being erected, that had become possible. Accordingly, it became a principal ecumenical task to preserve and deepen contact with Christians in Eastern Europe. It was seen to be necessary that considerate respect between churches take precedence over both critiques of ideology and public denunciations of totalitarian systems and their violations of human rights. It was more important to support member churches and help them to survive in countries where everything else was controlled by Communist authorities.

In 1967 the Albanian government declared the country to be the world's first atheist state, and all public expressions of religious faith were deemed totally illegal. In Poland, the Baltic nations, Czechoslovakia, Armenia, and other countries behind the Iron Curtain, the churches, while severely restricted, did find a kind of *modus vivendi*. They adjusted to the circumstances, cooperated with the authorities, and publicly supported Soviet foreign policy. In Bulgaria, the church suffered from a shortage of clergy and from severe inner conflicts. In Romania, the church was threatened by the plans, equally grandiose and mad, of Nicolae Ceauşescu to move the population to "urban agro-industrial centers." The best conditions for the church were in the German Democratic Republic (East Germany), where the provincial churches were a part of the Evangelical Church in Germany until the end of the 1960s, when they formed their own federation. These churches were, however, constantly dependent on economic support from the West. They quickly became smaller in size as fewer children were baptized; they were, like all parts of society, drawn into a system in which everyone exercised surveillance over everyone else.[8]

In the midst of Krushchev's persecution, the Russian Orthodox Church in 1961 became a member church of the World Council of Churches; it also sent observers to the Second Vatican Council. It thus took on a significant role in public cultural and interreligious relations. Young Metropolitan Nikodim of Leningrad was the church's most prominent international spokesperson. He skillfully diverted every debate concerning oppression and insufficient religious freedom in the Eastern countries, eagerly assisting in turning the attention of the WCC in other directions. He became one of the Council's presidents in 1975. He also had exceptionally good connections with the Vatican and wrote a book about Pope John XXIII, whom he regarded most highly. In 1978, at the age of forty-nine, he died suddenly in the arms of Pope John Paul I.

The World Council of Churches, the Lutheran World Federation, and the Vatican in practice contributed to the support of the Russian Orthodox Church's uncertain, risk-filled, and always questioned policies. The Church opposed the Russian state's official atheism by its celebration of Divine Liturgy wherever possible and it also, in spite of censorship, published a number of journals, books, and on occasion Bibles. Its political position also helped other churches in the Soviet Union and its orbit to maintain limited contact with the "outer world." They were not entirely unaware of ecumenical and theological developments. The small Protestant communities received official recognition from the state provided that they adjusted to the prevalent ideologies, which leaders such as the Lutheran bishop in Hungary, Zoltan Káldy, and his Reformed counterpart, Károly Toth, did not fail to do.

The ecumenical organizations expressed virtually no public criticism of the Soviet Union or of Cuba without the permission of local church bodies. This position gave rise to disappointment among dissidents in the East and criticism in the West. In spite of steady discussions concerning human rights and freedom of religion, the WCC never made statements directly addressing Communist dictatorships.[9] Nevertheless, many informal and strongly critical discussions took place between church leaders and representatives of society, especially concerning the limitations being imposed on freedom of religion. The voluminous correspondence with churches in Eastern Europe which has only recently been made available demonstrates that the WCC and other ecumenical organizations were far from clueless fellow travelers as critics have charged. But, to be sure, they did not have a firm and consistent attitude to socialist politics, and the staff of the organizations held to a variety of attitudes regarding socialism and the church politics of Eastern Europe.[10]

This public silence shook the integrity of the ecumenical movement, but the alternative of intruding in the affairs of Eastern European churches would have been no better. The Russian bishops were fully aware of what it could cost to shield their churches. More than a hundred bishops had been imprisoned and killed. Those who remained were forced to exercise their office under constant compromise. Not seldom, their lives became a long, drawn-out, gray martyrdom.

The Czech Reformed theologian Josef Hromádka advocated for cooperation and dialogue with Marxism-Leninism. He had studied in foreign universities and taught at Princeton Theological Seminary in the U.S. After the end of World War II he returned to Prague as a professor of systematic theology. He was well known for his debate on capitalism and socialism at the first WCC assembly in Amsterdam in 1948 with the future American secretary of state John Foster Dulles. At Amsterdam the WCC chose a kind of "third way," i.e., to defend democracy and human rights and to make global justice the objective of all economic development, but also to refrain from criticism of Eastern European socialism in the hope of contributing to internal change.

Hromádka was critical of Western civilization and had sharply separated himself from Nazism. He sympathized with Marxism and was convinced that history was on the side of socialism. He held that communism needed reform but in contrast to capitalism, which embodied imperialism and belonged to the past, it served peace. In order to survive, the church must choose the way of dialogue and cooperation. Accordingly, Hromádka was instrumental in the establishment of the Christian Peace Conference, which held its first assembly in Prague in 1958 and which gathered church leaders from all over Europe, China, North Korea, Vietnam, India, and several African countries. Among those leaders some were well known in ecumenical circles — K. H. Ting from China, Leopoldo Niilus from Argentina, Julio de Santa Ana from Uruguay, and Paulos Mar Gregorios from India. The goal of the conference was to develop constructive forms of cooperation between Christianity and state socialism which most people at that time believed had arrived to stay. Disarmament and decolonialization were high on the agenda.

The Prague Conference, as the Christian Peace Conference came to be known, was the only officially recognized ecumenical organization behind the Iron Curtain. However, in August 1968, when the tanks of Warsaw Pact nations just after the Uppsala assembly crushed the "Prague Spring," Hromádka's hopes to bring Marxism and Christianity together were also crushed. He died in 1970. The conference, marked by inner contradictions, continued its work in close contact with ecumenical organizations in Geneva. Their persistent restraint in respect to any criticism of socialism stood in stark contrast to their pronouncements concerning the United States and especially South Africa, where local church bodies strived for the formation of international opinion and consensus.

The Third World Leads the Debate concerning Development

At Uppsala it was not Eastern Europe but rather the Third World that shaped the debate concerning freedom, development, and human rights. Colonialism was on the decline. Many nations had obtained their independence in orderly fashion, although in southern Africa a drawn-out and bitter struggle continued. Many wished to believe that an open, humane, and democratic socialism was possible. Experiments such as President Julius Nyerere's collectivist *ujamaa* villages in Tanzania gave rise to a great deal of interest. Socialist freedom fighters like Eduardo Mondlane of Mozambique, Robert Mugabe in Zimbabwe, and Nelson Mandela, who was still imprisoned in South Africa, had the undivided support of youth and the sympathy of many elders. Young people in the West were also inspired by the dedication of Red Guards in China's Cultural Revolution, by the North Vietnamese who held the Americans in a stalemate, and by the struggle of the Sandinistas in Nicaragua. In the late 1960s there were many advocates of political revolution.

If theologians from the Western world were occupied with the church's catholicity and theology of mission or concerned with secularization, the leaders of Third World churches spoke rather of racism, the struggle against poverty, the population explosion, and relations with other religions. They based their arguments on experienced reality, not on the traditions and doctrines of the church. They interpreted the Bible in relation to their own social situation, urging theologians from the North to use more inductive methods. There was a need for open space where insight and experience could be shared and a common understanding of life's relation to faith could be formulated. The WCC was prepared to provide such space.

The Council's charter referred to the triune God in its theological basis. This opened a wider theological perspective than the Reformed-hued christocentric universalism which Visser 't Hooft and his generation represented. A Trinitarian theology made it possible to focus on humanity's responsibility for creation and also on the Spirit's role in the world. Mission became more than the proclamation of Christ; mission was rather understood as creating in every way the conditions for a life of dignity.

The section of the Uppsala assembly that worked on the theology of unity had "The Holy Spirit and the Catholicity of the Church" as its theme. One could not speak of the unity of the church without speaking of the Spirit who renews the church's faith and bestows the gift of unity. This, however, is the same Spirit that gives life to all creation and holds destructive powers in check. The Spirit is not limited to word and sacraments, but is active everywhere for freedom and justice. This section's report asserted that "[w]e have come to view this world of men as the place where God is already at work to make all things new, and where he summons us to work with him."[11]

The Lutheran teaching of the Christian's vocation to live a common, worldly life dedicated to the needs of the neighbor influenced this report, as did the Orthodox emphasis on the Spirit as life-giver. The report summoned Christians to social and political responsibility in the company of all people of good will. The churches possess moral substance since they do not have power. Olof Palme, Prime Minister of Sweden, emphasized this in his address to the Assembly:

> Mr. Palme spoke of the new situation in which "both the temporal and spiritual powers are compelled to reconsider radically our main duty towards suffering mankind. For the temporal power this involves a new recognition of the rights of the oppressed; for the churches it means the end of an era in which they were the guardians of a pattern of life which secured not only the power of the Church but the immutability of a social order." How seldom man has the power to surrender power. "Yet today the churches are surrendering their ego in order to serve to the ends of the earth." Both the secular and spiritual powers, faced with a world in need, are required "to approach the conditions of history in order to change them."[12]

In a "church for others" the need of those others determines the priorities. This was emphasized strongly, a reflection of the positive evaluation of secularization that was current at the time of the Uppsala assembly. The Lutheran theologian Dietrich Bonhoeffer had written even before World War II of "man come of age" and "religionless faith." According to him, a Christian must live a deeply worldly and disciplined life, face-to-face with death and resurrection in the midst of an existence where one's solidarity with the oppressed is tested.[13] The gospel liberates humans from oppressive social, economic, and religious structures so that they can stand up for their fellow human beings. When the world writes the agenda for the church, it is a sign that the church is set free from its self-preoccupation.

Secular Theology Wins the Day

In the 1960s theological debate moved quickly. Secularization, it was often claimed, did not necessitate a weakening of Christian civilization. Rather, it could be interpreted as a fulfillment of the desacralization of society and nature which began in the time of ancient Israel. Ultimately, it was a consequence of the Bible's message. To gain adherents to an isolated religious society, the thinking went, is not the primary task of the church; its primary task is rather to confess the God who leads history forward and thus unmasks the innermost essence of the world. It is the church's responsibility to prepare humans for a civilization that is spiritually and materially new. Secularization declares humanity to be of age. This includes a liberation from oppressive religious structures, and it must lead both to a thoroughgoing renewal of the church's outer forms and to its unreserved participation in the life of the world.[14]

The assembly section on worship in a secular age took its distance from secularism as a closed, one-dimensional worldliness, but in spite of the objections of Orthodox and Asian delegates it nevertheless accepted the intentions of secular theology. The anthropocentric character of that theology, however, raised questions about the content of "holy mysteries," and it did not take many years before spirituality, prayer, and the sacramental life again stood in the center. The 1970s became the decade of the charismatic revival, of new ecclesial movements, of fundamentalism, and of resurgent world religions. That shift was certainly not anticipated by the proponents of secular theology at Uppsala, who, led by Western Protestants, made the entire ecumenical movement move in the direction of a "secular ecumenism" even over Orthodox, Catholic, African, and Asian objections.

Debate on the Mission of the Church

The International Missionary Council was integrated into the WCC in 1961. The task of mission had to be formulated in a way that was congruent with other dimensions of the ecumenical enterprise, relevant to the post-colonial world, and in agreement with the biblical mandate. Discussions under such themes as "mission on six continents," "the church for others," and *"missio Dei"* (the mission of God) had been carried on for a long time. In preparatory material for the Uppsala assembly, the goal of mission was described as "a new humanity" and "God's *shalom.*" Conversion was for the sake of fellow human beings rather than for one's own salvation. Alterations in local and international structures designed to bring about social justice, national independence, and human rights on occasion justified the use of revolutionary means. The encounter with people of other faiths required sensitive dialogue, not a one-sided proclamation of the gospel.

The old mission societies, however, were still strong. Many of them had opposed the integration of the International Missionary Council with the World Council. They had difficulty accepting the view that mission was not just theirs but rather an integral task of the whole people of God. The church did not *have* a mission; it *was* mission. Bishop Lesslie Newbigin, who was the first director of the Council's unit on mission, always argued that the whole church shared in the task of mission. D. T. Niles maintained persistently that the Asian and African churches themselves had responsibility for mission in their own lands.[15] Nevertheless, many Western mission organizations defended the traditional role of the foreign missionary and could not agree to an expanded understanding of the goal of mission.

Opposing sides, therefore, formed at Uppsala. In the preparation of a report on mission, Nordic delegates failed in an attempt to propose traditional formulations. The debate was divisive and sharply polarized. Even if the final report was a self-critical compromise which presented a rather traditional view of mission, it pointed toward a more open, inclusive, and social interpretation of the task:

> Mission bears fruit as people find their true life in the Body of Christ, in the Church's life of Word and Sacrament, fellowship in the Spirit, and existence for others. There the signs of the new humanity are experienced and the People of God reach out in solidarity with the whole of mankind in service and witness. The growth of the Church, therefore, both inward and outward is of urgent importance. Yet our ultimate hope is not set upon this progress, but on the mystery of the final event which remains in the hand of God.[16]

The church should not cease its preaching of conversion, but it was also the church's task to change the world's economic and social structures.

The evangelical Anglican John Stott, who was to become one of the primary advocates of the Lausanne Movement, stated with disappointment, "The World Council confesses that Jesus is Lord. The Lord sends his Church to proclaim the Good News and make disciples. I do not see that the assembly is very eager to obey its Lord's commands. The Lord Jesus Christ wept over the city which had rejected him. I do not see this assembly weeping similar tears."[17] For Lesslie Newbigin, too, the assembly was an unnerving experience when questions of economic and social justice obscured the church's essential calling. He found the atmosphere hostile, the emotional temperature high, and the arguments frightening. Those who argued for a more traditional understanding of mission were "shaken over the abyss of hell."[18]

The Uppsala assembly invited the conservative evangelical movements to participate in the ecumenical endeavor in a way that would be acceptable to both sides. That invitation did not help. The evangelicals' criticism of the World Council of Churches was sharp. They described the assembly as deceitful vis-à-vis the missionary movement's biblical principles and goal. With Billy Graham at the helm they began to create other forms for international cooperation in mission.

The Church's Responsibility for a Just World Order

After the World Conference on Church and Society held in Geneva in 1966 on "Christians in Our Time's Technical and Social Upheavals," the words *renewal, change, development,* and *revolution* became lodestars in the field of social ethics:

> If our false security in the old and our fear of revolutionary change tempt us to defend the status quo or to patch it up with half-hearted measures, we may all perish. The death of the old may cause pain to some, but failure to build up a new world community may bring death to all.[19]

The world was divided into super-affluent societies occupied only with themselves, on the one hand, and marginalized societies that did not receive the assistance they needed for development, on the other. The global economy with its unequal apportionments of wealth gave rise to insistent political and moral questions. Countless human beings lacked daily employment and food. This was caused by the way societies were organized, which laws guided economic life, how the ownership of property was shared, and what kind of trade agreements prevailed. Such problems could not be solved by charity. International relations had to be changed. Rich countries were in the midst of a technological and scientific revolution while poor nations were boiling with expectations. They could meet if — as the Indian economist Samuel Parmer expressed it — they adopted a world perspective and created adequate political structures at the global level. Indifference and denial of the world's needs equaled heresy.[20] Having knowledge of the world's critical situation and also possessing the means to alleviate the causes of the crisis, they had no excuse for not taking action.

But the rich nations that were not economically dependent on the poor ones were unwilling to share their wealth. This led to an immense loss of life and dignity for both parties. No one should be surprised that people living in poverty in their desperation took to violence. The moral responsibility for such violence lay largely with the wealthy. The churches naturally wanted to minimize the use of violence in revolutionary social change, but had to acknowledge that there were situations in which violence was the only alternative. Earth is humanity's only home and all nations must share responsibility for its future. Such insight must permeate education, worship, and social action, and the churches must commit themselves to an alternative global development. Time was short, but it was not yet too late.

The Civil War in Nigeria Awakens Strong Feelings

Literally, the time was short. The armaments race seemed to have no end, and the war in Vietnam went on year after year. It was another conflict, however, that gave rise to great opposition at the Uppsala assembly. A merciless civil war raged between Nigeria and its breakaway state in the east, Biafra. Francis Akanu Ibiam, who was not only the first African governor in eastern Nigeria but also one of the presidents of the WCC, had been forced into exile. He supported his people when the much stronger Nigeria cruelly sought to starve Biafra out. Ibiam's old friend from the Student Christian Movement, Bola Ige, led the Nigerian delegation to the Uppsala assembly. For his part he defended the central Nigerian state against all accusations of cruelty, corruption, and instability. Delegates discussed the war in light of their own national and ethnic loyalties. The very word *Biafra* could not be included in a much debated resolution concerning the war because of the strong feelings to which it gave rise. The WCC attempted to avoid taking an openly political position, but the situation in eastern Nigeria was such a humanitarian catastrophe that in practice it was not possible to refrain from taking the side of the weaker party.[21] Both Caritas, the Roman Catholic relief organization, and the World Council airlifted food into Biafra under extremely difficult circumstances. The debate at Uppsala clearly demonstrated the enormous difficulty churches on different sides of an acute political crisis faced in maintaining solidarity and contributing to justice and reconciliation.

Uppsala '68: Summing Up

Uppsala '68 was a church historical event comparable in certain respects to the Second Vatican Council. This assembly changed the entire ecumenical movement. Previously, Protestant church leaders from the North Atlantic area in close contact with academic scholars almost completely dominated international ecumenism. The WCC, well established in Geneva, was seen as a respected and modern international organization with certain similarities to the United Nations. All the Orthodox churches were involved, although they played a more reserved role. The Roman Catholic Church was on the outside. But in 1968 the Orthodox began to find their feet and gained a hearing for some of their most basic issues, and the Roman Catholics participated vigorously in all the discussions. At the same time, women and above all youth were heard as never before. The World Council became theologically, humanly, and religiously a more inclusive fellowship.

Even more importantly, a long list of churches from Africa and Asia participated in the assembly with newly won self-confidence, successfully raising their own questions. The churches encountered the impatient Third World not only as an abstraction to be discussed but also as a tension-filled presence at the heart of the Uppsala assembly. The focus shifted from church theology to social ethics, from evangelization to interreligious dialogue, and from "law and order" to the revolutionary transformation of society's structures. Trinitarian theology opened up both the perspective of creation on issues facing society and the activity of the Spirit even outside the church. Secularization was interpreted as a liberation of persons to assume responsibility for renewing the church and for changing the world. The goal of mission was defined as a renewed humanity. The unity of the church was not intrinsic to itself but a sign of the unity of the human community. The struggle against racism became the point where the church's credibility was to be tested and the cost of solidarity paid.

At Uppsala environmental problems were barely touched upon,

while population explosion was considered the great threat of the future. The prognosis was that the world's population would double by the turn of the century — which actually happened. In contrast to the Roman Catholic Church, Protestant communions supported family planning and birth control. There was nearly unlimited confidence in technological and medical development and in economic growth. No one was yet discussing "the limits of growth." Good will and charity could not produce social development and economic justice. A comprehensive transformation of structures was so urgently required in many countries that violent revolution was unavoidable. Humanity was given a face and many began to interpret history "from the underside," from the experience of losers and with the belief that some form of socialism was the shape of the future.

These changes in perspective were so pervasive that they could be described as a paradigm shift.[22] Christocentric universalism lost its convincing power, although it survived thanks to the fact that the Orthodox and Roman Catholic Churches applied brakes to the Protestant infatuation with "secular ecumenism." The structure of the WCC remained nearly unchanged and its member churches continued life in their ingrained ways. Their adjustments to each other continued and church unions were consummated in several countries. At Uppsala there were three decisive new shifts in the center of gravity: from north to south, from a deductive to an inductive theological method, and from church ecumenism to secular ecumenism. It would no longer only be common tradition and teaching that would show the way in ecumenical work. To such would be added local experience and the actual conflicts of the world. The contexts of the church became as important as her catholicity, her relation to the here and now as urgent as returning to common sources. Ecumenism deals not only with the unity of the church but also with the unity of the whole human community.

CHAPTER 3

God Loves the Poor

You cannot dry another person's tears without getting your fingers wet.

MANAS BUTHELEZI

Nearly ten thousand mourners had gathered at the modest church in Groutville in Natal, South Africa. It was a bitingly cold day at the end of July 1967. Albert Luthuli, who had received the Nobel Peace Prize in 1960 for his struggle against apartheid, was being buried. He had been run over by a train, but many took it for granted that the authorities had had a hand in the matter. The forbidden flags of the African National Congress (ANC) drooped. The security police stretched out their microphones when the author Alan Paton spoke: "History will show that it would have been best for all of us if Luthuli could speak. But he had the voice of a lion and therefore he had to be silenced. He was the voice of those who themselves could not speak." When the casket was lowered into the earth, someone began to sing the banned *"Nkosi sikelel'i Afrika,"* "God Bless Africa." The rocking, singing, weeping congregation understood that this was not just the burial of a leader but the end of his religiously based program of nonviolence. Nelson Mandela had been imprisoned in Robben Island for three years. Other black leaders had gone into exile. This was but one of a thousand burials of those who struggled for a life of dignity: schoolchildren in Soweto, Steve Biko, those hanged in Pretoria's prison — the list goes on. The conflict worsened with every passing day. The armed branch of the ANC was ready.[1]

Racism, nationalism, and ethnicity have been deep concerns of the ecumenical movement. The International Missionary Council at its world conference in Jerusalem in 1928 had declared that every discrimination against human beings on the ground of their race or the color of their skin and every human's selfish exploitation or oppression of another person is to deny the teaching of Jesus.[2] To stand against racism was, in other words, a *status confessionis,* a question of faith. The World Council of Churches was established just when South Africa's National Party, with its politics of apartheid, was coming to power. A statement against apartheid issued at a "Church and Apartheid" meeting in South Africa in 1960 brought about division between the churches: 80 percent of the participants agreed with taking a strong stand against racial separation, while three Dutch Reformed Churches in South Africa repudiated the statement and withdrew from the World Council.[3] When Botswana and Lesotho became independent nations in 1966, followed by Swaziland, the noose was tightened around South Africa. The deportation of blacks to "townships" and "homelands" was designed to hasten what was called "separate development." The wrath of the blacks, however, only grew, and the conflict worsened. For a long time the churches hoped for a peaceful solution, but when the pain and sorrow became too great, good will was no longer effective. The churches had to choose between active opposition and continued attempts to mitigate the effects of racism. Violence was seen to be the last resort, and when the churches could no longer exclude the use of weapons, they had to justify their position. Racism was an obvious sin, and every attempt theologically to legitimate apartheid was to be rejected. The resistance of the poor, the oppressed, and women was justified in the eyes of God. Those who possessed power must be called to account. The WCC initiated its "Program to Combat Racism."

WCC General Secretary Eugene Carson Blake received a clear mandate at the Uppsala assembly. This veteran activist who had played a leading role in the American civil rights movement refused to adopt a "wait and see" position. At a consultation at Notting Hill, London, in 1969, led by the American presidential candidate George McGovern with the cooperation of the exiled ANC leader Oliver Tambo, the goal was made more precise. Exactly like slavery, racism could and must be abolished. Racism was global and took many forms, but the accumulation of power and wealth in white hands was reason enough to concentrate on the white racism that marked many nations, societies, and churches. Solidarity with those who suffered discrimination required a redistribution of political and economic power. Only then would fundamental cultural self-determination make sense.

Financial Support to Liberation Movements

The WCC chose to utilize economic pressure. It decided to give financial support to the humanitarian work of liberation movements through a special fund. At the same time it worked to discourage foreign investment in South Africa and to get financial institutions not to grant loans. This decision gave rise to strong protests. In South Africa there were virtually hysterical reactions. When the first grants were paid in September 1970, South Africa's prime minister, John Vorster, called a press conference. He was alarmed that persons who called themselves Christians would support those who murdered and terrorized innocent people in his country. The foreign minister of South Africa heightened the rhetoric: the World Council of Churches stood behind violently criminal acts — assassinations, murders, and armed robbery — against the civilian population, including women and children.

The money that was given out — a total of more than $12,000,000 from 1970 to 2001 — came mostly from Sweden, Germany, and the Netherlands. The grants were largely symbolic and intended for humanitarian work, but they were administered with no controls. Their purpose was to make concrete the solidarity of churches with those who struggled for national freedom and human rights, but critics claimed that the funds were actually released for weapons.

In spite of pressure from the government, most of the churches in South Africa remained members of the World Council. Debates concerning religion and politics, morality and violence, raged in the mass media, especially in Germany and the United Kingdom, countries which had strong ties to South Africa. *Reader's Digest*, with nearly eighty million readers, attacked the ecumenical movement with headlines such as "Karl Marx or Jesus Christ? Which Master Is the World Council of Churches Serving?" and "The Gospel according to Karl Marx — Why Have the Interests of the WCC Strayed So Far Afield from Christianity? Top Secret KGB Files Suggest One Reason." Conservative writers hammered out the message that the ecumenical movement had forsaken its original and purely religious goals and was now guided by Communist interests.[4]

Racism was marked by structural forms maintained for political and economic reasons, and transnational business interests provided local elites with weapons and mercenaries, and therefore the system must be exposed and undermined. One way to do this was to convince transnational companies to cease their investments in South Africa. Churches themselves broke off working with banks that gave loans to the South African government. The WCC made public a list of industries that had large interests in South Africa. European and American churches single-mindedly stimulated public opinion to force withdrawal from South Africa. The campaign for sanctions was successful. As repressive violence increased, with thousands of political prisoners being taken and hundreds of executions being carried out, Western economic powers became reluctant to be identified with the apartheid government, and investments decreased significantly.

Lutheran churches supported the Program to Combat Racism even though the Lutheran teaching concerning the "two kingdoms" often made Lutherans into mere observers politically. The Lutheran World Federation actually went farther than the World Council of Churches. A 1977 statement on "confessional integrity" declared any attempt to unite apartheid with the Christian confession to be impossible. Persons must be able regardless of skin color to celebrate Holy Communion together. The question of race was thus declared to be *status confessionis*, a matter of faith. All Lutheran churches were urgently admonished to reject apartheid unconditionally.[5] Two white member churches, one in South Africa and one in Namibia, refused to take action against apartheid, and their membership in the LWF was suspended. The opposition of the Confessing Church to Nazism in Germany was seen as an example of a Lutheran tradition of active protest. That example was now followed in South Africa.

It took twenty years of armed struggle, isolation, and sanctions before the South African government ceased its war against its own citizens, set Nelson Mandela free, and held democratic elections. The impact of church opinion and moral pressure, within and outside South Africa, is not to be underestimated. After being set free, Mandela traveled immediately to Geneva to express thanks to the World Council of Churches. He also came to the Eighth Assembly of the WCC in Harare in 1998, where he once again gave prominence to the churches' significance:

The [World Council of Churches'] support exemplified in the most concrete way the contribution that religion made to our liberation. From the days when religious bodies took responsibility for the education of the oppressed because it was denied us by our rulers, to support for our liberation struggle, whenever the noble ideals and values of religion have been joined with practical action to realize them, it has strengthened us and at the same time nurtured those ideals within the liberation movement.[6]

Can Violence Be Justified?

The Program to Combat Racism demonstrated the ecumenical movement's dilemma. Reality forced a choice between an unjust peace and armed struggle. It was, however, no simple thing to hold together tension-filled churches and at the same time take a prophetic and extremely controversial stance in the societies of the world. M. M. Thomas put the question well:

> How can we be at once messengers of peace in a world of strife, and messengers of strife in a world of false peace: that is without breaking the fellowship into messengers of peace and messengers of strife, and without breaking the structure of the Council into instruments of charity and reconciliation on the one hand and instruments of provocation and of conflict for the sake of justice on the other?[7]

What made the program so controversial was the fact that the churches accepted the use of violence and also included the right to rebellion within the traditional "just war theory." The WCC was formed in the shadow of two world wars, and questions about the legitimacy of violence were persistently being raised. As a matter of principle, radically pacifist Christians, such as Quakers and Mennonites, constantly held this issue before the established churches. Delegates to the Amsterdam assembly in 1948, who bore World War II fresh in their minds, made a simple and clear statement that "war as a method of settling disputes is incompatible with the teaching and example of our Lord Jesus Christ. The part which war plays in our present international life is a sin against God and a degradation of man."[8] All were in agreement that everything about war stands in opposition to Jesus' teaching and example, but the question still could not be evaded as to whether war was an inevitable final resort in the defense of human rights and national freedom.

There are other forms of violence and other ways to encounter violence. The term *structural violence* comes up often in analyses of how social and economic systems prevent blacks, the poor, and especially women from full participation in the life of societies. The civil rights movement in the United States broke down segregation and forced new legislation by nonviolent means. Latin American liberation theology taught the poor to study and analyze their situation in the light of the gospel in order to demand their rights by action, but without violence. At a 1974 conference held in Berlin on "Sexism in the Seventies," the WCC put discrimination against women on a par with racism as it initiated a lengthy but steady campaign for the full participation of women in church and society.[9]

As long as structural (or "systemic") violence was countered with peaceful methods, all was well and good. But to grant financial backing to armed liberation movements was something else. It meant that member churches that had made no formal decision were implicated in armed insurrection and supported revolution. This was so provocative that some member churches that could not be accused of racism, the Salvation Army for example, decided to leave the World Council of Churches.

The Churches Oppose Nuclear Weapons

While all this was going on, the superpowers continued the armaments race. The threat of an all-out atomic war cast its shadow over the world. Deep concern was expressed at the Uppsala assembly, but in 1983, when new warheads were replacing the old and there was talk of "star wars," the WCC unambiguously took a stand in opposition to atomic weapons. Yet militarism spread. Was the just war theory still applicable after Hiroshima? Was not "deterrence" itself also a way for the superpowers to prevent necessary social and economic changes? Was it reasonable to put so much money into armaments when half the world was starving? Instead of getting answers, the churches were criticized for their double moral standard and inconsistency since they accepted violence "from below," but were opposed to national military buildups.

In 1983, when world peace was seen to be most threatened, the Nordic churches, at the initiative of Archbishop Olof Sundby of Sweden and with the support of the Swedish government, invited both sides of this debate to a Life and Peace Conference in Uppsala.[10] The discussions primarily concerned atomic weapon buildups in a global context. Thanks to the work of Ambassador Olle Dahlén, who was chair of the Commission of the Churches on International Affairs, a unit of the WCC, church leaders, peace researchers, and politicians from sixty countries gathered. The conference was a complicated enterprise which required considerable diplomatic skill. It dealt with politically sensitive questions, and up to its conclusion it was uncertain if it would produce any substantial results. In the last hour the delegates came to a compromise:

> Most of us believe that from the Christian standpoint reliance upon the threat and possible use of nuclear weapons is unacceptable as a way of avoiding war. Some are willing to tolerate nuclear deterrence only as a temporary measure in the absence of alternatives. To most of us, however, the possession of nuclear weapons is inconsistent with our faith in God, our concept of creation and with our membership in Christ's universal body. Nuclear deterrence is essentially dehumanizing, it increases fear and hatred, and entrenches confrontation between "the enemy and us." Most of us therefore believe that the existence of these weapons contradicts the will of God. For all of us obedience to that will demands a resolute effort within a specified time-limit for their total elimination.[11]

Some months later the Vancouver assembly of the World Council of Churches took the same position:

> We believe that the time has come when the churches must unequivocally declare that the production and deployment as well as the use of nuclear weapons are a crime against humanity and that such activities must be condemned on ethical and theological grounds.[12]

The churches held fast to their view that war can be justified only if it involves the defense of national independence and is carried out with conventional weapons. Waiting for binding international agreements on disarmament, some churches, however — for example, Lutheran churches in the U.S. — supported a policy of deterrence by atomic weapons. Radical pacifists in the "peace churches" had a hard time finding support for their views. In the Third World the question of atomic weapons was often seen as a Western problem; for the poor, justice was more of a concern than disarmament.

Ecology Is Placed on the Agenda

The WCC's Department for Church and Society, which stood behind the Geneva conference of 1966 and prepared the ground for a new orientation in ecumenical social ethics, continued its work on questions of human survival. After the 1972 United Nations Conference on the Human Environment, held in Stockholm, and the report of the Club of Rome on "Limits to Growth," questions regarding social and economic development took on new dimensions.[13] Development was to be "sustainable" and it must not ruin the earth. The far-sighted Syrian Orthodox theologian Paulus Mar Gregorius from India had raised the issue in Geneva already in 1966, but environmental and ecological issues did not take hold in the WCC until its fifth assembly, held in Nairobi in 1975. At that event the Australian biologist and process theologian Charles Birch gave a lecture which led to a comprehensive discussion concerning the environment, sustainable development, and climate change. The global society must be so organized that both humans and animals are enabled to live balanced lives. This cannot happen unless the lifestyle of human beings is adapted to the whole environment, resources redistributed, the ecological balance restored, and all realize that they are a part of a greater, albeit extremely vulnerable, ecological system.[14]

Sustainability became a principal but politically loaded concern. Should the wealthy countries take greater responsibility, diminish their use of limited resources, and safeguard the environment, or should those in poverty once again pay the price by having brakes put on their industrial and economic development? Was it possible to unite economic growth with sustainable development? Was not "sustainable community" a better criterion than "development" for the life-affirming and moral alternative culture that some ecumenical visionaries dreamt of?

In seminars on gene technology, energy, militarism, and the environment, researchers and church leaders encountered one another. At a 1979 conference in Cambridge, Massachusetts, on "Faith, Science, and the Future," half the participants were physicists and other natural scientists, while the rest were theologians, sociologists, politicians, and leaders of industry. The nuclear reactor had just broken down on Three Mile Island in Pennsylvania, and that fact put nuclear energy at the center of the debate. The problem was not only one of safety and the storage of waste; in addition, high technology in general tends to increase injustice rather than foster what is good for all. Nuclear power was a concrete example of the problem, since the rich countries were determined to prevent developing lands from building nuclear plants on the grounds of risks to safety in the enrichment of uranium. The churches could not prescribe ethical standards for either research or international relations, but they hoped to minimize the conflict between different interests through insightful dialogue.[15]

Superficially, it appeared that the Protestant and Roman Catholic churches were not much different in respect to social questions. There were similarities in their views on human rights, economic development, and technological and social change, and it was Roman Catholics who first spoke of God's love for the poor and of the church as a sign and sacrament for the world. Rome's membership in the WCC had been put on ice, but cooperation around doctrinal questions and mission was well established when a Joint Committee for Society, Development, and Peace (SODEPAX) was formed in 1968. Its work covered the field from research and education to economy and disarmament. This work was, indeed, promising, but when the curia in Rome turned in a more conservative direction and expressed its opposition to liberation theology, basic differences in theology and ecclesiology became apparent. The Vatican and the World Council were not comparable as organizations and they represented different cultures. Rome was accustomed to taking its time and speaking carefully and in general terms, while in Geneva it was normal to address specific questions quickly with the claim of being prophetic. In Rome, SODEPAX was understood as being all too independent; in Geneva, it was seen as having its hands tied. This contributed to the conclusion of this cooperation in 1980.[16]

Bureaucrats Set Theology to the Side

Experts and specialists began to have less influence in the World Council of Churches. They were criticized for being tools of the industrialized lands and for a lack of activism. This was also true for academic theologians who had previously played such an important role. Contact between natural science and theology, which had been the special gift of Paul Abrecht to the World Council, diminished at the time when the churches from the Third World began to determine the agenda. It was also a consequence of the "quota system" that began to be followed in 1971. When young people and women received places in all deliberative organs, the number of ecclesiastical figures and academic theologians — and even of laypersons who represented research, law, and politics — was diminished. As a result, prominent church leaders often lost interest. The WCC became, like many other ecumenical organizations, more of an interchurch bureaucracy than a theological forum. Those who were employed took every opportunity to set their mark on the programs.

Many were distressed at this development. They were of the view that the World Council had lost both competence and trustworthiness; it no longer did justice toward the complexity of problems, toward alternative solutions, and toward the many existing forms of social thought. Instead, an ideologically determined "orthopraxy" excluded divergent interpretations. Whether concerning globalization or the environment, social ethical questions in reality required better informed and more nuanced actions. Indeed, it was a near disaster that the ecumenical movement came to be seen as a political instrument. This stood in sharp contrast to the conviction that although the church could not change the world, it could, thanks to its long experience and broad anchorage, be heard and through its own renewal be a convincing sign of God's future.

The Churches' Responsibility for a Just Social and Economic Development

After the Uppsala assembly, the churches' strategy regarding social questions was marked, despite all the talk of revolution, by trust in gradual social and economic development. Such trust was in fact characteristic of all ecumenical organizations. The World Council of Churches, the Lutheran World Federation, and Caritas International channeled steadily increasing contributions to various development projects and to the relief of natural catastrophes. This led to an intense discussion regarding "root causes" of poverty, sustainable development, public mobilization, and the contributions of women to social change. This discussion stretched from an idealistic faith in foreign aid in the 1960s to a confrontation with neoliberal overconfidence in growth and free markets in the 1990s. No one minced words in criticizing this; witness the statement of the WCC's seventh assembly, held in Canberra in 1991:

> Growth for growth's sake . . . is the strategy of the cancer cell. . . . Growth for growth's sake is increase in size without control, without limit, in disregard for the system that sustains it. It ultimately results in degradation and death. Development, on the other hand — like the strategy of the embryo — is getting the right things in the right places in the right amounts at the right times with the right relationships. Development, while supported both by growth and *reduction* of its parts, results in a self-sustaining whole.[17]

The churches desired to go from a welfare state to a welfare world by having nations reciprocally share resources with each other, giving the poor the possibility of providing for themselves, for example, through microcredit. But development carried with it unavoidable conflicts, since it also demanded major changes in international structures and power relationships. Injustice had long camouflaged itself with "law and order." When people stood up to demand their rights, it was difficult to steer clear of unrest.[18]

In 1970, the World Council of Churches instituted a special Commission on the Churches' Participation in Development (CCPD).[19] Alongside the Program to Combat Racism, it became the most visible sign of the turn of the tide that took place at the Uppsala assembly. The commission undertook a heavily ideological analysis of the causes of poverty that allowed virtually no other interpretations. All international relief and diaconal work was to be judged by the question of its effects on long-range changes in the situation of the poor. Recipients were to have genuine influence and all aid was to be guided by a comprehensive social view. Questions were sharpened as to whether massive contributions of foreign aid for social and technological development and international cooperation could really help the poor as long as the global economic system simultaneously increased the power of those who were already powerful. A possible solution was to be found in Latin American theories regarding how poor nations could be set free from the exploitation and dominance of the industrialized ones, and how impoverished people could be liberated from profiteers.

Paulo Freire's book *Pedagogy of the Oppressed* became a kind of manual in this effort.[20] Freire was driven by a passion that the poor had a right both to their own story and to naming their own world. They must be made conscious of this right and encouraged to take things into their own hands. *Conscientization* became a word on everyone's lips. Freire, who came to Geneva as a political refugee from Brazil, became the WCC's most well known staff person; he quietly guarded against development being corrupted into a new form of oppression.

God Loves the Poor

Talking of God's "preferential option for the poor" evokes a particular image of God, a key to reading the Bible, and a chosen perspective on history contained in the idea that God is partisan and takes sides. Jesus was poor, born of simple parents, had his life threatened by a dictator, and was a refugee in a foreign land. He found his home on the edges of society, identified himself with prostitutes and rejects, pleaded the cause of children and women, and gave new value to those whom he encountered — before he himself became destitute and was tortured and executed.

It was easy for the poor in slums to identify with such a savior, and it was tempting for theologians to undertake an analysis of society which agreed with such an interpretation of Scripture. This narrative about Jesus became an instrument for the changing of social and political history. Liberation theology desired to "decolonize" institutional Christianity and set the church free to become the church of the poor. This sociologically determined ecclesiology ultimately was not acceptable to traditional Roman Catholic views, but it attracted many Protestants.

Even though the WCC never took an official position in favor of either the predominantly Latin American analysis of social and economic dependency or liberation theology's contextual and social interpretation of the content of salvation, the ecumenical movement nevertheless became permeated by these views. Theologians who read history from the "underside," in order to see the world and the church with the eyes of women and the poor, set their stamp on nearly all ecumenical debate. Although there were no signs that Orthodox and traditional Protestant member churches would give up on the ecumenical movement, there was an obvious risk of a polarization that could lead the large Western churches to lose interest in the face of institutional "liberation ecumenism." Social ethics based on traditional church teaching and confession and this contextual analysis of society went in such opposite directions that it was difficult to hold the ecumenical movement together. Christocentric universalism as described above in Chapter 2 was more and more called into question both by the reality of religious pluralism and by the fact that it did not reflect the depth of the alienation of the poor. It was often held that one universal history of salvation could not do justice to the experience of the many cultures and nations. A church united was no automatic solution to problems of sexism, racism, and exploitation. The idea of a "responsible society" could not be expanded to include the new challenges. Nor, in the end, did liberation theology itself have much to say about the ambiguity of technology or the global threats to the environment.

Justice and Peace: "An Imperative for Our Time"

Fifteen years after the Uppsala assembly it seemed absolutely necessary to channel together the different streams — those which came from church tradition and those that came from the experiences of the poor and of women. At the 1983 sixth assembly of the World Council of Churches in Vancouver the social ethical program was concentrated into one theme. This became, practically speaking, the end of the "realistic" social ethics that went back to the 1930s but which had begun to give way already at the Geneva conference of 1966.

When the Vancouver assembly took place, the World Council was at its strongest. It had, in spite of all ideological and ecclesiological antagonisms, nearly undivided support from the large American and European churches and also considerable trustworthiness in Africa, not least thanks to the Program to Combat Racism. It was permeated with contextual theology from Asia and Latin America. The Orthodox churches participated on their own terms, and work with the Roman

Catholic Church continued in spite of the crisis surrounding SODEPAX. The Commission of the Churches on International Affairs (CCIA), which had been established in 1947 as an official link to the United Nations and other international organizations, gained high respect for its integrity, even though its early forms of quiet and professional diplomacy had given way to more controversial and confrontational positions taken in favor of the Third World.[21] Critics, however, argued that the CCIA thus sacrificed its competence and influence even though it had mediated peace in southern Sudan, cooperated in the process that led to the Helsinki Accords of 1975 (the Final Act of the Conference on Security and Cooperation in Europe), and had spoken with nuance and insight on a host of international questions.

There were tensions within — between the different programs of the World Council, between the institutions and the movement, and between North and South — but these tensions were manageable. The programs needed better coordination, and the fellowship had to be strengthened. Justice and peace (in that order) overshadowed questions regarding unity and mission, and the ecumenical goal was summed up as *Justice, Peace, and the Integrity of Creation* (JPIC).[22] Together with the Roman Catholic Church, various peoples' movements, and nongovernmental organizations, the member churches of the WCC embarked on a "conciliar process" to deepen a comprehensive understanding of the world and to establish a mutual "covenant" between the churches which would set justice, peace, and the inviolability of creation as first priorities. The background to this was the dismal picture presented by the world, with its arms race, unjust orders, and risk of total self-annihilation. Christians must stand up for their faith and do what they can to avoid disaster. Peace and justice was not just one alternative among others but an "imperative for our time."

The churches should not merely translate the values of God's reign in different social contexts; they themselves should live the gospel and thereby demonstrate an alternative way of structuring society. To confess Jesus Christ as the life of the world was to choose sides against all the powers of death. There was to be no distinction between the spiritual and the worldly. It was not enough to speak of Christian ethics — the churches must practice those ethics by actively encountering forces of dehumanization. The incipient globalization of financial markets, production of goods, and mass media was looked upon as one of many destructive forces. In Europe, where the conciliar process had its beginning in the months before the fall of the Berlin Wall,[23] the anthropocentric way of looking at things, which characterized the WCC after the 1968 assembly, was, however, questioned from an unexpected direction. "Mother Earth" deserved integrity and her own rights. Humans were, biologically, one among many created entities and must act according to ecological conditions. Creation became humanity's dialogue partner.

The European churches which gathered in Basel in the spring of 1989 around the theme "Peace with Justice for the Whole Creation" asserted that peace, justice, and the preservation of the natural environment were three indistinguishable challenges. For the first time in nearly a thousand years, the Orthodox, Roman Catholic, and Protestant churches of Europe met together and made common cause. Ten thousand participants expressed their commitment to building a responsible Europe that was open to the world. The time, however, was not ripe for the binding ecumenical council of which many delegates dreamed. And a "covenant" between churches proved more problematic than expected. The word itself not only referred to God's covenant with humanity, but it had taken on a particular meaning in the Calvinist tradition. Debate about what was actually involved in "covenanting" caused the vision from the Vancouver assembly nearly to come to a halt. The Roman Catholic Church withdrew from the global process. The planning of a world convention in Seoul, South Korea, in 1990 on "Justice, Peace and the Integrity of Creation" as the culmination of the process proved more difficult than expected.

The Ecumenical Social Ethic Loses Much of Its Credibility

The road to Seoul was bumpy, and what happened was more a liturgical event than a conference of binding commitment. The final document could be read as a moralizing summary of ecumenical positions of the 1980s.[24] Clearly the rubrics of this document were uncontroversial assertions that cost nothing to support although they had a more challenging subtext:

- all exercise of power is accountable to God
- God has an option for the poor
- all races and peoples are of equal value

- male and female are created in the image of God
- truth is at the foundation of a community of free people
- peace comes from Jesus Christ
- God loves all creation
- the earth is the Lord's
- human rights are given by God.

In solidarity with the poor and oppressed, delegates to the Seoul conference signed an agreement that with great seriousness they would work for

- a just economic order and for liberation from foreign debt,
- true security for all nations and peoples,
- a culture that can live in harmony with creation's integrity, and
- the eradication of racism and discrimination.

There was not much new in this apart from an emphasis on nonviolence which some years later became the starting point for the "Decade to Overcome Violence: Churches Seeking Reconciliation" (2001-2010). Those who had hoped for an authentic and theologically motivated decision in favor of the protection of the environment were disappointed. The Seoul conference distinguished itself from earlier meetings in which experts prepared the way for a "realistic" social ethic. Instead, at Seoul Bible studies and personal testimonies gave direction and content to the discussions. There was no breakthrough for an integrated and comprehensive environmental theology or for an ecclesiology determined by social ethics. By the seventh assembly of the WCC in Canberra, 1991, the whole JPIC process had to a great extent been lost. It was doubtful that a universal consensus in matters of social ethics could ever be reached.

The wall dividing East and West had fallen, and the Cold War was over. A deconstruction of political ideals was well under way, and utopian visions were fading away. Without common points of reference, ecumenical social ethics were in disarray. In this situation questions as to the nature of the fellowship shared by churches in the ecumenical movement were sharpened. Could ecclesiology and ethics be united in such a way that what the local church *was* agreed with what it *did*? Could the church become an open and inclusive moral fellowship charged with the task of protecting the varieties of life and cultures?[25]

Everything was open, the way forward unknown. Economic expansion overloaded the environment and globalization created new barriers, even between churches. Social ethics, which for decades had been the strength of the ecumenical movement, had become its weakness. Paul Abrecht explained the situation by asserting that the ecumenical model for a new world order, which had been spoken of so much since the beginning of the 1970s, had been some kind of socialism. The theology of revolution of the 1960s had been transformed into a theology of liberation which led to a struggle against global capitalism. When socialism collapsed in 1989, the churches were totally unprepared. They came to Seoul with a populist ideology which no longer had support or relevance. Ecumenical social ethics found itself in a hopeless situation when, torn from its theological and historic roots, it was forced to acknowledge that revolutionary change of the world's economic and social order was an illusion.[26] But what was the alternative? Charles West, an American social ethicist, asked if the world could be saved by replacing one power structure with another. Does not all power stand under the judgment of God?[27] In a sweeping criticism of the conciliar process's "mantra-like combination of ideas" which could lead "to yet another level of abstraction for purposes of conceptual convenience," thus becoming "a sort of crypto-metaphysical overview designed to make complex reality graspable," Julio de Santa Ana demanded that the ecumenical movement return to humankind's local, concrete, and historical reality.[28] No one could say which way the churches should choose or even if it were any longer possible to formulate a social ethic behind which most people could stand.

It took time for the churches to free themselves from the way of thinking that was at home in the world of the Cold War. That world no longer existed, and now it was the ecumenical movement that had to change. The World Council's assembly in Canberra in 1991 had as its theme "Come, Holy Spirit — Renew the Whole Creation." This was a prayer for guidance in a confused time when the ecumenical movement itself became shaky, and individualistic questions, above all those concerning human sexuality, began to cast shadows over the churches' social responsibility and threatened to devastate the ecumenical fellowship of churches.

CHAPTER 4

The Decolonization of Mission

The old kind of language just could not be used any more.

LESSLIE NEWBIGIN

At New Year's 1973, a world mission conference took place in Bangkok. At the same time, American B-52s were lifting off from a nearby base and flying toward Hanoi loaded with new bombs. It had been nearly a year since President Richard Nixon had visited Mao Zedong in China in order to receive assistance in getting out of the Vietnam War, but that war had continued with greater and greater losses on each side. In South Africa apartheid was the rule, in Latin America the generals were in charge, and in Europe there were still no cracks in the wall.

The 1968 assembly of the World Council of Churches in Uppsala had not succeeded in solving the opposition between those who saw the message of mission as being primarily the forgiveness of sins, reconciliation with God, and eternal life; and those who asserted that mission was just as much to work together with the God of history for justice in the world. Now at Bangkok the theme was "Salvation Today." The conference aimed directly at this theological dichotomy and the polarizing logjam between the individual and social dimensions of the Christian message:

> The salvation which Christ brought, and in which we participate, offers a comprehensive wholeness in this divided life. We understand salvation as newness of life — the unfolding of true humanity

in the fullness of God (Colossians 2:9). It is salvation of the soul and the body, of the individual and society, mankind and "the groaning creation" (Romans 8:19). As evil works both in personal life and in exploitative social structures which humiliate humankind, so God's justice manifests itself both in the justification of the sinner and in social and political justice.

As guilt is both individual and corporate so God's liberating power changes both persons and structures. We have to overcome the dichotomies in our thinking between soul and body, person and society, humankind and creation. Therefore we see the struggles for economic justice, political freedom, and cultural renewal as elements in the total liberation of the world through the mission of God. This liberation is finally fulfilled when "death is swallowed up in victory" (1 Corinthians 15:55).[1]

Criticism of the World Council's Understanding of Mission

A Lutheran scholar of mission from Tübingen, Peter Beyerhaus, who had himself been a missionary in South Africa, was extremely critical of ecumenical developments in general and heavily involved in opposition to the Program to Combat Racism. He endeavored to bring together persons who stood in opposition to the World Council of Churches, conservatives who saw the Council as involved in "horizontal" questions while ignoring Jesus' command to make disciples of all nations. The theological crisis of the mission movement must be taken seriously, he asserted, even though African and Asian church leaders dismissed his agenda as largely irrelevant to the Third World.

Beyerhaus represented evangelical mission organizations whose goal was to reach the "unreached" so that they would be converted, baptized, and live as Christians. There were over two billion such persons in the world, and the task was urgent. To describe salvation as a liberation to a better life on earth was seen by evangelicals as a betrayal of both "classical" missionary endeavor and the original calling of the ecumenical movement. Thus the Lausanne Committee for World Evangelization was formed in 1974 as an alternative to the WCC's Commission on World Mission and Evangelism. The Lausanne movement was originally sponsored by the Billy Graham Evangelistic Association.

These conservative Protestants were not alone in their view that the

World Council represented an all too "this-worldly" interpretation of the gospel. The Holy Synod of the Russian Orthodox Church, led by its patriarch, Pimen, wrote in a sharp letter of August 1973 that the Bangkok world mission conference had had nothing to say concerning either the ultimate goal of salvation, namely, eternal life in God, or Christian morality, which is the presupposition for reaching that goal.[2] This communication led to a number of consultations with the Russian Orthodox Church, which brought about the formation of important and enduring Orthodox contributions to an ecumenical theology of mission.[3]

A great deal had happened since the integration of the International Missionary Council into the World Council of Churches in 1961.[4] A conference on "Mission in Six Continents," held in Mexico City in 1963, had affirmed that the church's task was the same in all places and that the boundary between faith and unbelief went directly through all nations and churches. A respected journal, the *International Review of Missions,* had changed its name in a scarcely noticed but highly symbolic way: an *s* fell away, and *Missions* became *Mission*. Mission was now not only the contribution of Western and Asian missionaries to other lands, but a task shared by all the baptized regardless of where they lived. Mission was the task of the whole church to pass on the whole gospel to the whole of humanity throughout the whole world. Mission was not a thing reserved for specialists, officials, or charismatic Christians. The church *was* mission, through its sacramental life, its public proclamation, and through service, *diakonia,* of every sort.

The debate concerning mission took a new turn when church leaders from Africa, Asia, and Latin America entered seriously into the discussion; this is what happened in Bangkok in 1973. They rejected the Western influence over churches in the Third World, emphasized the need for social change, and argued that salvation was not just righteousness before God and eternal life but also decent living conditions here on earth. Some Africans, with the Kenyan Presbyterian John Gatu in the forefront, urged the Western churches at least temporarily to stop sending missionaries and funds to the Third World. A moratorium would give the Third World churches the opportunity to find their own theological and cultural identities, discern their own missionary vocation, and clothe the gospel in local garments. The call for such a moratorium was attractive even though it was not easily implemented. It did, however, take on meaning insofar as relations of dependency were reconsidered, the number of Western missionaries became smaller, and new forms of cooperation were developed. The "receiving churches" in many cases assumed direct influence over the priorities of the "sending churches." Many churches were invited to "mission in return," which increased mutual reciprocity and equality.

Solidarity with the Poor Becomes Decisive for the Credibility of Mission

At the Uppsala assembly in 1968 the church's mission had been localized at certain pressure points in society: revolutionary movements, universities, industries, large cities, and the suburbs. At such places the "new humanity" was to come forth, and there the churches had the task of making a reality of God's will. Faithfulness to the gospel should be judged by three questions: Does mission contribute to placing the churches on the side of the poor, the abused, and the forgotten? Do Christians have the confidence to show solidarity with the concerns of other people and to use the issues and structures of others as vehicles for change? Does mission help Christians to read the signs of the times and move with history toward the realization of a new humanity?[5]

The WCC Commission on World Mission and Evangelism also affirmed that solidarity with the poor was the decisive criterion for the faithfulness of mission. The world mission conference of 1980, meeting in Melbourne under the theme "Your Kingdom Come," emphasized that the Kingdom belonged to him who was sacrificed "outside the city gate" (Hebrews 13:12), a fact that testified to mission's proper location. The way was to share with the poor in their struggles. The church could not proclaim the reign of God without deep empathy and identification with those who live in spiritual, material, and physical need. It must stand on their side and work to change all political, economic, and cultural structures that deprived them of self-respect and limited their freedom. A church was best equipped "to bring good news to the poor" (Luke 4:18) if it itself was poor. Therefore, a primary responsibility for mission must lay in the hands of churches that are themselves poor. The Western forms of mission, which had arisen in the "awakenings" of the eighteenth and nineteenth centuries and had marched hand-in-hand with colonialism, were exhausted and must be phased out. Evangelization and the expansion of the church was to be a matter for local initiative.

So began a gradual dissolution of old missionary structures. The care of the sick had been a concern for the church ever since apostolic times and had been carried out by individual Christians, cloisters and monasteries, congregations, and diaconal organizations. In Africa, hundreds of mission hospitals were either taken over by local churches or nationalized. The WCC established a Christian Medical Commission in order to help with new structures, increase medical competence, and deepen theological reflection about wholeness and health. Western medicine was not to be the privilege only of the wealthy. The policies of pharmaceutical companies in poor nations must be closely examined. Good experiences with traditional medicine and indigenous health care must be taken seriously. Every Christian community could become a locus for healing. When the HIV/AIDS crisis arose in the 1980s, the World Council, working closely with the World Health Organization, took responsibility to inform people, break down prejudices, coordinate efforts toward alleviation, and gradually work through the difficult ethical and pastoral problems to which the epidemic gave rise. In June 1986, when the crisis was still at an early stage and there was great uncertainty concerning both its origins and its contagion, the WCC held a first consultation aimed at strengthening the church's responsibility to be a healing fellowship. The message to those who were struck by moral panic could not be misunderstood: "AIDS is an illness and must be treated as such. . . . God, who loves all humankind, cares for the health and welfare of all his children and never sends sickness as punishment."[6]

Beyond health and the care of the sick, evangelization and education had been seen, since the days of the early church, to be areas of concern for mission. Schools by the tens of thousands and education in its widest sense had laid the foundation both for the independence of African nations and for the meaningful involvement of women in social development. The schools, however, were mostly shaped to educate students to serve the prevailing social and political systems. Accordingly, the World Council took it upon itself critically to review different pedagogical and ideological attitudes and to advance a view of education which was strongly influenced by Paulo Freire and the Austrian philosopher Ivan Illich.[7] They were proponents of a pedagogy of individual responsibility and social change. At the Council's assembly in Nairobi in 1975, a holistic view of teaching was strongly advocated.[8] The challenge to educate for cultural integration, change, and liberation was met with great enthusiasm. This fervor died down, however, when it became apparent what a gigantic task it was to alter people's attitudes toward education. The network for alternative schooling subsequently thinned out. But the conviction remained that no pedagogy was ideologically neutral and that personal and social liberation required far-sighted and enduring education.

Solidarity with the poor was to be tested in the slums that surrounded large cities such as São Paulo, Bangkok, and Nairobi, and among landless workers in countries like Brazil and the Philippines. In such places groups, often comprised of volunteers who wanted to share the circumstances of the poor in order to help them gain better living conditions, took countless initiatives to lessen alienation, establish human dignity, and assist people in organizing themselves socially and in labor unions. Some of these initiatives were inspired by post–World War II European industrial missions and movements of worker-priests; others had the characteristics of labor and political movements. The World Council formed a network, Urban Rural Mission, in which volunteers shared experiences that sharpened their awareness of the fact that struggles against unbearable working conditions, child prostitution, or the abuse of women were a part of God's mission. Established churches were often hostile to this kind of mission, and those involved frequently came into conflict with the military, police, and multinational corporations. The Urban Rural Mission was often unable to distinguish itself from groups with purely political goals and thus frequently found itself in alliances with various leftist movements. It desired to be the forerunner to the church, which tended to be unwilling to stand up in struggles for land for the landless, the right of workers to organize unions, or the right to a decent home. In some situations Urban Rural Mission found it difficult both to dissociate itself from leftist movements and to maintain any structured form of Christian life and regular worship. The difference between Sunday meetings for tired volunteers with threadbare Bibles on the outskirts of Seoul and the charismatic worship in some of the inner city's packed and shining megachurches could not have been greater. Urban Rural Mission was the 1970s' most radical expression of the ecumenism of solidarity.

It had many inspiring models. Mother Teresa in Calcutta gave new dignity to the dying. Dom Helder Camara in Recife chose the side of the poor in the favelas. Abbé Pierre in Paris organized homeless rag pickers. Metropolitan Irenaeos in Crete built schools for the children of farmers. Brother Roger in Taizé taught thousands of youth to unite action with contemplation. Archbishop Tutu in South Africa ridiculed the white holders of power. Wolf Biermann in East Germany sang protest songs. These were all Christians who expressed their faith through action. When they helped the poor they were called saints; when they spoke of the root causes of poverty they were accused of being communists. Thanks to mass media, they became icons of goodness for the whole world.

A Dialogue between Religions Begins to Take Shape

For the renewal of mission it was crucial to move from one-sided proclamation to mutual dialogue. This was a large step for Christians accustomed to believing that God had revealed himself only in Christ and had given saving faith only to Christ's followers. Other religions were still regarded as futile, human strivings for insight and meaning. Many saw virtually no points of contact between religious faiths; each religion was a unique weaving of its own myths, rituals, and spiritual insights. The nineteenth-century missionary movement, to be sure, brought the world religions into the discourse of academic research, and many Christians approached other religions with admiration, respect, and love, but they could not renounce their conviction that the revelation in Christ was unique. Church fathers of the third century had provided their basic view: "Outside the church there is no salvation." Jesus' own Great Commission (Matthew 28:18-20) was as unequivocal as the statement in the Acts of the Apostles that "[t]here is salvation in no one else, for there is no other name under heaven given among mortals by which we must be saved" (Acts 4:12).

Interreligious dialogue as it is currently understood began to arise toward the end of the 1960s. The Second Vatican Council's Declaration on the Relation of the Church to Non-Christian Religions, *Nostra Aetate,* provided some important theological foundations.[9] The text was concerned primarily with the Jewish people, but it emphasized that God has created all humans in his image and given them their longing for truth and meaning. There is a transcendental consciousness in every person and all religions contain elements of truth. Regardless of confession, all people on earth belong to one humanity. Christians must, therefore, acknowledge that there are elements of truth and spiritual value in all communities of faith and work with them for justice, peace, and freedom without giving up the proclamation of Christ as the way, the truth, and the life.

In the report from the section on mission at the Uppsala assembly in 1968, which evangelicals saw as being all too vague concerning the proclamation of Christ, there was a part which dealt with interreligious dialogue that passed without debate.[10] It made a distinction between proclamation and dialogue, although it also held that dialogue is an element in Christian witness. A first consultation with Muslims, Hindus, Buddhists, and Jews in 1967 had taught participants that dialogue required both openness and seriousness if persons together wished to seek the depths of human existence and work for the good of humanity. The WCC gave an Indian theologian, Stanley Samartha, responsibility for leading a new sub-unit on Dialogues with People of Living Faiths and Ideologies, which was started in 1971. Even though this dialogue was seen as a part of the Christian witness, it was not to be structurally combined with mission and evangelism. This work was begun with the support of other South Asians, including Paulos Mar Gregorios, M. M. Thomas, Russell Chandran, and Lynn A. de Silva. These persons knew from their own experience how important good relations were between the world's religions. Europeans, who at that time seldom shared life with persons of other faiths, found this more difficult to understand. At the World Council Assembly at Nairobi in 1975, for example, Bishop Per Lønning of Norway dismissed interreligious dialogue as a denial of both the missionary task and the ecumenical movement. Christian exclusiveness was placed in opposition to religious pluralism, apologetics to openness, and church ecumenism to wider religious fellowship. The last word, however, went to the Asian theologians who defended the necessity of dialogue on the basis of the church's freedom, credibility, and spiritual maturity.[11]

While the dialogue program was being established in the WCC, a debate concerning the presuppositions and goals of the encounter of world religions continued in the Council's member churches. Even if one admits the value of open contacts between different faith communities, it remains difficult to unite dialogue between religions with the many biblical assertions that give Christianity an exclusive character. A Christian can, in principle, relate to other religions in three different ways. The first is to hold that one's own faith is the only true faith, thus denying that the experiences of others are authentic or that their view of life possesses universal applicability. God's revelation in Christ is unique. The church should proclaim that revelation so that its universal content is realized. One's own religious identity is formed by distinction and separation from that of others, even at the cost of isolation.

The second way of relating is to acknowledge that the spiritual experiences of others can also be genuine and that there are other valid views of life than the Christian view. Humans can express an authentic relation to God in different ways. This, however, does not rule out that one can hold one's own tradition of faith to be true and thus in the end best for all people. Evangelization can be motivated by the faith that ultimately Christ is the valid answer for the aspirations of all religions and that the grace of the gospel is intended for all people. Christianity is a religion of revelation. It would be a betrayal of the Christian faith to give up the conviction that all things will be summed up in Christ. Interreligious dialogue must not relativize truth or water down the command to mission.

The third way of relating is to question whether there is any faith, Christian or otherwise, that could claim universal truth. In postmodernity it has become more and more common that people not only tolerate but actively accept and affirm the faith, prayer, and religious life of others. No God worth the name can be the God of only some persons, and no faith community can claim to possess total knowledge of the way of salvation. Everyone has a right to his or her own image of God. The plurality of religions and religious experiences is not to be seen as a problem but rather as a possibility for the mutual enrichment of one another and for the acquisition of new spiritual insights. No one needs to give up their own convictions, but everyone must be prepared humbly to listen to the experiences of others and to test inherited and ingrained positions. A genuine pluralism can lead to a positive and interactive interpretation of religious multiversity. To wrestle with and to attempt to understand the questions of others presuppose confidence in one's own faith and devotion to a God who is always greater and who transcends all human concepts. Recognizing that genuine encounters with God take place in all communities of faith, people can in their depths together contribute to humanity, peace, and justice. God's Spirit works in surprising ways and at places where one least expects it.[12]

At the Canberra assembly of the World Council in 1991, representatives of Australia's aboriginal people performed some of their indigenous rites. The Korean theologian Chung Hyun Kyung in the Assembly's main lecture, "Come Holy Spirit — Renew the Whole Creation," made reference to Buddhism and called on spirits of the departed who had experienced degradation, suffering, and death.[13] These events received great attention and led to a vigorous debate concerning syncretism. The Orthodox churches began seriously to consider leaving the World Council of Churches.

At the same time, the first Gulf War was sharpening the conflict between the Western world and Islam. Increasing terrorism made interreligious dialogue simultaneously more problematic and more urgent. Within Christian, Jewish, Muslim, Hindu, and Buddhist communities of faith, strong and self-confident "fundamentalist" forces were asserting themselves, with the result that there was considerable talk of an inevitable global clash between irreconcilable civilizations.

After twenty years, interreligious dialogue was acknowledged and began to take shape. "Theology of religions" became a major academic discipline. Many initiatives were taken to bring religions closer to each other, and one interreligious movement after another arose. The insight that one cannot separate religious positions from social and cultural relationships matured — even in religiously blind old Europe. In the encounter of religions it became possible for everyone to reflect on their own identity. Migration, the mass media, and the internet contributed to a perforation of the boundaries between faith communities, and their complexity became apparent. In ancient Christian countries like Ethiopia and France, other religions demanded greater "civil space" and conflicts quickly flared up. In lands like Indonesia, Egypt, and Iraq, conflicts had an obvious religious dimension. In light of this, the WCC took as its task the exercise of a kind of "religious diplomacy" in situations of conflict, urging religious leaders to use their moral authority to preserve order in societies and, where necessary, to prepare the way for political initiatives. The Council's 2006 assembly in Porto Alegre, Brazil, held that interreligious dialogue more than ever before demonstrated that a fundamental task of the WCC was to engage itself in the world, solve conflicts, create peace, and protect both human dignity and the rights of religious minorities.[14]

The Decolonization of Mission

The Lausanne Movement: An Alternative to the World Council of Churches

The World Council of Churches made a clear distinction between mission and evangelism — which had its own commission and a central place in the organization — and interreligious dialogue. In spite of the distinction, there was a split in the international mission movement. The Lausanne Committee for World Evangelization was organized by the conservative evangelical wing of American Christianity and its offshoots in other parts of the world. Its intention was to defend a traditional understanding of mission, which was seen to be biblical and in conformity with the commission given by Christ. The Lausanne movement differed from the World Council in its view of Scripture and its concentration on personal conversion and the forgiveness of sins for Jesus' sake, as well as in its greater concern for church growth rather than for efforts to change the unjust structures of society.

It was the evangelist Billy Graham who in 1960 had gathered conservative evangelical leaders from around the world in order to develop a common strategy for global evangelization.[15] At the same time as he himself pursued one "crusade" after another throughout the world, he also persuaded the World Evangelical Fellowship, which had been founded in 1951 and numbered more than one hundred sixty million evangelical Christians, to stand behind an International Congress on World Evangelization held in Lausanne, Switzerland, in the summer of 1974. At this congress, Donald McGavran, professor at Fuller Theological Seminary in California, had great influence by virtue of his theories concerning church growth. The Anglican John R. Stott, who was so critical of the World Council's Uppsala assembly, represented a more intellectual interpretation of Christianity and was himself not averse to social applications of the gospel. Certain Latin American theologians — René Padilla, Samuel Escobar, and Orlando Costas — conveyed a somewhat positive estimate of liberation theology. It was, however, American perspectives and experiences that left the deepest marks on the Congress and its continuation committee. In the "Lausanne Covenant," which was prepared under the leadership of John Stott and which the delegates signed, is to be found the movement's theological basis.[16] This basis is founded on a view of the Bible as divinely inspired in all its parts, on christocentric universalism, and on a conviction that a new missionary era is approaching. The young churches, largely of the Third World, were expected to play a major role in the evangelization of the world in anticipation that Jesus Christ would soon return to the world "personally and visibly, in power and glory, to consummate his salvation and his judgment."

The Lausanne Committee for World Evangelization desired to offer a clear alternative to the theology of mission associated with the ecumenical movement. Its view of evangelization was built on methods taken from sociological and anthropological research and crafted for communication by mass media. The Lausanne leaders saw themselves as the legitimate heirs of the World Missionary Conference held in Edinburgh in 1910.[17] In their eyes, the World Council of Churches had lost both its goal and its credibility under the influence of secular humanism and Marxist liberation theology. If in Geneva there was talk of social justice and Christian witness as two sides of the same coin, in Lausanne, thirty miles away, there was talk of the conversion of the heart and the salvation of the soul which in the best of cases leads to taking social responsibility:

> To evangelize is to spread the good news that Jesus Christ died for our sins and was raised from the dead according to the Scriptures, and that as the reigning Lord he now offers the forgiveness of sins and the liberating gifts of the Spirit to all who repent and believe.... The results of evangelism include obedience to Christ, incorporation into his Church, and responsible service in the world. (*The Lausanne Covenant* 5)

The Lausanne movement challenged the World Council of Churches more than any other entity during the 1970s. Emilio Castro, who was director of the Commission on World Mission and Evangelism before he succeeded Philip Potter as WCC general secretary in 1985, was known as a stirring preacher who steadily referred to the Bible. He had a deep feeling for the message of the evangelicals and held all doors open for conversation, but he could not relinquish the wider interpretation of the gospel's message, which he had appropriated from his native Latin America.[18] The criticisms of the Lausanne movement found a certain receptivity among the Orthodox churches; in Africa, Asia, and Latin America evangelical churches grew considerably. The World Council had no other choice than carefully to adapt to a more conservative theology of mission, taking every opportunity to play down conflicts. The text on mission and evangelism which in 1982 summarized the Council's work on the theology of mission since the 1968 assembly, is introduced by a very explicit statement concerning the individual person's right to hear the gospel and its call to conversion from sin to a life for others, but it then lays emphasis on bearing the good news to the poor "in Christ's way."[19]

The Gospel Must Be Translated in Local Contexts

In spite of the fact that the ecumenical movement early on was aware that the gospel must be clothed in the garbs of culture and interpreted in contextual terms, it was, paradoxically, the Lausanne movement that first began seriously to work with questions concerning the gospel and culture. Adaptation to local customs and traditions, i.e., inculturation, had taken on a new actuality because of both Vatican II and the cultural and religious renaissance that followed decolonization. To translate the gospel into local terms was seen to be requisite for its advancement, but the gap between a ready-packaged gospel and syncretism was narrow. The Lausanne Committee initiated comprehensive work on this set of problems, utilizing tools of anthropology and sociology. This resulted in more concerted ventures and a more effective evangelism in different parts of the world. At the same time, however, there remained a startling lack of awareness of how completely the entire evangelical movement was colored by American culture.

Several years later, in 1983, when it adopted "Gospel and Culture" as a programmatic theme, the World Council of Churches did not follow the same instrumental view of inculturation or contextualization. Its approach was not to adapt in order to reach "the unreached" or simply to have missionaries settle down in local conditions; rather, local Christian communities should feel free to use their own stories, music, and symbolic worlds as trustworthy signs of Christ's presence in their cultures. It was important to defend cultural diversity, preserve common memories, and insure the right to identity and dignity. Under the pressure of globalized media, mass tourism, and standardized patterns of consumerism, a general leveling out of cultural differences was occurring. Therefore, a strengthening of religious and cultural diversities became necessary.

It was seen as obvious that the church of Christ must include women and men of different skin colors, ethnic origins, sexual orientations, and cultural backgrounds. Varieties of these sorts were given by God in creation and must also characterize the church as the body of Christ. The principle of diversity had often been violated, as in Germany by Nazism or in South Africa by apartheid. The ecumenical movement held fast to the principle that authentic unity was something totally different than uniformity.

Unity is to be built upon the reconciling grace which breaks down every barrier of race, color, cast, tribe, sex, class, or nationality without destroying diversity. Unity is to be expressed in tension between universality and contextuality. When globalization levels out cultural differences, it is the church's responsibility to defend the riches of diversity, but that must not happen at the cost of the common treasure of faith, *depositum fidei*. A more positive view of the church's diversity requires "the reconfiguration of our theological basis, our liturgical expression and our institutional expression."[20]

Old Western attitudes toward mission have survived in the Lausanne movement, whose strategies have shown themselves to be successful. While many member churches of the World Council more or less discarded their traditional mission work in favor of diaconal programs, many evangelical and charismatic churches, largely from the United States and South Korea, sent thousands of missionaries to nearly all countries to establish new congregations.

The centennial of the Edinburgh World Missionary Conference took place in 2010. Roman Catholics, Pentecostals, and evangelicals participated in planning the centennial event. This did not, however, prevent the Lausanne Committee from holding its own conference on the future of missions in Cape Town, South Africa, in the same year. The confrontation between the World Council of Churches and the Lausanne movement has calmed down, but the two ways of describing and realizing the church's mission to the world live on.

CHAPTER 5

Unity in Diversity

No church can be church in the full meaning of the word apart from the other churches.

KONRAD RAISER

The Pacific Ocean surged toward its high shores as the World Council of Churches held its sixth assembly in Vancouver in 1983. The theme of the assembly was "Jesus Christ — the Life of the World." A native arbor was set aside on the campus of the University of British Columbia, and nearby a sacred flame burned for the duration of the assembly, an invitation to engagement and reconciliation with Canada's indigenous cultures. Not far from there, worship was held in a multicolored tent that was topped by fluttering banners. Hymns, prayers, and symbols borrowed from different traditions were woven together into a rich liturgy. Diversity made itself apparent within a deep experience of togetherness. Worship of this sort was something new. At previous assemblies, worship was always celebrated according to the established order of one or another particular church. Now a transconfessional congregation appeared, an anticipation of the unity of the church. This worship made a deep impression on the delegates. As pilgrims at a temporary resting-place, they sensed the fragrance of heaven and glimpsed their ultimate goal.

In the tent the archbishop of Canterbury presided at the Eucharist, assisted by female and male clergy from different churches. Many thousands of worshipers brought the world to God in their prayers. Orthodox and Roman Catholic Christians, who were unable to receive the Holy Communion, participated in the readings and in the kiss of peace. The doors of heaven were ajar to the white-clad hosts from all peoples, tribes, nations, and tongues standing before the throne and the Lamb. The liturgy was an echo from the time of the undivided church. It confirmed that there is much more that unites the churches than there is that divides them. Participants shared a eucharistic vision: all of Christianity should with thanksgiving bear humanity and all creation to God to receive reconciliation and new life from the death and resurrection of Christ:

> Christ — the life of the world — unites heaven and earth, God and world, spiritual and secular. His body and blood, given us in the elements of bread and wine, integrate liturgy and diaconate, proclamation and acts of healing.... Our eucharistic vision thus encompasses the whole reality of Christian worship, life and witness, and tends — when truly discovered — to shed new light on Christian unity in its full richness of diversity. It also sharpens the pain of our present division at the table of the Lord; but in bringing forth the organic unity of Christian commitment and of its unique source in the incarnate self-sacrifice of Christ, the *eucharistic vision* provides us with new and inspiring guidance on our journey towards a full and credible realization of our given unity.[1]

Unity Rooted in the Mystery of Faith Is a Sign for the World

The Second Vatican Council and the Uppsala assembly each described the church as a sign and sacrament for the world. Many in ecumenical circles have spoken — in a manner some consider pretentious — of the church as a "prophetic" sign. In the middle of the world's shrinking boundaries, antagonisms, and conflicts, the church lives as a eucharistic fellowship of extremely diverse people who through baptism are united with Christ and each other and are thus a sign of the unity of humanity.

Fellowship or, rather, communion *(koinonia, communio)* is the key ecclesiological concept. Since this notion, to be sure, risks being restricted by dogmatic qualifications or churchly structures, its inner dynamic must constantly be recaptured in human communities reflecting the creative, loving, and unchanging relations of the triune God, Father, Son, and Spirit. No verbal translation does justice to the content of *koinonia*. The term refers to a fellowship that is rooted in the perfect unity of God. It is more sacramental than sociological; it unites faith and ethics, and it encourages diversity both in ecclesial structure and worship. With God's *koinonia* as the source and model for unity, there is a potential for ecumenical progress, since unity is thus anchored in the deepest level of the mystery of faith without requiring uniformity. The churches live in a real, though imperfect, communion. The ecumenical calling is to realize, deepen, and make visible a *unity* which remains always and completely a gift of God.

In the churches of both East and West people have for ages spoken of unity with God and each other as *koinonia*. This expresses both an understanding of the church which Protestants do not always easily grasp and a dynamic theology which does not quickly lend itself to scholasticism or institutionalism. Influential theologians like the Roman Catholic Henri de Lubac, the Anglican Rowan Williams, and the Orthodox John Zizioulas have taught the ecumenical movement that the Eucharist "makes the church." In the celebration of the Eucharist, *koinonia* with God — through the ages and in the present — becomes visible.

The Apostle Paul writes, "The cup of blessing that we bless, is it not a sharing in the blood of Christ? The bread that we break, is it not a sharing in the body of Christ? Because there is one bread, we who are many are one body, for we all partake of the one bread" (1 Corinthians 10:16-17). This is an assurance that the "many" become one body as they share the same cup and break the same bread. A congregation at worship is a gathering of "the dispersed children of God." They are made into one fellowship, even into "one body" (John 11:52).

When Paul writes of baptism he develops what he means by "many": "As many of you as were baptized into Christ have clothed yourselves with Christ. There is no longer slave or free, there is no longer male and female; for all of you are one in Christ Jesus" (Galatians 3:27-28). "Many" is thus not a numerical entity; it refers rather to the community's actual and observable cultural and social diversity. If a congregation were to strive for uniformity by excluding those who are different by culture, gender, sexual orientation, or social status, its basis for unity and catholicity would be something other than Christ. That all become "one" (actually, "one person") in Christ does not depend on their empathy for each other, their solidarity, or even their common understanding of faith; it depends solely on their sharing the bread which is Christ's sacramental body. When "many" break bread together, their union with Christ through baptism is realized (1 Corinthians 12:13). The Holy Spirit brings together differing people, and their gifts and abilities are transformed for the building up of the community. The Eucharist anticipates the reign of God and is celebrated openly as a sign for humanity. *Koinonia* is made manifest in the midst of a shattered world. The world's brokenness is there exposed and it is taken into the death and resurrection of Christ for reconciliation and restoration.[2]

Unity takes shape in the Eucharist. This starts not with the many who are united, but rather with the One who in himself unites the many. Ecumenism does not deny or neutralize differences. Rather, it acknowledges and celebrates the rich variety that unity enfolds. Ecumenism does not intend to bring about unity by human means; it means, rather, that the unity already existing in Christ is being uncovered and made visible. Every local congregation belongs to the universal church, but that is not primarily a matter of organization or of active relations. It is first of all a matter of the hidden unity with each other in Christ becoming visible to ourselves and the world in the Eucharist. A congregation is not merely a fragment of the universal church, and the universal church is more than the sum of all local congregations. The one, holy, catholic, and apostolic church comes into sight in its sacramental fullness in every place where the Spirit unites the living and the dead who through baptism are grafted into the body of Christ.

When Paul develops his picture of the church as one body (1 Corinthians 12), he emphasizes both the body's wholeness and the different and separate functions of its parts. If the whole body were an eye, what would happen to hearing? Differences are necessary, but all parts of the body are mutually dependent on one another. The eye cannot say that it has no need of the hand. The individual parts must complement each other if the whole body is to live.

In the same way, the church is simultaneously a universal and local fellowship of individual communities which are dependent on each other for their lives. It is hardly noteworthy when a kind of unity arises between humans who think and act in similar ways and have common interests. The world is full of such groups. But the church is something else. Every congregation points toward the reign of God not on the basis of similar points of view, common moral outlooks, doctrinal agreements, or absence of conflicts. On the contrary, it points toward the reign of God by the unbreakable communion between persons of differing backgrounds, views, and lifestyles, who through baptism belong to Christ and in the Eucharist make that membership visible. They do not need either to agree or act in the same way in order to be one. But they must together celebrate the memory of how God liberated his people from slavery and estrangement and thus share in the foretaste of the future which rests on God's promises.

Eucharistic Sharing: An Unattained Vision

The eucharistic vision emphasized at the Vancouver assembly in 1983 disappeared even before it reached the churches. Roman Catholic and Orthodox Churches were (and continue to be) unable to open their communion tables to all the baptized until common understandings of faith, ordination, and papal primacy are reached. As the inspiring vision which integrates the various dimensions of the ecumenical movement began to fade, many lost the belief that a visible unity between the churches is really possible. The ecumenical high summer was over; autumn was already on the way.

The possibility of celebrating the Eucharist together remains the central ecumenical question and the one which concerns people in the pew the most. Orthodox and Roman Catholics look upon the Eucharist as the culmination of unity in faith, doctrine, and confession, and thus they reject other Christians or apply extremely restrictive rules for participation in the Eucharist. Most churches of the Reformation invite all baptized persons to the sacrament since it is the Lord's table, and a common Eucharist is seen to be a way to deepen the unity of the church. Thousands of Christians break the churches' rules every week, but there is no sign that the churches themselves are close to changing those rules. Since the Eucharist both theologically and practically is the place where the unity in Christ of "the many" becomes visible, the divided communion table is a huge scandal that stands in brutal opposition both to Jesus' prayer and the basic motivation of the ecumenical movement.

Baptism, Eucharist and Ministry

According to the WCC Commission on Faith and Order, "unity" must have the following characteristics: a common understanding of the apostolic faith and a desire for common confession of that faith; a mutual acceptance of each other's baptism, Eucharist, and ministry so that worship can be celebrated together without reservation; and forms for joint decision-making and authoritative education in the faith. Churches still have a long way to go, but it appeared in the early 1980s that a few of these conditions were close to being realized. Faith and Order, in which both Roman Catholic and Orthodox theologians join with those of other traditions, after many years of work approved the groundbreaking text *Baptism, Eucharist and Ministry* (BEM).[3] This document, adopted in Lima, Peru, in 1982, continues to be widely regarded as the most significant ecumenical step in decades. The text has been translated into more than forty languages, spread throughout the world, and discussed by nearly all church bodies. Simultaneously the "Lima Liturgy," subsequently used at the Vancouver assembly of the World Council, was developed. The BEM process continued for a number of years with responses from churches, theological studies, research, and worship. It prompted theological and liturgical developments in many churches and laid the groundwork for innumerable dialogues between churches.[4] In some churches the reception of *Baptism, Eucharist and Ministry* was euphoric, recalling the great advances of the Second Vatican Council.

In contrast to conciliar texts, BEM was a "convergence text," open to supplement and correction. *Convergence* is a dynamic and optimistic term which suggests an ongoing movement in which the partners come near to each other, yet without having reached their goal. The text did not express complete agreement between the churches and gave no definitive answers to longstanding church controversies. It was not the result of negotiation on actual dogmatic differences; it rather emphasized the churches' common heritage from the early church. The text was carefully framed and, like conciliar texts, heavily dependent on contemporary patristic research, which has increased our knowledge of the early church's theological and sacramental life as well as its first steps in forming tradition.

For the sake of unity the churches must simultaneously be re-rooted, renewed and updated *(aggiornamento)*. Ecumenism involves simultaneously holding fast to the church's tradition, which stretches back to the earliest church, and answering contemporary challenges. The quest for consensus in respect to baptism, Eucharist, and ministry is an example of the former even as controversies which have arisen in history are boldly faced. By looking back to the early church, common understandings became more possible than previously anticipated. Orthodox and Baptists, Catholics and Lutherans, Anglicans and Pentecostals recognized each other in the lives of the first Christian communities and consequently were able to reflect together on the faith of the early church.

When *Baptism, Eucharist and Ministry* was forwarded to the churches of the world for reactions, the early euphoria had already begun to fade. A number of critical questions were raised, but for the most part the responses were positive. Some churches from the more radical wing of the Reformation tradition thought that too much "sacramentalism" had been smuggled into the text. Others could not agree to its view on ordination. The chapter on the Eucharist received the least criticism. The eucharistic awakening which touched so many churches during the second half of the twentieth century had brought with it a new understanding of the central place of the holy mysteries in the life of the church, but separation at the Lord's table, a great concern since the time of the apostles (1 Corinthians 11), remained. That the whole people of God could not together participate in the sacrament of the altar persisted as the ecumenical movement's most painful deficit.

Sociological and Theological Views of the Church

The starting point for theological reflection on ecclesiology is the assertion of the Nicene Creed that the church is *one* in the same way that it is *holy, catholic,* and *apostolic*. This unity — like the church's holiness, catholicity, and apostolicity — must constantly be recaptured and made visible. God's self-revelation in Christ has universal scope and decisive meaning for all humanity. Christ is the Redeemer and Lord not only of Christians, but of all.

Yet many in the ecumenical movement would question such claims. Can one truth really apply to all? Is not the church as we know it merely one of many equally acceptable communities of faith? Does not love imply that there must be space for different and even contradictory expressions of faith? Is not any claim regarding the unity of the church on specific terms yet another form of oppression? The defense of the uniqueness of God's revelation in Christ and the assertion that there is but one way to salvation are open to accusations of conservatism, Eurocentrism, even fundamentalism. But Faith and Order has in principle held fast to its calling to seek the visible unity of the whole church and to its task of clearing away the theological barriers to such unity. Faith and Order does not accept any separation between truth and love.

There always has been a tension between the theological and social programs of the ecumenical movement and a tendency to distance them from one another. In spite of the fact that it has undertaken an experience-based project on "The Community of Women and Men in the Church"[5] as well as a broadly based study of the relationship between the unity of the church and the unity of humankind,[6] Faith and Order has suffered a certain marginalization in the WCC. In the 1970s its theological work was seen as irrelevant in a world in need of revolutionary social change. Since then it has been criticized for not taking seriously either the social dimension or the contextuality of the life and teachings of the church. Even though many church bodies have expressed strong support for the work of Faith and Order, they have contributed very little to the financial well-being of that work. The largest portion of their support for the ecumenical organizations has been earmarked for social causes.

This tension has ultimately boiled down to a conflict between a more theological and a more sociological understanding of the church and its unity. Sociologically seen, the disunity of the church is a consequence and reflection of the unjust ordering of the world with its sharp divisions between rich and poor, races, cultures, and peoples. Work for the visible unity of the church must, accordingly, begin with joint efforts for a just world and contributions to the reconciliation and renewal of the whole human community. Seen from a more traditional theological perspective, however, church divisions primarily reflect differences of doctrine, sacraments, and ministry. Unity as an integral mark of the church has its own integrity and must be attained in order for the church to be church in accordance with its historic confessions of faith. Therefore the dialogue on doctrine, pastoral praxis, worship, and ecclesiology is absolutely indispensable.

Since church divisions had their origins in ancient disputes in the

Middle East and Europe, they have not been felt to be equally burning by those who do not share the history of the Mediterranean countries but who now take their stand in the Third World's struggle for political and economic freedom. Gustavo Gutiérrez of Peru, perhaps the leading liberation theologian, has dismissed theological work for the unity of the church as a relic of the past, like others likening it to a "marriage between senior citizens," that is, between persons who have lived together but feel it important to be married before they die.[7]

In an earlier time, the connection between the church's unity, mission, and social responsibility had been seen to be indisputable. It was unthinkable to separate work for the unity of the church from work for the unity of humankind even if individual churches laid the accent a bit differently. But after the World Council's 1968 assembly in Uppsala it became difficult to hold ecumenism's three dimensions together. The Pontifical Council for Promoting Christian Unity directed nearly all its attention to ecclesial-theological work while the WCC was mainly preoccupied with social-ethical questions. Even if many church leaders held fast to the original and integrated ecumenical vision, leaders of the relief organizations which received the greater portion of financial support saw to it, with help from the church of the South, that questions of justice came first. The report from the Vancouver assembly of 1983 stated that, for some,

> The search for a unity in one faith and one eucharistic fellowship seems, at best secondary, at worst irrelevant to the struggles for peace, justice, and human dignity; for others the Church's political involvement against the evils of history seems, at best, secondary, at worst detrimental to its role as eucharistic community and witness to the Gospel.[8]

Being organized in a number of separate units, the WCC gave the impression that the unity of the church and the vision of a just world were alternatives rather than two sides of the same coin. The programs "Justice, Peace, and the Integrity of Creation" and "The Unity of the Church and the Renewal of Human Community" had difficulty in finding each other. Social ethics and ecclesial self-understanding tended to go their separate ways.

Church Union and Church Fellowship

Definitions of "unity" and opinions as to how it is to be attained differ widely. Before the Roman Catholic Church entered the picture, work for unity was largely motivated by the conviction that it would add effectiveness and trustworthiness to Christian mission. The goal was organic unity between different churches and communions. If such entities had sufficient agreement regarding doctrine and church order, it was felt that they could come together to form a united church. The first such union was the Church of South India, formed in 1947.[9] This was followed by a number of church unions, mostly between Presbyterian, Reformed, Methodist, Congregational, and Anglican churches. United Churches were established in Zambia and Jamaica, Papua New Guinea and Pakistan, Australia, Canada, the United Kingdom, and in many other lands. Other church unions had been formed even earlier for political reasons, as in Germany, Japan, and China. If there were several church bodies of the same confession in a country, they often came together, as did Lutherans in India, Hong Kong, Australia, Tanzania, and the United States. Thanks to these united churches, millions of Christians entered a larger and richer fellowship, even as certain dimensions of the inherited spiritual legacy of old communions were lost when theological and liturgical practice was smoothed out.

Lutheran churches, receiving considerable support from the Lutheran World Federation (LWF), were seldom parts of unions with other churches. During the intensive debates of the 1970s concerning "models of unity," the Lutherans championed one of "unity in reconciled diversity."[10] This model was based on the view that theological agreements, reciprocal recognition of ministries, cooperation, and even some form of mutual decision-making are possible without the confessional identities of partners being eroded. Confessional variations can be seen as legitimate since they are largely a consequence of historical circumstances. Similarly, a common church organization would be no guarantee against loveless division. In the churches of the LWF, traditional structures, names, and confessional identities are therefore not seen as barriers to authentic church communion. Churches can be ecumenical, open, and inclusive without giving up their distinctive characters. This "reconciled diversity" model of unity has been sharply rejected by others who stand for organic unity, as well by those who seek a conciliar fellowship based on unity in faith, teaching, and confession.

"Reconciled diversity" has been seen by some as a smokescreen set up to preserve the status quo. It leads to a reunification that requires no repentance or renewal but rather gives the churches the freedom to live in practice as they always have.[11]

A large number of church fellowships have, however, been built on the notion of "unity in reconciled diversity." This has not affected the organization of individual churches, but it has brought about full sacramental communion, the mutual recognition of ministries, the free movement of communicants between churches, and even a certain conciliar decision-making. The best example of this is the agreement concerning "pulpit and altar fellowship" established at Leuenberg, Germany, in 1973 between Lutheran and Reformed churches of Central Europe; it has since expanded to include over one hundred church bodies around the world.[12] Twenty years later, nearly all of the Nordic Lutheran folk churches concluded an agreement in Porvoo, Finland, with the Anglican churches of Great Britain and Ireland for full church communion. This agreement required the attainment of far-reaching common views, especially in respect to the episcopacy.[13] It has profoundly influenced the self-understanding of the major churches in Northern Europe. There are many other examples of such interchurch agreements, not least in the United States. These proceedings, which are very much inspired by a *koinonia* ecclesiology, might over time lay the bases for more comprehensive "communions of communions." These many bilateral agreements between churches with varying requirements for doctrinal accord have been the fruits of the enduring multilateral work of Faith and Order.

For Orthodox churches, such church fellowship, arrived at by adjustment to each other, has for reasons of principle not been of any interest. The dialogue between Oriental and Eastern Orthodox churches has led, after 1500 years of controversy over questions of Christology, to a fundamental agreement on questions of liturgy and spirituality, the Trinity, the Incarnation, the Spirit, and the church, but this has in practice changed little. The Roman Catholic Church has entered into no binding reciprocal settlements with other churches. Unity, for these churches, could in no way be a matter of negotiation. Unity could be reached only by the conversion of all partners in the dialogue, spiritual renewal, and a common theological insight concerning the truth.

A committed conciliar communion between churches which share faith and life was the model which set the tone of interconfessional dialogues after the 1968 assembly. At that time there was boldness to speak of the World Council as an instrument to realize a true universal, ecumenical, and conciliar form of common life and common witness and finally to launch a vision of an authentically universal council which could speak for all Christians and show the way forward.[14] This vision had its background in the ecumenical councils of the early church and in the Second Vatican Council, but also in the Russian teaching of *sobornost*, which referred to a deep spiritual (and national) unity within the inherited Christian tradition. A divided Christianity should be reconciled and renewed through prayer, deliberation, and resolve under the Spirit's guidance to the fullness of truth and love. Such conciliarity was seen as a process rather than a specific event. The section on "What Unity Requires" at the 1975 Nairobi assembly of the World Council approvingly quoted a Faith and Order statement concerning "conciliar fellowship":

> The one church is to be envisioned as a conciliar fellowship of local churches which are themselves truly united. In this conciliar fellowship, each local church possesses, in communion with the others, the fullness of catholicity, witnesses to the same apostolic faith, and therefore recognizes the other as belonging to the same Church of Christ and guided by the same Spirit . . . they [the churches] are bound together because they have received the same baptism and share in the same Eucharist; they recognize each other's members and ministries. They are one in their common commitment to confess the gospel of Christ by proclamation and service to the world. To this end, each church aims at maintaining sustained and sustaining relationships with her sister churches, expressed in conciliar gatherings whenever required for the fulfillment of their common calling.[15]

The Roman Catholic Church in Dialogue

The gap was wide between churches with minimal requirements for church fellowship and churches that insisted on full agreement not only in doctrine but also in structures of ministry, organization, and practice. No other church measured up to the standards of the Roman Catholic Church. For that reason interconfessional theological dialogue aiming at deepened unity became for a number of decades the dominant form of ecumenical work. Vatican II, with its unambiguous pronouncement that relations to other churches should be deepened with visible unity as the ultimate goal, gave wings to such dialogue. The Catholic Church placed conversation with specific church families high on its agenda. Soon about twenty official dialogues were under way, with Lutherans and Pentecostals, Copts and Seventh-Day Adventists, Anglicans, Armenians, and many others.[16]

When the Pontifical Council for Promoting Christian Unity invited confessional organizations to bilateral dialogues, these organizations took on a new role in the ecumenical movement.[17] The "Christian World Communions" had begun to take on organized form at about the same time as the World Council of Churches. The Lutheran World Federation (LWF), which was founded in 1947 in Lund, Sweden, was the most prominent of these confessional organizations with units for theological studies, interchurch cooperation, communication, and an extensive program of relief and development. With an independent institute for theology and ecumenism (in Strasbourg, France) and with the support of wealthy and ecumenically committed churches in Germany, the United States, and the Nordic lands, the LWF became a significant actor in the ever more complex ecumenical movement. When the Lutheran churches decided in 1990 to upgrade their federation to become a genuine church communion *(communio)*, they became, even as they preserved independence, more responsible to each other, determined not to go their separate ways in respect to important questions. This also had a certain limiting effect on their ecumenical freedom.[18]

The Christian world communions for a long time were criticized for strengthening the confessional identities of church bodies at the cost of greater ecumenical fellowship. This criticism was especially strong in Asia, where it was directed toward the LWF, since Lutheran churches had chosen to remain outside church unions in both India and Indonesia. Even though the LWF consisted largely of church bodies that took great responsibility for the WCC, there was at times tension between the two organizations. That tension persisted even in the 1960s when the two organizations had the same moderator.[19]

In the official interconfessional dialogues after Vatican II, the LWF became the first partner of the Roman Catholic Church. The theological conversations with Rome changed the self-understanding and ecumenical role of the confessional organizations. All identified themselves with the larger Christian tradition, but each esteemed its own tradition in the conviction that it had lasting value for all of Christianity. The organizations had certain ecclesial traits, but their authority over member churches was not clear. As a consequence of their contact with the Catholic Church, the Christian World Communions (CWC) became independent actors in the ecumenical movement. This situation prevailed until 1998 when the World Council of Churches formally "recommended that a process be initiated to facilitate and strengthen the relationships between the WCC and CWCs."[20]

These dialogues, which developed into an extensive network and were pursued at all levels, deepened churches' understanding of each other and increased their insight into the complexity of the ecumenical project. Participants recognized themselves in the history of others and thus could correct mistaken preconceptions, judgments, and misunderstandings. The Leuenberg Agreement toward church fellowship between many Reformation churches was a fruit of intense theological conversation. The dialogues presupposed that each church family should revise and clarify its theological starting points and pastoral positions. This has led to increased awareness both of particular identities and of what is indispensable in particular traditions. Paradoxically, the dialogues have also contributed to a heightening of boundaries, a hardening of positions, and a sharpening of profiles over and against others.

In spite of growing agreement in respect to many doctrinal questions, the dialogues have not achieved as much as many had hoped.[21] The churches received reports from the dialogues and were expected to incorporate results into the bases of their own confessions if they did not clearly contradict those confessions and if they were in agreement with the biblical tradition. The process of "reception" took a long time — if it ever took place.[22] Dialogue presupposes that the churches recognize each other as churches. Thus it appears easier for Protestant churches to make the conclusions of the dialogues their own than for the Roman Catholic and Orthodox Churches. Yet many dialogue documents remain unattended to. Outside the circles of academic theologians and bishops there are few who know the contents of these documents. The conversations have raised many new questions and controversies remain which need continued work. The dialogues have institutionalized an open, listening attitude in the churches and influenced their theology through actual agreements, but the actual implementation of a deepened church communion still awaits.

Unity in Diversity

The *Joint Declaration on the Doctrine of Justification*

Only one dialogue text has been officially adopted by the Roman Catholic Church. This is the *Joint Declaration on the Doctrine of Justification*, signed by the general secretary of the Lutheran World Federation, Ishmael Noko, and the president of the Pontifical Council for Promoting Unity, Cardinal Walter Kasper, on 31 October 1999 in Augsburg, Germany.[23] This agreement was the result of decades-long theological dialogue which reached the point where the sixteenth-century mutual condemnations over the doctrine of justification were no longer seen as applicable or church-dividing. The Declaration has not brought about any practical consequences, such as intercommunion between Lutherans and Catholics, but symbolically it is extremely significant that the great dispute of the Reformation has come close to settlement. Dialogues between the two bodies have continued with new presuppositions and new energy.

For Martin Luther, humanity's salvation through faith by the grace of Jesus Christ was the article "by which the church stands or falls." He criticized the Roman Catholic Church, of which he was a priest, for having compromised the pure gospel by making salvation into a question of self-righteousness and a decent life. Only God can bestow righteousness, which is a gift of grace to be received in faith. This dispute reached dimensions that split the church. In the heat of the argument the matter was simplified: faith or works, God's gift or human efforts, the word of the Bible or that of the church.

The doctrinal discussions of the past decades between the Roman Catholic and Lutheran churches have given the matter greater nuance. Even if the two churches employed different formulations and gave varying weights to the questions, they have shown themselves to be in basic agreement, reaching the point of a common interpretation and description of the doctrine of justification. By distinguishing between unchanging truth and its description, and thus between necessary agreement and legitimate differences, they have reached a common position that does not contradict either's doctrine. The *Joint Declaration* was epoch-making, not only because it dealt with the most central and controversial question of the Reformation, but also because it has shown that unity does not presuppose uniformity in every formulation or complete agreement about the importance of the matter itself. The *Joint Declaration* is the crown of the entire twentieth-century effort to heal the wounds caused by the Reformation for the whole Western church.[24]

Fundamental Differences Remain

At the beginning of the twenty-first century there remains a long way to go before a *koinonia* exists in which the churches recognize in each other the fullness of the one, holy, catholic, and apostolic church and express that communion in conciliar decisions, sacramental life, and common witness and service. Only the churches of the Reformation have taken concrete steps toward unity among themselves. Ecclesiological differences have prevented sacramental communion even between Roman Catholic and Orthodox Christians. In spite of the 1964 embrace between Pope Paul VI and Ecumenical Patriarch Athenagoras in Jerusalem and all subsequent dialogues, these churches have not been able to implement their communion, even though doctrinally they are close enough to recognize each other as "sister churches." Their relation continues to be marked by a mixture of affection and suspicion. A genuine reconciliation, after a separation of a thousand years, remains distant.

A feeling of disillusionment and resignation has replaced the euphoria that marked the time after Vatican II. The ecumenical vision that inspired the churches after the two world wars has been met with so many institutional obstacles that many are now asking whether unity through theological dialogue is at all realistic. Should one expect unity to come in a totally different way which we have not yet identified? Has the ecumenical movement betrayed its own calling by devoting so much attention to the world's questions? The World Council of Churches has been impaired in recent years. The eagerness and sense of direction to which Pope John Paul II gave such eloquent expression in his 1995 encyclical *Ut Unum Sint* ("That They May Be One") and in his ecumenical encounters and symbolic acts have been toned down by his successor. One must acknowledge that there are enduring and fundamental differences that no dialogue seems able to overcome in the foreseeable future.

The Roman Catholic Church has chosen to meet the postmodern relativization of truth by strengthening its own claims, its centralized structure, and its self-sufficient ecclesiology. Some Orthodox churches have returned, after decades of persecution, to pre-revolutionary attitudes and self-understandings. Protestantism wavers between its catholic heritage and a freedom and individualism reflecting the market economy and the liberal society. At the same time a "Fourth Church" has emerged that is not bound by old institutions and codified confessions, but rather is contextual, charismatic, and adaptable. The ecclesial landscape is swiftly being altered, and the ecumenical movement is becoming more and more complex and difficult to grasp. But Faith and Order, which for many years had played a comparatively minor role, was again placed in the center of the ecumenical movement after the World Council's assembly of 2006 in Porto Alegre, Brazil. The whole ecumenical house may once again be rearranged.

CHAPTER 6

The Ecumenical Landscape

The future of ecumenism depends on how willing we are to recognize that there is dignity in diversity and difference.

Sam Kobia

When the ecumenical movement began, the world was still neatly arranged. The Catholic Church was thoroughly centralized and directed from Rome. It possessed the same organization and educational system everywhere, and it always worshiped in the same way, with Latin as the chief language. Its missions grafted new Christians in Africa, Asia, and Latin America into the structure, spirituality, and values of the Western church.

Likewise, Protestant churches around the world reflected Western history and experience. The Reformation had taken place in Europe as a consequence of the sixteenth century's theological and political upheavals. Other cultures had nothing to do with this, but were brought into it through colonialism, missions, and emigration. Leading theologians were all educated at European or American universities. Missionaries for the most part had an Anglo-Saxon background. Many were inspired by revival movements which blossomed at the edges of established churches, while others came from sectarian groups. Protestant Christianity arrived divided in Africa and Asia, and it would become even more divided. This diminished the credibility of the missionary movement, but it also provided motivation for the ecumenical movement.

The Ecumenical Landscape

The Eurocentric outlook of both Catholic and Reformation churches permeated ecumenism up to the 1960s. Only then did the ecumenical movement become truly global, taking on a complexity that none of its pioneers could have foreseen. The Orthodox churches of Eastern and Central Europe, the Middle East, India, and Ethiopia had an outlook at once broader and more limited than other churches. The identification between church and state in Eastern Europe limited the Orthodox vision, and life under harsh dictators and as minorities in Muslim countries gave them a humility lacking to Western Christians. Most churches walked out of step with each other and at times even with their own age. When European civilization was shattered by World War I and empires crumbled, Orthodox and Protestant churches realized that they needed each other. But Catholics were not encouraged to seek any fellowship in faith, and even less did the powerful Roman Catholic Church seek partnership with other Christian communities.

Individuals such as Germanos Strenopoulos (Germanos of Thyatira, 1872-1951), Nathan Söderblom (1866-1931), John R. Mott (1865-1955), and Joseph Oldham (1874-1969) were among those who first took the ecumenical initiative.[1] Yet they had differing motivations. The Protestants desired to coordinate mission endeavors and efforts for peace and social justice even as they also desired to come to terms with scandalous church divisions. The patriarchate in Constantinople desired to create a "league between the churches" comparable to the League of Nations in order to preserve the churches' interests when emperors and czars were overthrown and freedom threatened.[2] The Orthodox and Protestant traditions were strangers to one another. If crises in their environments had not arisen, they would scarcely have united around common goals and created ecumenical organizations.

Mainline Churches in North America

State churches in Europe were different from the North American church bodies that came into the ecumenical movement. The latter were voluntary associations, immigrant churches, and classified as denominations. As they became integrated into American society and left behind their national-cultural identities, some of their confessional differences were also leveled out. Competition for members in a "religious market" resulted in a low profile being given to doctrinal matters. Churches attaching themselves to the ecumenical movement comprised central elements in American church and social life and thus became known as "mainline churches." When the Catholic and Orthodox Churches, in time, became major forces in America and the ranks of conservative evangelicals grew, they came also to be called "middle churches."[3] They preserved open relations toward each other, in large measure accepted modernity and the historical-critical study of the Bible, and they also — by American standards — adopted liberal political views, recognizing the responsibility of the state for basic social security, education, and health care. Each of these churches, however, also included strongly conservative elements.

In the 1960s these mainline churches began to lose ground. Secularization increased, church membership decreased, and financial resources began to dry up. This decline went on for four decades with a slight leveling out only at the turn of the millennium. In 2005 only ten of the twenty-five largest church bodies in the country belonged to this group.[4] The base of the ecumenical movement thus had been dramatically weakened. Mainline churches could not influence public life as before. They became preoccupied with their own problems, and their interest in the wider world and wider church suffered. For decades they had been the self-evident home for the middle class; now they had to defend themselves against aggressive conservative bodies. They also had difficulty controlling internal tension over ethical questions and conflicts. The National Council of the Churches of Christ in the U.S.A., which in addition to the Episcopal, Lutheran, Methodist, Presbyterian, and Reformed churches included a number of Orthodox and African American churches, became increasingly dependent on secular charitable foundations and funds for its work; in 2007 only a fifth of its income came from member church bodies. At that time, furthermore, questions of unity were overshadowed by issues of peace and justice.

The ecumenical churches not only lost members but also were threatened by a kind of balkanization when some — not all — of them began to ordain women and later openly homosexual persons and in the eyes of many adopted all too liberal positions on questions of social, political, and international affairs. Conservative evangelical groups and independent congregations grew accordingly. These also had their roots in Protestantism and held fast to the four pillars of the Reformation — Christ alone, Scripture alone, faith alone, and grace alone — but less as reforming principles over against Catholic theology than as support for biblicism, individualism, and moralism. These groups supplied the base for the influential "religious right" in American politics. American church geography has been further complicated in recent years by millions of Christian immigrants to America from different parts of the world who have organized their own ethnic churches and congregations.[5]

The Weakening of Old European Churches

In Europe, new expressions of religious life have been more moderate than on the other side of the Atlantic. Conservative Christian movements have not gotten a strong foothold, even though the number of congregations marked by low-church, evangelical, and charismatic convictions has increased, not least in Great Britain. A conversion-oriented, Jesus-centered, and biblicist Christianity does not seem to provide a real alternative to inherited, open, and more liturgical expressions of faith.

The weakening of the traditional churches, most of which in the past were organized as state churches, has been even more dramatic in Europe than in the United States. In Germany alone more than three million Protestants and two million Catholics left their churches between 1990 and 2004. In England the number of baptisms per year has dropped by a third, and the Church of England has lost its majority status. In the Church of Sweden a loss of members was seriously felt at the beginning of the twenty-first century, when that church was largely separated from the state. German reunification in 1989 required enormous economic contributions by the churches, with the result that much less financial support has been left over for international ecumenical work. Indeed, throughout all of Protestant Europe today most young people have nearly no contact with church life, and the communal knowledge of faith has been lost. The World Council of Churches, which in large measure was financed by German, Nordic, and American churches, felt these changes immediately and has had to reduce or terminate many programs and make do with a far smaller staff.[6]

Nazism and Communism had determined the frontiers for ecumenism in Europe. The German Confessing Church *(Bekennende Kirche)*, before and during World War II, became the principal model for a critical relation between church and society. The ecumenical movement became from its very beginning a protest movement against undemocratic structures, ideological limitations on human freedom, and industrial society's devastation of creation. The involvement of a committed laity maintained a creative tension between people-based movements and ecumenical institutions such as the World Council of Churches and the Lutheran World Federation.[7]

When the Soviet Union fell, churches in Eastern Europe received a new freedom. In Russia, which was threatened by chaos and disintegration, the Orthodox Church was restored to its former national role and became a source of continuity, national identity, and moral leadership. Its showdown with the fallen order of things also led to a reevaluation of its ecumenical relations. The Orthodox Churches in Georgia and Bulgaria suspended their membership in the WCC, while the churches in Romania and Albania took on a leading role in international ecumenism. When the dictatorship of the military junta in Greece began to heal, the Greek Orthodox Church both reestablished its relations with the Roman Catholic Church and renewed its full participation in ecumenical cooperation.

Tension within the Catholic Church

While the European Community became more solidified by the signing of the Maastricht Treaty in 1992 and the upheavals in Eastern Europe speeded the European Union processes, the churches were not as willing as governments to give up some of their independence for the sake of greater unity. But they could not avoid being affected by the political processes of integration.[8] Pope John Paul II, who played a dominant role in the collapse of Communism, desired to insure that the new Europe acknowledged its Christian roots and preserved its spiritual and moral heritage. He said that Europe must "breathe with both lungs," referring to the continent's Slavonic and Latin parts. East and West must cooperate if the union were to survive. He gathered the European Catholic bishops in order to interpret "the meaning of this moment for the Christian faith and the history of Europe." The bishops called for a "reevangelization" of Europe. This was interpreted by many Protestants as an attempt to strengthen Catholic values, but the Catholic bishops were very much aware that dialogue and cooperation with other Christians, Jews, and all people of faith were necessary.[9] The Roman Catholic Church, which for two thousand years had been the strongest unifying factor in Europe, welcomed European integration but was concerned that it could limit the freedom and responsibility not only of nations, but also of families, and individuals. The principle of subsidiarity must be maintained: all decisions should be made at the lowest possible organizational level. The pope wanted a European Union built on Christian values with respect for freedom of religion and for the moral consequences of Christian faith. He proclaimed Catherine of Siena, Birgitta of Vadstena, Cyril and Methodius, and Edith Stein (Teresa Benedicta of the Cross) patron saints of Europe along with the traditional Benedict of Nursia, symbolizing his efforts to hold the whole continent together.

The Second Vatican Council had set loose contradictory forces in the Roman Catholic Church. Many Catholics wanted to go farther than the Council Fathers in adapting the church to the modern world; others felt betrayed by what they termed the "radical" Council and locked themselves in reactionary attitudes. "Progressives" wanted to allow married clergy, the use of contraceptives, and the toleration of homosexual persons. For them, the 1968 encyclical of Pope Paul VI, *Humanae Vitae,* came as a slap in the face. That encyclical upheld the Church's traditional view of sexuality and birth control. It put an end to the early enthusiasm when the Curia, theologians, and dioceses worked together to implement the Council's decisions by reservation toward and actual opposition to reform. Paul VI was not able to meet the expectations of the "progressives," and their situation became even worse when John Paul II and Joseph Cardinal Ratzinger took over.[10] They silenced Latin American liberation theologians who, with the help of the concrete experiences of the poor, exposed the interests of those with political power, and they also told the Jesuits in India not to express more openness toward the truths in other religions than could be accepted by the Curia. In many places there were conservative bishops and laity who held fast to the old ways and desired to continue celebrating the Tridentine Mass in Latin. Archbishop Marcel Lefebvre of France, who was one of the most extreme traditionalists, ordained four bishops in 1988 without the approval of the Vatican. He was subsequently denied his right to exercise the episcopal office and excommunicated. Until his death in 1991, however, Lefebvre saw himself as an upholder of the true Catholic Church. In 2009 Pope Benedict XVI lifted the excommunication of the four bishops Lefebvre had ordained.

The Vatican had to find a middle way between those who supported a radical renewal of the church and those who formed a reactionary opposition to the Council's decisions. Its sympathy was, however, doubtlessly with the conservative forces. Brakes were applied to much of the new thinking brought about by the Council. John Paul II appointed virtually only conservative and unfailingly loyal bishops. "Progressive" theologians lost their right to teach in Catholic institutions, while the reactionary group Opus Dei in 1982 was granted status as a personal prelature and its founder, Josemaria Escrivá, was in 2002 canonized as a saint. In the United States the positions of the Curia received support from such influential persons as Richard John Neuhaus, Michael Novak, and George Weigel, who moved in position from active leftist opposition to the Vietnam War to neoconservatism allied with the religious right in support of the Iraq War.[11]

Polarization within the Roman Catholic Church was most acute in the Netherlands. Under the leadership of the forward-looking Cardinal Bernardus Alfrink, Council decisions were put into effect. A new *Catechism* was published, and for the first time the laity were given genuine influence in the Church. Social and political barriers between Catholics and Protestants were torn down. Many Catholic organizations became ecumenical or even secular. The Catholic Church joined the National Council of Churches, and baptism was mutually recognized. But the movement for reform met strong opposition, and conflict threatened to split the Catholic Church in the Netherlands. The number of Roman Catholics diminished greatly, and participation in Sunday Mass shrank to one-fifth of what it had been.

During the turbulent decades after Vatican II, approximately 50,000 men around the world left the priesthood, many in order to be married. Vocations diminished over forty years to a tenth of what they had been. In 2005 in the United States there were only 454 priests ordained, compared to 994 forty years earlier, although the number of Roman Catholics had increased during the same period by eighteen million persons. In Europe the shortage of priests was even more serious: in Ireland, which had been accustomed to supplying priests the world over, only 15 men were ordained in 2005; Poland alone continued to have a surplus of ordained priests. Scholars spoke of "a continent without priests." Those who remained in service were often older men — at the turn of the century the average age of priests in some countries was over seventy. This was somewhat ameliorated by the fact that the number of married deacons increased.[12] Religious left their orders for secular work, and monasteries and convents were closed. At the same time new ecclesial movements were formed, base communities grew like mushrooms out of the earth, liturgical experiments blossomed everywhere, and contextual theologies took root. It seemed as if the old structures were crumbling and being replaced by new, more youthful, and possibly more relevant forms of Catholic life.

The Conference of European Churches in a New Situation

The three major ecclesial traditions in Europe have not marched in step. While many Orthodox churches have continued to live largely with a theologically premodern understanding of the world preserved during their long oppression in communist lands, the Roman Catholic Church somewhat reluctantly adjusted to the modern world. Many of the Reformation churches, on the other hand, have had to face a deep crisis of authority accompanied by a postmodern suspicion of ready-made answers. Religion has increasingly become a private matter. The churches have had to choose between being marginalized or adapting themselves to a liberal public opinion, especially in respect to ethical questions.

Different approaches to and views of the churches' task created, as we have seen, considerable difficulties in ecumenical cooperation once the initial enthusiasm which followed Vatican II and the 1968 assembly of the World Council of Churches passed. After the fall of the Berlin Wall in 1989, considerable differences came to light which strained the solidarity between churches almost to a breaking point. It was then, however, that regional ecumenical work in Europe received an impetus, the Conference of European Churches was renewed, and many national councils of churches were given new strength.

The Conference of European Churches was formed in the 1950s in order to preserve contact between churches in Eastern and Western Europe. It was a fragile organization, gradually complemented by other agencies for coordinating the work of study centers and lay academies, giving the churches a voice in deliberations at Brussels, drawing attention to questions of immigration and to the Helsinki Agreement — the 1975 act of the Council on Security and Cooperation in Europe which also monitored the status of human rights and religious freedom. In

Europe, in contrast to other parts of the world, ecumenism became a matter of widespread public urgency stimulated by the German Church Days *(Kirchentag)*, gathering several hundred thousand participants; communities such as Taizé in France, Iona in Scotland, and Corymeela in Northern Ireland; and networks such as *Kairos Europa*. The European churches had long relied on the world ecumenical organizations based in Geneva and thus were slow to develop their own regional cooperation.

Two events, both occurring in 1989, changed this. The first was that the Conference of European Churches became a regional partner in the worldwide conciliar process of "Justice, Peace, and the Integrity of Creation" which had been initiated at the WCC's 1983 Vancouver assembly. A European conference in Basel in 1989, in which Protestants, Orthodox, and Roman Catholics all took part, actually became the high point of the whole international process. The second event was the fall of the Berlin Wall, which occurred a few months later. This brought about a totally new but uncertain situation for European church cooperation. Roman Catholic bishops called for the "reevangelizing of Europe," while the Orthodox, more humbly, wished for a return to "Christian Europe." Protestants, who valued the positive aspects of secularism and individual freedom, were less inclined to claim a larger role for the institutional churches. The Conference of European Churches, however, united at its meeting in Graz, Austria, in 1997 around *Charta Oecumenica: Guidelines for the Growing Cooperation among the Churches in Europe,* a document of great importance. It was signed at Strasbourg in 2001 by the presidents of the Conference of European Churches and the Council of European Bishops' Conferences. To be sure, relations between the Orthodox, Roman Catholics, and Protestants later became more difficult, but the third meeting of the Conference, in Sibiu, Romania, in 2007, again brought together leading spokespersons for all these churches. This time "spiritual ecumenism" was the main point on the agenda.[13]

The ecumenical movement has its deepest roots in Europe, where divisions between churches began. Political changes in Europe in the closing years of the twentieth century also were the most dramatic in the world. Secularism, the loosening of state control over the churches, the loss of members, and the shortage of clergy have changed the churches, but so have the many spiritual and social renewal movements, a democratization of old institutions, and the ordination of women priests and bishops. Yet the weakened European churches can no longer determine global ecumenical theology and priorities, and their financial support of the worldwide ecumenical organizations is much less than in the past. Europe has become one region among others. It remains distinct in light of its long institutional, spiritual, and intellectual Christian history, but today also distinct as the only region in the world where Christians are actually decreasing in numbers because of both secularism and an aging population.

Regional Ecumenical Councils outside Europe

Regional ecumenical councils were formed from 1959 to 1982 in Asia, Africa, the Mediterranean, the Middle East, and Latin America. As in the United States and Europe, Protestant and Orthodox churches participated in all of them; the Roman Catholic Church was a full member in three such councils. These councils have the same theological basis as the WCC but are totally independent, with many variations between them. They are financed, like virtually all ecumenical work, chiefly from North America, the Nordic countries, and Germany, and during their best years they carried on comprehensive programs for peace and social development. As with the world confessional organizations, there has often been a certain degree of tension between the regional councils and the World Council. In the middle of the 1970s, when controversy concerning the funding was at its height, a crisis arose which developed to the point that certain of the councils questioned whether the WCC should have direct contact with their member churches. This created a need both for a common vision and for agreements concerning cooperation and shared responsibilities. At the turn of the century, a Common Understanding and Vision of the Ecumenical Movement was adopted, leading all ecumenical organizations to coordinate their activities. A reconfiguration of the entire ecumenical movement became necessary in order not to sacrifice the movement to its own success.[14]

    This regionalization of ecumenism followed the independence which churches in Asia and Africa received as colonialism came to an end and a strong emphasis on the contextualization of theology and church life ensued. It was possible to establish regional councils thanks to public funding for development channeled through church relief organizations such as *Brot für die Welt* in Germany and *Lutherhjälpen* in

Sweden. Such financial support was given on condition that regional councils of churches directed their attention to social and economic development.

The Churches in Africa

In the 1960s Africa was the continent of hope. Nearly all of its countries had become independent, and many were convinced that general well-being was within reach. A Pan-African movement was under way, and the Organization of African Unity (OAU) was established. However, national boundaries were often the unnatural constructions of colonialism, and conflicts spread throughout the nations. Faith in the future suffered hard shocks from misuse of power, corruption, and internal conflict. Churches nearly collapsed under the burden of maintaining hospitals and schools left behind by mission organizations. Thousands of "African Instituted Churches" were established, centered around charismatic leaders and prophets who clothed the Christian faith in African garb but at times were also at the edges of heresy. Evangelists promising healing, miracles, and a brighter future set up new and aggressive missionary enterprises. The churches in Africa were more divided than in any other continent. African Christians had never experienced the church in any other way. They were accustomed to living with all kinds of denominations, sects, movements, and parachurch organizations and often did not view such splintering as a scandal but rather as *shaura la Mungo*, something to leave up to God.[15] Was it even possible to unite the churches? Was it not more urgent to solve Africa's political and economic problems, overcome the remnants of apartheid, and concentrate on health care, especially where the AIDS pandemic struck?

The All Africa Conference of Churches was formed in 1963 in order to hold together the churches that were growing over the whole enormous continent. Ecumenism was often more identified with development work than with church unity. Faith and Order met with little response in Africa, and the Organization for African Unity's appeals for interfaith dialogue were not heard. It would not be until the 2000s that the African churches, with support from the Lutheran World Federation, together with leaders and politicians from other faith communities, took seriously questions surrounding the encounter of religions and the common responsibility of faith communities both in situations of conflict and in efforts to build societies.[16] By that time many mosques and churches had been burnt and hundreds of lives had been lost. Struggling countries like Sudan and Somalia suffered for decades from wars and communal conflicts with religious overtones.

Yet Africa remains on the way to becoming the Christian continent of the world. Churches have grown rapidly, and their solidarity has been increased in the struggle against colonialism and apartheid. Leaders such as Desmond Tutu and José Chipenda in the 1980s strengthened the role of the All Africa Conference of Churches, even as multi-party states simultaneously grew in number and increased in economic strength. But the genocide in Rwanda in 1994 and ongoing war in Central Africa took millions of human lives, and the nation of Zimbabwe soon sank into economic and political chaos. Today, the African churches are large and vital, but they lack the unity, economic resources, and organization required to meet unending crises, whether caused by hunger, HIV/AIDS, corruption, war, or environmental disaster.

Christian Theology in Asian Contexts

In Asia the situation is different. In spite of church growth, Christians are a decided minority in nearly all Asian countries, the Philippines being the only exception. Even if denominational structures characterize most Protestant churches, they are conservative, often ethnically based, and bound to their traditions. The number of charismatic and independent communities are increasing, not least among Chinese in Southeast Asia, and megachurches have multiplied in countries such as South Korea.

After nearly thirty years of isolation, oppression, and near-extinction, the church in China rose anew in 1979, showing itself to have amazing resilience. In a few decades the Protestant church, which is organized according to the patriotic "three-self principle" in the China Christian Council, gained tens of millions of new members.[17] Divisions along confessional lines had been given up as early as the 1950s, and the church today identifies itself as "post-denominational." In spite of great efforts to train clergy and laity, the church cannot offer the kind of religious education that the large influx of new Christians requires. New converts to Christianity often read the Bible in a literal way, and the growing congregations are frequently marked by both charismatic and fundamentalistic elements. Leaders of the churches have accommodated themselves to the conditions of the communist society, while the large number of "house churches" outside the registered organizations often take a more critical position toward the communists. The Catholic Church suffered the imprisonment of many bishops and hundreds of priests during the Cultural Revolution of 1966-1976. For a long time the Catholic Church in China seemed to be untouched by the Second Vatican Council, but that has changed. Today it is comparatively well organized and is growing at a steady pace. Still, it has no official link with the Vatican. Catholics in China have little contact with Protestants, and the state even defines the two traditions as two different religions.

All of the great world religions have their origins in Asia. Relations with people of other faiths stand high on the ecumenical agenda. Buddhism, Hinduism, and Islam have each taken on new meaning in people's lives as vitalized and politicized forces. Interfaith dialogue is absolutely essential. The religions live side by side and must together contribute to forming society with space for diversity and mutual respect. Asian artists have depicted a Christ "with an Asian face," and theologians such as Kosuke Koyama, Raimundo Panikkar, Stanley Samartha, and M. M. Thomas have ventured to show that Christ is greater than all Christian images of him and that he has been present in Asian religions and cultures long before he was recognized and acknowledged. The encounter with others who worship God has influenced the Christian understanding of both salvation and hope. Indeed, the Asian experience largely determined the approach when the WCC seriously took up the question of the religions.

In Asia, as in Latin America, "the people" are defined as the powerless, marginalized, deprived, and oppressed; thus, "the people" became a major theological theme in the 1970s. When the Communists spoke of the people, they spoke of party members or the proletariat, and Mao Zedong admonished the Red Guards to "serve the people." This emphasis was paralleled in Christian theology and praxis. Sinners were those who made the poor destitute, and, to be sure, at times their struggle was idealized to such an extent that "the people" took on messianic characteristics.[18]

The Korean word for "people" is *minjung*, while experiences of oppression and unjust suffering are summed up in the concept of *han*.

The Korean variant of liberation theology is called "minjung theology," and it is clearly political in emphasis. It makes use of ancient cultural symbols and expresses *han* in music, dance, and drama.[19] It was this notion that Professor Chung Hyun Kyahn used at the Canberra assembly of the WCC in 1991 when she described how the Holy Spirit works through *han*, using the Buddhist figure of Bodhisattva Kwan In, goddess of compassion, as a picture for the Spirit.[20]

She was far from the only one who referred to human experience using the wider culture to interpret and communicate the gospel. But in conservative churches those who advanced an ecumenical theology conditioned by Asian terms were seen as perpetrators of sheer provocation, as were those who presented Christian faith through Asian music, art, and architecture.[21] The Christian Conference of Asia supported such persons, but it paid a price for this position as well as for its support of political action groups and protest movements. Some member churches left the organization, and in 1987 it was banned from Singapore where it had its headquarters. Authorities there charged it with supporting liberation movements in other countries as well as subversive elements in Singapore. The Christian Conference of Asia first moved its headquarters to Hong Kong and then eventually to Thailand, where its priorities have changed considerably.

Liberation Theology in Latin America

If Christians in Asia have lived in the shadow of other religions, so the Protestant minority in Latin America has been overshadowed by the Roman Catholic Church. Conflicts became sharp when the Catholics defined the Protestant communities as sects and the Protestants, in turn, accused the Catholics of superstition and collaboration with corrupt oligarchies. Vatican II changed things. It aroused great sympathy among the many bishops who wished to show the Church's solidarity with the poor through concrete social programs. Liberation theology, thousands of base communities — *communidades ecclesiales de base* — and popular, public opposition to military dictators led to several decades of renewal and church struggle throughout Latin America, which in turn influenced the ecumenical movement around the world.

During the industrialization of the 1950s, which happened with the help of considerable foreign investment, the large cities grew. Slums, *favelas,* climbed up the sides of hills and both destitution and criminality increased. Labor unions and the student movement each became more radical. Their suspicion of market economy increased when economic growth failed to create social integration but rather widened the gap between rich and poor. The military coup in Brazil in 1964 introduced a state terrorism which burdened the whole continent well into the 1980s. Dictatorships in Chile, Peru, Paraguay, El Salvador, Ecuador, Argentina, and other countries dampened hopes for social change. Human rights were blown away. The opposition gathered in base communities and organizations such as Christians for Socialism. Several ecumenical centers were founded for reflection on social issues and for Christian-Marxist dialogue.

Liberation theology was characterized by the fact that it interpreted concrete human experience in the light of the gospel narrative. It was contextual and inductive and invited the poor to reflect over God's presence in the struggle for sustenance and human rights. Liberation meant to be freed from international and local structures which lead to dependence and misery, and to be able to take life into one's own hands in order to contribute to a more just society for all. The Peruvian Roman Catholic Gustavo Gutiérrez, the Brazilian Presbyterian Rubem Alves, and the Argentinean Methodist José Míguez Bonino were among the first liberation theologians, and they were followed by hundreds of others. Seldom has a theological current made such an impression. The method and direction of liberation theology inspired *minjung* theology in Asia, black theology in South Africa, and perhaps above all feminist theology in the North Atlantic countries.

The Roman Catholic Bishops Conference of Latin America gathered in 1968, in the presence of Pope Paul VI, and coined the phrase "God's preferential option for the poor." It met again ten years later in the presence of John Paul II, when a reaction against liberation theology already was in the wind. The bishops, to be sure, did confirm their solidarity with the poor and with the indigenous people once again, and they also expressed support for ecumenical cooperation. But criticism of liberation theology was sharpened and conservative forces gained ground. The pope, who was extremely suspicious of everything that had the slightest odor of Marxism, proceeded to name only conservatives as new bishops. Liberation theologians such as Leonardo Boff were marked for critical examination by the Congregation for the Doctrine of the Faith. When liberation theology had actually spread throughout the world, that Congregation in 1984, led by Cardinal Joseph Ratzinger, issued a much debated "Instruction on Certain Aspects of 'Theology of Liberation'" in which he warned against ideologization and laid down principles for the Church's understanding of freedom and liberation.[22]

The Latin American Council of Churches (CLAI — Consejo Latinoamericano de Iglesias) was established by Protestant churches in 1982.[23] The Council included a number of Pentecostal churches. Its constituting meeting took place the same year as the Faith and Order meeting in Lima, Peru, where the document *Baptism, Eucharist and Ministry* was adopted. The Council, however, was not primarily concerned with such theological issues. Archbishop Oscar Romero had been assassinated in San Salvador in 1980, and his murder was followed by hundreds of others, especially in Central America. The crimes of the military regimes and the assaults by armed opposition movements were too numerous to be counted. Under these circumstances, it was inevitable that peace, democracy, and human rights as well as the protection and survival of indigenous peoples would take precedence over ecclesial and theological matters. Roman Catholic and Protestant sociologists made similar analyses of economic and social structures, but constructive cooperation between the churches slackened when the Curia and its loyal bishops began to distance themselves from liberation theology. At the 1992 Bishops Conference, held in Santo Domingo, Dominican Republic, and again in the presence of the pope, the Protestant observers withdrew when the Roman Catholic Church claimed to be the only spiritual and moral force that could shape the future of Latin America. The bishops at this time supported the prevailing economic order, hoping to humanize it with the help of traditional Catholic social doctrine. Simultaneously they directed their attention toward wider cultural matters rather than struggling directly to overcome unjust social conditions. Latin American Roman Catholicism moved from confrontation to accommodation and cooperation.

The Pentecostal movement which had come to Latin America during the 1920s was well established. Some of the older Pentecostal churches participated in regional ecumenical work and were also members of the WCC. In the 1970s their growth accelerated, and they lured away large numbers of nominal Catholics. Hundreds of conservative evangelical congregations were also formed. Glittering megachurches were built in the large cities, and they attracted large crowds. The Roman Catholic Church felt threatened by this new Christendom, and this had an effect on cooperation with Lutherans, Methodists, Anglicans, and Presbyterians. At the turn of the century, liberation theology had been severely weakened and Latin America had nearly disappeared from the global map of ecumenism.

The Middle East Council of Churches

Of all regional organizations, the Middle East Council of Churches for a long time was the most effective. For many years its general secretary was Gabriel Habib, a venturesome and visionary Eastern Orthodox layman who had contact with all of the political leaders in the region and the full backing of bishops and patriarchs. The Council developed into a dynamic cooperative organization for all churches from Iran to Cyprus and Armenia to Egypt. Over the centuries, the Eastern and Oriental Orthodox, Roman Catholic, and Protestant church families have shared responsibility for maintaining the Christian presence in the Holy Land. They have analyzed reasons for the emigration of Christians, raised the spiritual and theological levels of the churches, set them loose from their social and cultural isolation, fostered Christian unity, and — in spite of internal resistance — set forth a common witness to peace and reconciliation.[24] Constant war, the unbearable plight of the Palestinians, the large-scale exodus of Christians from war-torn Iraq and their vulnerability within the Muslim world have all brought the churches together. Their weak position has given them humility in relation to the political powers, while the complicated rules for the care of holy places in Jerusalem have created unending conflicts.

Yet in spite of external difficulties there has been a thoroughgoing inner renewal in many churches. This is most evident in the Coptic Church in Egypt, where monastic life prospers and Christian education, social initiatives, and a renaissance of icon painting have given the Christians a new sense of self-esteem, although events since the "Arab Spring" of 2011 may have jeopardized even their safety. The Eastern Orthodox Church in Lebanon has established a modern university and brought the training of priests up to date. Armenians play a prominent role in international ecumenism. Relations with the Roman Catholic Church, which includes parishes of both Latin and Eastern rites, have improved, not least because of papal visits (Paul VI in 1964; John Paul II in 2000; and Benedict XVI in 2012) which fixed the world's attention on the significance of a continued Christian presence in the region. The small Protestant church bodies at times have served as mediators between the ancient churches, and Lutherans in the Middle East have become well known for their Palestinian schools.

In this boiling cauldron, where confessions, politics, nations, and cultures cannot be distinguished from each other, the Middle East Council of Churches has sought to draw a boundary line between religion and politics. This has been necessary in order to preserve the integrity of the churches in relation to political Judaism and Islam, but in practice it has proven impossible. To maintain Jerusalem as an open city for all three Abrahamic faiths, to temper the religious extremism which rankles both the powerful and powerless, to support refugees from Iraq and more recently from Syria and serve the large communities of migrant laborers in the Gulf, and to preserve the churches' common witness to peace and reconciliation are the most urgent concerns of this ecumenical council.

The Ecumenical Movement at the Turn of the Century

The regional ecumenical organizations are facing different challenges. All, however, must pay considerable attention to theological education in order to give the coming generation of priests, pastors, and church leaders an ecumenical vision as well as knowledge of the life of other faith communities. Priorities have for several decades been determined by poverty in Africa, interreligious relations in Asia, military dictatorships in Latin America, political integration in Europe, threats to the environment in the Pacific, right-wing politics in the United States, the Palestinian question in the Middle East, and the legacy of colonialism in the Caribbean.

In addition to these regional organizations there are twenty or more global confessional organizations — Christian World Communions — each of which has its own theological and social concerns,[25] more than one hundred national Christian councils, and a large number of specialized groups such as the United Bible Societies. International ecumenism is difficult to survey and nearly impossible to coordinate. These many organizations struggle to preserve their own interests, maintain their bureaucracies, and secure access to common sources of church funding.

When the Cold War came to a close, the World Council of Churches attempted to gather these organizations around a new and better coordinated understanding of their common task. All of them had begun to grow weaker. Their level of support for the integrated program of "Justice, Peace, and the Integrity of Creation" was disappointing to the World Council. The Lausanne movement had the initiative regarding evangelization and mission, and the Lutheran World Federation maintained its own programs parallel to those of the World Council of Churches. Faith and Order had difficulty uniting around its priorities. Understandings of ecumenical social ethics were deeply confused. The Christian World Communions concentrated on strengthening their internal relations, and the WCC, hit by financial and theological crises, was no longer seen as the "privileged instrument" of the ecumenical movement. On the contrary, at the turn of the century the organization appeared to be a confused and disillusioned organization marked by sinking morale and receding support. Moreover, after having overestimated its own importance in both church and society, the Council now clearly tended to underestimate itself. Its Central Committee was torn in different directions. Some wanted to strengthen its traditional theological work; others wanted to transform the WCC into more of a non-governmental organization (NGO) focused on social questions. Everywhere there was talk of an ecumenical "winter," a "cul-de-sac," or a betrayal of the original vision.

This crisis had its parallels in the United Nations and nearly all other international organizations. They had all been established under post–World War II presuppositions, and they had flourished as long as "the modern" did not erode. Now they were required to find new forms in a world where political and economic as well as religious and intellectual conditions were so different.

The ecumenical movement needed a well-grounded, united, and forward-looking vision. The 1990s were devoted to developing that vision. Since its assemblies of 1998 and 2006 stood behind "A Common Understanding and Vision of the Ecumenical Movement," the WCC, in concert with others, has begun to play the more active role of the coordinator of the whole multifaceted ecumenical movement.[26] Indeed, with its breadth and good name, its base in the churches, and its "trademark," it was self-evident that the World Council had to take on this responsibility. It was also necessary to strengthen its relation to the Roman Catholic Church, to involve the Pentecostal churches, and to

The Ecumenical Landscape

move ahead with plans to develop a meeting place for all Christians, a "Global Christian Forum."[27]

Yet the ever frostier attitudes toward ecumenism in some of the old and traditional churches were ominous. Questions about biblical interpretation, inclusive language, gender equality, ordination of women as priests and bishops, and especially human sexuality became extremely thorny.[28] The greatest challenge to the global ecumenical movement, however, is the large number of new forms of Christianity which have sprung up in all parts of the world. The "Fourth Church" has been born, and it clearly has a future. But it stands virtually completely outside the ecumenical movement.

CHAPTER 7

The Fourth Church

Christianity exercises an overwhelming global appeal, which shows not the slightest sign of waning.
PHILIP JENKINS

On 9 April 1906, a handful of poor customs workers and domestics gathered for prayer in a simple house in Los Angeles. A thirty-six-year-old itinerant preacher, William Joseph Seymour, had for weeks assured the group that if they prayed with sufficient fervor they would experience a new Pentecost. He was a controversial figure from Louisiana who had been shut out of one church after another because of what were perceived to be his delusions, but his little congregation prayed and prayed — and then it happened. The fire of the Spirit came on them, and they broke out in shouts of joy and in dancing. Many more came, and the house was soon too small. Seymour then rented an abandoned ramshackle church on Azusa Street. The revival went on for a long time, and thousands of persons found their way there. The first newspaper article about this remarkable movement appeared in the *Los Angeles Times* on the same day as the devastating earthquake that shook San Francisco, 18 April 1906. That blacks and whites worshiped together and that even women prophesied was a sign that the Second Coming of Jesus was near, but it was also a clear provocation in the racially segregated United States. In a few weeks the congregation had many hundreds of members, received international attention, and began to branch out. That same fall it sent its first missionaries to Liberia

The Fourth Church

and Angola. Within two years congregations had been started in Mexico, Canada, Europe, the Middle East, Africa, and Asia. The global Pentecostal movement had been born.[1]

The movement sprang out of the eschatological atmosphere that prevailed among some Christian groups at the beginning of the twentieth century — in particular the African American churches and the Methodism of lower-class whites. To them the earthquake had confirmed that the end of the world was near. The Lord delayed things, but the revival continued and the Pentecostal movement became, alongside the ecumenical movement, the most innovative element in twentieth-century church history. The two movements, however, went their separate ways. They did not encounter each other until the 1960s, when the old churches realized that millions of people lived their Christian lives outside all established traditions of faith. A "Fourth Church" had appeared alongside the Orthodox, Roman Catholic, and Reformation believers. It was comprised of a jumble of congregations, difficult to comprehend, challenging, and divisive, yet it confidently shared the fundamental Christian confession that Jesus is Lord.

The Pentecostal Revival Spreads throughout the World

The Pentecostal revival had distinctive features: the gift of the Spirit confirmed by speaking in tongues; the message that Jesus is the eternal savior and king; and a certain distance from the unfaith and delusions of the older churches. Its adherents considered their revival movement to be a completion of the Reformation and the birth of the true church. Ordinary Christians dismissed the Pentecostals as disruptive and antidoctrinal, shunned their emotionalism, and accused them of setting their own experience above the words of Scripture. The Spirit stood against the letter, the movement against the institution, and the Pentecostals did not give in. People who could refer to a personal experience of God had nothing to fear from those who only offered dogmas.

The Pentecostal movement has been attacked, contradicted, and rejected. It has also been torn asunder from within. But it appears as though rejection and division have contributed to the spread of the movement. Its message has touched people and brought them into contact with that elemental spirituality that has been called "primal religion." In his rich study of the Pentecostal movement, Harvard University professor Harvey Cox has sympathetically pointed out that persons at a deeply personal level recaptured three dimensions of spirituality: speaking in tongues as the heart's free and intimate speech, piety in its most elementary form marked by a kind of "universal grammar of the Spirit," and a hope for a radically different world.[2]

Pentecostal congregations often have similar pastoral structures, but they have developed in many different ways. For some, "baptism in the Spirit" has been a "third blessing" after being born again and sanctified. This is characteristic of the Church of God in Christ, an African American denomination which has grown to become the fifth-largest church body in the U.S. Others, including the largest Pentecostal church body in the world, the Assemblies of God, interpret baptism in the Spirit as a second blessing that confirms conversion. A number of Pentecostal churches do not acknowledge the doctrine of the Trinity and baptize only in the name of Jesus.[3]

The Pentecostal message has appealed largely to the poor and uneducated. It is concrete, accessible, and straightforward. Instruction, visions, and prophetic utterances are received with hand-clapping, dancing, and speaking in tongues. Committed people on the basis of their own spiritual experiences have founded new congregations. Bible schools and the formal training of clergy were not introduced until the third and fourth generations of Pentecostals.

The movement has grown most dramatically in Latin America; its ability to adapt to different cultures is one of its strengths. It has helped people meet what was for them an unknown world. People who had severed their social roots and migrated to urban areas were given a new community to which to belong, support for family life, encouragement for the education of children, and a new sense of personal identity. Dutiful loyalty and sobriety contributed to social advancement. In a generation or two, many Pentecostals escaped poverty and entered the lower middle class. They gave up their former church membership, rejected secularism, and made the Pentecostal movement a third alternative. They repudiated academic theology and dogma in favor of mystery and ecstasy. Pentecostal spirituality provided a spiritual and social space where people, in spite of difficult external circumstances, could experience inner freedom.

This was a religion for people in transition, and in large measure it was a women's movement with many outstanding female evangelists. Since the Spirit blows where it wills, Pentecostalism was chronically uncontrollable both in organization and in teaching. In Latin America, it became a kind of popular Catholicism without priests. In Africa, it was similar to the "African Instituted (Independent) Churches" which were formed around colorful prophetic figures. In East Asia, some Pentecostal preachers appeared as shamans in suits. Many leaders presented themselves with an authority bordering on despotism. In the worst of cases, some of them claimed themselves to be Messiahs. The Pentecostal movement quickly became the dominating element in what might be called the "Fourth Church."[4] A hundred years after its birth, the Pentecostal movement has come to encompass one-fourth of Christendom.[5]

Christianity's Center of Gravity Shifts to the Third World

Charismatic expressions were also significant in the indigenous Christian movements and emerging local churches in Africa. Thus they are often counted as belonging to the Pentecostal family. In the late seventeenth century, a woman in the Congo, Kimpa Vita (Dona Beatrice), was one of the first who proclaimed a black Jesus and opened an African way to God. She was burned at the stake in 1706, accused by the Roman Catholic Church of superstition. Her movement did not last long, but she had many followers who united Christian faith, native African religion, and local customs. Many of these movements began during World War I, when prophets such as William Wade Harris in Liberia, Simon Kimbangu in the Congo, and Daniel Nkonyane in South Africa were active.[6]

In 1981 the Africa-originated churches accounted for 15 percent of the Christian population south of the Sahara. Since then they have grown by at least a million followers each year and now are said to number a hundred million adherents.[7] The rites, symbols, music, and proclamation of these churches represent a reaction against the Western forms of the historic churches and in fact are part of an African cultural renaissance. They are similar to the Pentecostal movement insofar as they often attach greater significance to the Holy Spirit than to Christ, who is seen to be comparatively distant since he has ascended to heaven. The Spirit shows its power when people are healed, freed from demons, speak in tongues, and convey a prophetic message. The Spirit creates a new community which has a certain continuity with traditional religion.

This widely shifting movement is radically biblicist. All of the Bible's books are given the same importance. The account of Israel's slavery in Egypt can be read as a history of the situation of blacks in South Africa. Other texts lend legitimacy to polygamy. Drums and visions which are spoken of in the Bible are recognized again in African culture. The Bible gives support for a strong sense of community and dependency on relatives. The congregation can be seen as a new "tribe" or "family" for those who have been forced to leave their homes to find work and other opportunities.

For the past five hundred years, the history of Christianity has been coupled with the history of the West, and this has determined the ecumenical movement's theology, perspective, and organizational structure. At the beginning of the twentieth century, the majority of Christians were white. The "Christian civilization" of the North Atlantic area gave colonialism its ideological base. Christianity was the religion of the industrialized countries, but with modernity those countries became secularized. When other countries were modernized and industrialized, it was anticipated that religion would also lose its grip, but that did not happen. Churches in Africa, Asia, and Latin America had more vitality and proved more attractive than the churches of the Western world. In a few decades Christianity's center of gravity shifted from north to south. When colonialism eventually came to an end, the churches in the Third World grew at an altogether unexpected pace.

Geneva and Rome more and more resemble deserted parish churches far away from the world's actual centers of communication, finance, and population. Today cities like São Paulo, Nairobi, Manila, and Shanghai have larger Christian populations than do Moscow, London, or Chicago. A "typical" Christian at the beginning of the twenty-first century is a woman who works her *shamba* in Africa, a street peddler in Bogota, or a Philippine domestic who works in Dubai. Half of all who worship on a Sunday in London are immigrants from Africa and the West Indies. The Anglican Church in Nigeria, the Reformed churches in Indonesia, and the Presbyterian churches in Korea have many more members than their "mother churches" in Europe or the United States. There are more Christians in China than in Germany. Since church growth parallels demographic changes, the number of Christians is increasing most in countries like the Philippines, Mexico, and Ethiopia. Hundreds of thousands of persons every year also leave their old religions and attach themselves to Christian churches. This is most common in countries where religious practice has been forbidden, as in China. In the entire world there are nearly two billion Christians, who together comprise a third of the world's population. Only about eight hundred million Christians live in North America and Europe, while about one billion two hundred million Christians are found in Asia, Africa, and Latin America. If one extrapolates the numbers to 2025, there will be two billion six hundred million Christians in the world, far more than half of them being Asians, Africans, and Latin Americans.

The Roman Catholic Church is growing at the fastest rate since it already includes more than half of all Christians. Protestant churches are also growing, while the Orthodox churches, which largely are to be found in the old European and Middle Eastern countries of their origin, remain basically unchanged. The number of Christians throughout the world is growing except on one continent — Europe. There the population is aging and diminishing, fewer children are being baptized, and many are leaving the churches. Simultaneously, the number of Muslims in Europe is steadily increasing. Globally — for the foreseeable future — Christianity will hold its position and remain the world's largest religion, but it is moving south, being urbanized, and becoming more conservative and charismatic. This has profound implications for the ecumenical movement.

The Fourth Church: One Expression of the Renaissance of World Religions

The "Fourth Church" already includes 25 percent of all Christians. It is neither Orthodox, Roman Catholic, nor of the Reformation. It is, rather, charismatic, biblicist, evangelical — and practically untouched by modern ecumenism. It is a new kind of Christianity, at times aggressive in its missionary enthusiasm and at times also politically provocative, but for the most part more directed toward individual conversion and spiritual well-being than toward social renewal. The Fourth Church is anything but uniform, and it is constantly changing. The Bible provides its theological and liturgical connection to the early church, moral guidance, and basic norms. This is of crucial importance, not least when its leaders claim to receive their own revelations.

One of modernity's illusions has been that as secularization marches forward humans will reject the "irrational" notions of faith. But, to the contrary, Christianity itself is part of the renaissance of the world's religions. The Fourth Church has come into being and grows in protest against the traditional churches and their petrified institutions, fixed dogmas, liturgical formalism, and intellectual remoteness from the holy mysteries. In the Fourth Church there is room for emotion and feeling, spontaneous prayer, faith healing and exorcism, and the potential for new forms of political Christianity.

Established in 1958 by the Pentecostal pastor Paul Yonggi Cho, the Yoido Full Gospel Church in Seoul, Korea, soon after its founding had several hundred thousand worshipers each Sunday and is now said to be one million strong. With elements of positive thinking, prosperity theology, healing, speaking in tongues, and proselytism, the church has been the object of sharp criticism, but the congregation has also become the model for hundreds of personality-driven megachurches throughout the world. In Nigeria, the Redeemed Christian Church of God is one of many examples of a charismatic church dedicated to prosperity. It was founded in 1952 and grew explosively under the leadership of Enoch Adejare Adeboye. It now has nine thousand congregations in Nigeria and hundreds more in the rest of Africa, Europe, the West Indies, and North America. On Redemption Way in Lagos, nearly half a million persons sometimes gather for a "Holy Ghost Service." With its own radio station and highly professional internet presence, it is the aim of the church to win at least one member of every family in the world. To name yet one more example, Sunday Adelaja came from Nigeria to Belarus and later to the Ukraine to study journalism. In Kiev in 1983 he founded the Embassy of God, a Pentecostal church that now has more than thirty thousand members in Europe and North America.

To an even greater extent churches like these characterize the understanding of many as to what Christianity is. Can the Roman Catholic Church, which in contrast to Protestant communions stands undivided, withstand the pressure from such movements and uphold the marks of the church of Christ as one, holy, catholic, and apostolic? The "great tradition of the church," which for two millennia has been preserved by the historic churches together, is under threat. The missionary enthusiasm of the new Christians also seems to be bringing Christianity into direct conflict with other religions. Solidarity in faith transcends national and ethnic boundaries, and religion often provides a primary identity for people. If this religion is an aggressive, fundamentalist, self-confident kind of Christianity, is there reason to fear that its "crusade" will be answered by jihad? It is possible that we might see in Africa a development toward a more militantly committed and political Christianity, a *Res Publica Christiana*, which will confront the Muslim world, the *Dar al-Islam*.[8]

The growth of the historic churches in the southern half of the globe and the ascendancy of the Fourth Church can to a certain extent be explained by historical circumstances such as colonialism, oppression, and modernization, and by sociological factors such as population growth, urbanization, and migration, and also by the contextualizing of theology. But the fundamental presupposition for all religion is the universal need of all for comprehensive symbols which hold their universe together. This need is greater when existence is fragmented and social solidarity is fragile. The Pentecostal movement came into being in America's melting pot as the twentieth century dawned. It was a spiritual movement that showed itself capable of functioning through social change and in a variety of cultures. This was true also for conservative evangelical Christianity, which throughout the world has given birth to thousands of independent congregations, missions, and parachurch organizations during the latter part of the same century.

Fundamentalist Evangelicalism Keeps Its Distance from Ecumenism

The boundary between evangelicals and Pentecostals is no longer as clear as it was in the past. The two types of Christianity influence each other, and there are many similarities between their ways of viewing Scripture and congregational life. In spite of the fact that the conservative evangelical movements have their roots in the Reformation, it seems correct to include many of them within the Fourth Church, especially outside the United States. There are, actually, four reasons for this: (1) their basic ecclesiology or understanding of the church is decisively different from that of the Orthodox, Catholic, and Reformation churches; (2) as a rule they stand at great distance from the ecumenical movement; (3) they often are marked by elements of a "prosperity gospel"; and (4) they now have their foothold in Latin America, Africa, and Asia, where their theological and sometimes even political influence is considerable.

In April 1942, two hundred persons gathered in St. Louis, Missouri, in order to organize the evangelical movement, an act which caused American religion to change its course. They came from fundamentalist circles but assumed a more moderate stance in order to attract others. The most well known was Billy Graham, who was to become a world evangelist and a counselor to one American president after another. Thus the National Association of Evangelicals came into being.[9] They concentrated on making Fuller Theological Seminary in California the equal of Princeton Theological Seminary in New Jersey and *Christianity Today* the equal of the venerable *Christian Century*. A long list of theological seminaries, publishing houses, and parachurch organizations identified themselves with this new evangelicalism, which rejected both hard-necked fundamentalism and liberal Protestantism. A dynamic religious activism came to life; it so deeply influenced American church life that after fifty years twice as many American adults identified themselves as "evangelical" than as "mainline."

In the nineteenth century, practically all large American Protestant bodies were evangelical in the sense that they pursued traditional Reformation teaching and were also inspired by one revival after another. They took major responsibility in society in the confident faith that the Kingdom of God could be realized in the United States. During the conflict at the beginning of the twentieth century between modernists and fundamentalists, these evangelical Christians were split into two camps. Established, politically liberal Protestantism could no longer provide shelter to the militant conservatives who maintained a literal interpretation of the main elements — or fundamentals — of the Christian faith. Indeed, these conservatives were labeled "fundamentalists," and they became more and more uncooperative. The men who gathered in St. Louis wanted, in contrast, to save their version of evangelical faith from being caged in the literalism, pessimism, anti-Catholicism, and isolation of the fundamentalists. They thus seized the initiative while the fundamentalists were marginalized. From these margins the hard-line fundamentalists continued to struggle against everything that could be termed liberal or ecumenical.

Conservative evangelical Christians emphasize the Bible's authority and infallibility and the importance of personal conversion, but there is no official theological or doctrinal line between Christians identifying themselves as "evangelical" and other Protestants, even if evangelicals more readily turn toward churches that possess a clearly conservative profile. Manifestations such as biblicism, being born again, evangelization, family values, and opposition to abortion and same-sex marriage indicate what evangelicals in general stand for and against. They attend church more often than others, witness to their faith more easily, and often express a feeling that God speaks to them personally: "God wants me to . . ." or "God said to me. . . ." Most evangelical church bodies carry on extensive missions in other countries.

When the American "Christian right" began to wage its campaign against liberal theology, the teaching of evolution in schools, belief in global warming, abortion, and same-sex relations and gave its undivided support to the Republican Party, the "conservative evangelicals" came to center stage and gained a disproportionate share of the nation's electorate. That share amounted to one-third in the 2004 presidential campaign. Right-wing Christians had been a political force since the 1950s with Senator Joseph McCarthy's anti-Communist crusade, but the Christian right was truly born in the 1960s. It arose in reaction to movements for civil rights and against the Vietnam War, for sexual liberation, and the feminist and gay movements. The Christian right created a formidable alliance with popular, largely right-wing political action groups, think tanks, educational institutions, and legal aid groups. It enlisted television evangelists and media executives and formed a network of thousands of ministers. With its growing strength it also began to influence American foreign policy. It gave wholehearted support to Israel, endorsed Zionism, and emphasized the special role of the Jewish people in God's salvation history. It supported increased federal spending on HIV/AIDS prevention (albeit with considerable restrictions) and defended freedom of religion, provided that it included their own right to evangelize and proselytize. Republican politicians — from the president to mayors of small towns — had good reason to stand alongside this single-minded movement.[10]

The Christian right has had nothing to do with the ecumenical movement. Fanatical representatives of the right, such as Carl McIntire, who founded the International Council of Christian Churches in direct opposition to the World Council of Churches, and the North Ireland clergyman Ian Paisley, were familiar demonstrators at ecumenical conferences, referring to ecumenism as the work of the devil. When such fundamentalist Christians set foot in the Third World, they often carried with them extremely negative pictures of the ecumenical movement, accusing it of being sympathetic to communism, supportive of terrorists, and bearing a false gospel. The struggle between the ecumenical movement and this group from the Christian right was often bitter and at times even mirrored the polarizations of the Cold War.

The Pentecostal movement was also averse to the ecumenical movement, although without the same political overtones. Pentecostals considered that the ecumenical movement occupied itself in a futile human attempt to unite and renew churches that had already lost spiritual power and were more occupied with social and political matters than with the proclamation of the gospel. Nevertheless, in 1961 two Pentecostal churches in Chile joined the World Council of Churches, and in 2010 seven Pentecostal churches belonged to the Council. The fact remains, however, that while welcome in the WCC, the Pentecostal movement has remained marginal in it.

Nor have African Instituted Churches found a place in the ecumenical movement. Only two of the approximately six thousand such church bodies have affiliated with the WCC, namely, the Church of the Lord Aladura in Nigeria and *Eglise du Christ sur la terre par le Prophet Simon Kimbangu* (Church of Christ on Earth by the Prophet Simon Kimbangu) in the Democratic Republic of Congo. The Kimbanguist Church has been quite active in the WCC and was led for many years by the atomic physicist Bena Silu. When the church's founder, on the basis of a new revelation, included himself in the Holy Trinity, relations to the Council cooled but were never broken.[11] The African Independent Churches have developed their own ecumenical network, the Organization of African Instituted Churches, which was founded in Cairo in 1978 and registered in Kenya as an international organization. It is an associate member of the All Africa Conference of Churches and has a working relationship to the World Council

A Charismatic Awakening among WCC Member Churches

In the 1960s a charismatic revival broke out in a number of churches that belong to the WCC as well as in the Roman Catholic Church. It had many of the characteristics of the Pentecostal movement although in a tamer form; for a long time it was called by the name "Neo-Pentecostal." The movement began in an Episcopal parish in Van Nuys, California, where a priest named Dennis Bennett was rector. Many of his parishioners received the baptism of the Holy Spirit, and soon this renewal spread to a long list of American churches and groups. After a few years, this charismatic movement was also found in Protestant churches in Europe, Asia, and Australia, and it even struck in the Roman Catholic Church. The movement met a certain opposition from church leaders, which led to a critical discussion concerning both the relation of personal spiritual experience to the church's teaching authority and the relation between spirituality and social action. Large services of charismatic worship were held in the Episcopal National Cathedral in Washington, D.C.; and when ten thousand charismatics filled the Basilica of St. Peter in Rome and spoke in tongues before an amazed Pope Paul VI, the movement received greater acceptance. *Rinnovamento nello Spirito* in Italy soon had a quarter of a million members, and *Communauté Emmanuelle* in France was able to gather twenty thousand persons to its meetings.[12] Many traditional Pentecostals were, nevertheless, skeptical about this "socially acceptable" variant of their movement, which could always, they said, be trimmed and tailored by nail-biting bishops and ministers anxious to threaten no one.

Within ten years a large number of WCC member churches were being influenced by the charismatic movement. Many believed that a shared experience of Spirit baptism and speaking in tongues would break down the walls between the confessions and mediate a great ecumenical breakthrough. But the churches largely confined the charismatic movement within the boundaries of their own structures. It thus had a fairly limited impact on ecumenism, although it contributed to a high estimate of the Pentecostal movement, brought Protestants and Roman Catholics closer to each other, and gave pneumatology (teaching concerning the Holy Spirit) a more central place in theological discussion. When the WCC adopted "Come Holy Spirit — Renew the Whole Creation" as the theme of its seventh assembly in Canberra, Australia, in 1991, this was connected both to the charismatic renewal and to an emphasis on the Spirit's work in the world as seen in the Council's concentration on justice, peace, and the integrity of creation.

In 1975 the WCC initiated a program aimed at the renewal of congregational life. It was devoted to spirituality, the development of worship, and the coordination of work at evangelical academies and study centers worldwide. The charismatic movement stood at its peak and received special attention in this program. The churches shared their experiences and undertook comprehensive analyses of the theologies of charismatic groups, their ecumenical significance, and their relation to the established churches. A consultation — with WCC General Secretary Philip Potter, Professor Walter Hollenweger, Anglican Archbishop Bill Burnett of Cape Town, and the Dominican priest Kilian McDonnell in principal roles — admonished the World Council to take both the traditional and new Pentecostal movements with greater seriousness.[13] However, it took eighteen more years before an organized conversation with Pentecostals began. It was not easy to find persons who could navigate the multifaceted movement, and in fact the WCC did not show genuine interest in encountering such — from its ecumenical vantage point — conservative, inner-directed, divisive, and theologically unsophisticated Christians.

Yet the doors were opened by others. Latin America's regional ecumenical council had many Pentecostal churches among its members and also took a number of initiatives toward cooperation with evangelical churches. In the United States some Pentecostal churches demonstrated a modest degree of openness to ecumenical contacts — e.g., Pentecostal theologians participated actively in the Commission on Faith and Order of the National Council of Churches. Yet it was difficult to move to structured dialogue with clear goals. The Roman Catholic Church, however, was able in 1972 to undertake an official dialogue with the Pentecostal movement on the initiative of the South African David du Plessis. Internationally, he was the best known of the leaders of the Assemblies of God and participated personally in a number of conferences of the WCC. His connections with the Vatican were, however, controversial within his own group. Information about his ecumenical endeavors remained extremely sparse within the Pentecostal movement. The Pentecostal World Fellowship, in the formation of which du Plessis had participated, did not support any ecumenical dialogue. The Assemblies of God, however — albeit reluctantly — took responsibility for talks with the Roman Catholics to start. The early conversations dealt with how to understand and interpret the Bible, "continuing revelation" in the present, the work of the Spirit outside the church, Spirit baptism, adult baptism, and salvation. Walter Hollenweger, who devoted his life to studying the Pentecostal movement, has called this dialogue with the Roman Catholic Church "one of the most important events on the religion scene in our century."[14]

After the WCC assembly in Uppsala in 1968, which saw, according to an evangelical critic, "the crystallization of another gospel," and after the world mission conference in Bangkok in 1973, which according to the same critic "codified another mission for the ecumenical and conciliar movement," the evangelicals went their own way.[15] The Lausanne movement became their forum for mission theology and strategy. Yet during the thirty years that followed the two sides came nearer to one another, and at the WCC assembly in Harare in 1998 the evangelical delegates were prepared to agree that mission has both a social and personal dimension, but they forcefully called on the World Council to return to its original Bible-based, christocentric orientation to mission if evangelical groups were to participate in the ecumenical movement in a meaningful way.[16]

Greater Social Consciousness in the Evangelical Movement: A Breakthrough for Ecumenism

In the United States the number of socially committed evangelical Christians has been growing, largely in response to the Iraq War but also as a result of influences from more socially radical partners in Asia, Africa, and Latin America. Micah Challenge, an appeal issued in 2001 based on Micah 6:8 ("... what does the Lord require of you but to do justice, and to love kindness, and to walk humbly with your God?"), mobilized hundreds of evangelical organizations throughout the world in support of the United Nations' millennium goal to reduce global poverty by 50 percent by 2015. The World Evangelical Alliance has also declared its determination to work for just trade relations and for the writing off of international debt. Many evangelicals have kept their distance from the moralism of the Christian right and from much of the Republican Party's platform. Among them can be mentioned the former U.S. president Jimmy Carter and also Jim Wallis, who for a long time has had great influence through the journal *Sojourners* and its extensive network. Such persons desire to attack poverty at its roots, work for justice, bring an end to current wars, and engage the question of climate change. The National Association of Evangelicals, mentioned earlier in this chapter and now an umbrella organization for groups which together have approximately thirty million members, in 2004 admonished all American evangelical Christians to strive for justice for the poor, protect human rights, seek peace, protect God's creation, respect human life, and defend the family. Organizations such as World Relief and World Vision have for a long time worked to increase federal funding for development, to reduce international debt, and to bring about just trade practices. In 2006 eighty-six prominent evangelical leaders demanded that carbon dioxide emissions be diminished, among them Rick Warren, the author of the bestselling book *The Purpose-Driven Life* and now among America's best known preachers.[17] This increasing concern regarding global warming by evangelicals also indicates that neither opposition to abortion nor support of "family values" remains their sole social concern.

Yet in spite of this change of attitude in the direction of an integrated approach both to social, economic, and cultural questions and to the rethinking of mission and development, which large numbers of evangelicals are pursuing, attempts to move the evangelical movement as a whole closer to the ecumenical movement have been halfhearted at best.[18] Mutual stereotypes lie in the way. Political values have overshadowed the ecumenical imperative. And now other winds are blowing. In the United States, a new ecumenical entity, which at this point resists being called an "organization," has been formed, Christian Churches Together.[19] This entity is broader in scope than the National Council of Churches, since it includes nearly all church bodies in the country. The Christian right and conservative Roman Catholics find each other here. Similar developments are to be found in other countries as well. In India, the National United Christian Forum includes most communions. In Sweden, evangelical groups and the Pentecostal Church are now members of the Swedish Christian Council. Even the Russian Orthodox Church, in spite of internal political quarrels, is finding some common ground with Roman Catholics in their common quest to preserve traditional moral values. In all such initiatives ecclesiological differences are put in the background for the sake of common witness.

At the initiative of the WCC, a "Global Christian Forum" is being born. After several years of preparation, leaders of the historic churches, the Pentecostal churches, the African Instituted Churches, and evangelical groups gathered in 2007 in Nairobi with unified goals. This was an ecumenical breakthrough of considerable significance. Practically all Christians throughout the world — the First, Second, Third, and Fourth Churches — are on a journey toward a common platform. The churches desire first of all to learn to know and trust each other in order possibly to speak together in the name of all Christianity. The fact that there is now a forum for meeting can provide the groundwork for deepened ecumenical engagement, and the Fourth

The Fourth Church

Church can now more easily enter the ecumenical movement. The twentieth century came to an end in 1989 with the fall of the Berlin Wall, and since that time there has been more than merely a reconfiguration of the old ecumenical movement. A new ecumenism for the twenty-first century is taking shape, and it will surely be something very different from what we have known in the past.

CHAPTER 8

After the Wall

"Would you tell me, please, which way I ought to go from here?"
"That depends a good deal on where you want to get to."
"I don't much care where —"
"Then it doesn't matter which way you go. . . ."
"— so long as I get somewhere."

LEWIS CARROLL, *Alice in Wonderland*

After 8 May 1989, the police set up blockades on the roads leading to the St. Nicholas Church in Leipzig. The exits from the expressway were closed off each Monday when "peace prayers" were scheduled. The pressure increased week after week; persons were arrested on their way to the church, and more and more agents from the Stasi, the state security force, sat in on the services. The two thousand places in the church were not enough when Christians and atheists, the old who were resigned to things after decades of grayish socialism and the young who were inclined to leave the country, gathered together. The peace prayers had begun in 1982; they quickly became a kind of safety valve where critics of the government could meet and publicly identify the grim state of things in East Germany.

The German Democratic Republic, the DDR, observed its fortieth anniversary on 7 October 1989. It turned out to be a day of violence in Leipzig. Soldiers and police crushed defenseless citizens. Hundreds were loaded into trucks and taken away. The newspapers editorialized that the "counterrevolution" must come to an end, by armed force if necessary. The atmosphere was tense at the peace prayers two days later. The St. Nicholas Church was filled hours before the service began. More party functionaries and Stasi agents were present than usual. They listened, as on every Monday, to Jesus' Beatitudes concerning the poor, the humble, the peacemakers, the persecuted. It was an impressive, quiet service of worship which concluded with a call to peace and an appeal to nonviolence; afterwards, the bishop blessed the congregation.

Outside the church, tens of thousands had gathered with candles in their hands. They stood silently while the military and the police withdrew and the tension was relieved. The quiet, nonviolent demonstration following the peace prayers went on for several weeks without even one shop window being broken. One member of the Communist Party's Central Committee commented, shortly before his death, "We had planned for everything. We were prepared for everything. Just not for candles and prayers." After more chaotic days, the Berlin Wall fell on 9 November, but without violence.

The churches played a central role in the peaceful revolution that took place in Europe in 1989-1990. Pope John Paul II supported his homeland, Poland, and the Holy See participated in the entire diplomatic process leading to the fall of the Soviet Union. Protestants in East Germany and other countries in Eastern Europe had contact with churches in other parts of the world, and the message and actions of the ecumenical conference in Basel earlier that year were widely circulated. Possibly the decision of the churches to work from within for changes in governments contributed to their collapse.

When turning points in contemporary history are spoken of, the May Revolt in Paris in 1968, the fall of the Berlin Wall in 1989, and the terrorist attacks on New York and Washington on 11 September 2001 are always named. Some question whether the events of 1968, while they shook Europe and brought about changes in the values and lifestyles of a whole generation, were ultimately of such great significance. But all agree that the fall of the Berlin Wall not only symbolized a great upheaval but changed the direction of world history. The dramatic and unforeseen course of events was not simply the end of the long period during which communism dictated the future for half of the world's population. The dream of a secure and just society of equals which was the foundation of democratic socialism also suffered a shock. The welfare state found it necessary to adjust itself to a neoliberalism which proclaimed that market forces were superior to the national state even in the production of welfare.

In the months and years to come, the United States became the world's only military superpower. The Gulf War of 1991 launched a massive military presence in the Middle East, East Africa, and Central Asia. This, in turn, gave rise to an intense and often religiously inspired anti-Americanism. The European Union was strengthened, took in more member states, and undertook a new if still limited military role. The globalization of markets and media accelerated. The previously self-evident connection between democracy, the free market, and economic growth was shattered when China's totalitarian communist national order experienced unprecedented growth. Fragile democracies were set up in many countries. Wars in the Balkans, in Africa, and to a certain extent in Chechnya and Iraq were "new" wars which, in contrast to "old" national wars, were civil wars with confusing mixtures of political, ethnic, economic, and religious interests. These wars were not financed by taxation and were extremely profitable for weapons dealers, mercenary militias, security firms, and even organized crime. Armed conflicts not only changed in character; they were actually fewer than in the past, especially in Africa. In 2002 there were only half as many wars in the world as there had been ten years earlier. A number of conflicts were brought to a conclusion by negotiation rather than by victory. The peace efforts and the peacekeeping forces of the United Nations played a significant role in this development.[1]

The vitality and politicization of the religions that was clearly an element in these developments came as a surprise to those who believed that secularization was a natural consequence of prosperity and that Europe especially was leading the way toward a weakening of all religion. The 1979 Islamic revolution in Iran, the role of Buddhism in the conflict with the Tamils in Sri Lanka, the rise of the Hindu national party in India, and the combining of land with promise in Israel showed that things were, rather, the opposite. Europe was not the norm but the exception.[2] The influence of liberation theology in countries like Nicaragua, the support given by the Roman Catholic Church to Solidarity in Poland, and the undisguised political activity of the Christian right in the United States also demonstrated the ambiguous role of Christianity in society.

All religion can be transformed into ideology and misused for political purposes; Islam in particular has developed a reputation for being especially violent. People forget, however, both that all of the great world religions in principle reject violence in the name of God as a distortion of fundamental beliefs, and that religion in most cases serves as a protection for human dignity. In consequence of this forgetfulness, the ecumenical movement has consistently emphasized the constructive contribution of world religions to tolerance, peace, and social development. In 1986 Pope John Paul II invited religious leaders from all over the world to Assisi in Italy for a day of dialogue and prayer for peace. This gathering took on considerable symbolic meaning. Subsequently, the pope gave the Community of Sant'Egidio the task of continuing such religious encounters. With its active network of leading Muslims, Jews, Hindus, Buddhists, and Christians, Sant'Egidio has been able annually to coordinate large interreligious conferences that have received considerable attention in the media. This has been only one of many initiatives to build bridges and develop the common responsibility of the religions for the future of the world.

A New Starting Point for Social Ethics

For the World Council of Churches, as for many other international organizations, the decade of the 1990s was a time of uncertainty and reappraisal. Time had passed since the Council's 1968 assembly in Uppsala with its focus on the Third World, aid, development, and liberation from oppressive systems. Now the revolutionary movements had lost strength, and global economic forces were determining human conditions down to the smallest village. The WCC had, as always, difficulties in limiting its commitments, but it decided to devote its attention and resources primarily to four issues: to continue its concern for justice, peace, and the environment; to carry through its decade of "Churches in Solidarity with Women"; to develop its resistance to globalization; and to maintain its campaign to protect human rights.

Noble-sounding moral generalizations were not adequate for such commitments. The idealism which had given inspiration to social ethics in the time since 1968 had to give way to a "hopeful realism" grounded in local contexts. Social ethics could no longer be based on a metaphysical frame of reference or on universal norms or common human experience. There are far too many "worlds" in the world for that to be possible. Shortsighted commercial and economic interests had the power to influence basic values. Traditional cultures were being sacrificed for economic growth. The certainty with which people spoke of "the responsible society" was lost, but so also was the confidence that churches, as in the past, could come to agreement regarding "justice, peace, and the integrity of creation." The most common words in the ecumenically correct speech of the 1980s — justice, human rights, responsibility, solidarity with the poor, sustainable development, democracy, peace, equality — began to be emptied of their content. Generalizing idealistic terminology hid actual political and social conflicts.[3]

In a fragmented world, generally applicable social ethics had to be changed for the taking of positions in thousands of particular and unique situations. The concrete moral and political praxis in local circumstances caused more debate than a general discourse regarding values. It was not difficult to support the declaration of the World's Parliament of Religions, meeting in Chicago in 1993, which advocated a culture of nonviolence and equal rights for women and men, or to appreciate Hans Küng's powerful development of a global ethic based on the common values of the world's great religions.[4] But when such efforts come to be put into practice, difficulties come to light. It is one thing to desire to develop a culture of nonviolence, another thing to know how this might come about. The same basic values can and must be implemented in different ways in different situations. Nevertheless, general human ethical values which exist in all cultures offer a common framework and direction for differing contextual applications; diversity and pluralism do not need to lead toward a total relativism of values. It still is possible to gather the churches around certain ethical matters which have an impact on all humankind.

The superpowers had made a degree of peace with each other, so that weapons of mass destruction were no longer seen as the primary threat to civilization. Consequently, the ecumenical movement focused on economic, communication, and social globalization, which in those days was construed as a threat to the ecumenical visions of the unity of humanity and the whole creation and of a good life for all. The churches must on the basis of their faith, solidarity, and moral commitment work for an alternative world order which would not widen the gap between the poor and the rich, dehumanize humanity, or threaten the environment. For a long period of time the ecumenical movement had taken the side of the weak at the table where the struggle for power, resources, and livable space was negotiated, and it had many friends among those who fought against the negative consequences of globalization. The WCC participated actively in the World Social Forum, the annual meeting of civil society organizations first held in Brazil in 2001, desiring to be an open space where churches and social movements could freely test their thoughts concerning the future. If the mighty forces of globalization were to be steered in a direction that would benefit all human beings and the environment, it would be necessary for the churches to ally themselves with other faith communities, primarily those of the Abrahamic religions.[5]

The churches did not deny that globalization has its positive aspects; they themselves transcended all human and national boundaries in their mission to share their message, anthropology, and worldview with people in all lands and cultures. They participated actively in various actions of solidarity, such as development and relief aid, and they themselves utilized the communication technology that made the globalizing of financial markets, production, and consumption possible. No transnational corporation in the world could match the Roman Catholic Church with respect to international scope, unified organization, centralized leadership, and the exchange of corporate values. The ecumenical movement was itself global and dedicated to strengthen the churches' common faith and worldwide witness. Its horizon was a unified humanity.

An Unjust Global Economy Alarms the Churches

The problem, therefore, was not a heightened mutual global interdependence, but that the world economy was dominated by the wealthy and exploited the poor.

Early in its life, the ecumenical movement had been alarmed that transnational companies with their own rules had such a large role in the world's economy. Already in 1937, the Life and Work Conference held in Oxford had expressed its regret that it was difficult to attain democratic goals, since "the economic order in many countries [has] some resemblance to a tyranny, in the classical sense of that term, where rulers are not accountable for their actions to any superior authority representing the community over whom power is exercised."[6] In 1955 the WCC undertook a critical study of private industry in "the economically underdeveloped world." Questions about ambiguous investment practices in the underdeveloped world arose time and time again, and they led to the conclusion that transnational corporations with their enormous influence should be subject to international law and regulation. In 1975 at Nairobi a very sharp charge was formulated: transnational corporations "are a typical example of the ways in which capitalist forces in the international and national sphere join together to oppress the poor and keep them under domination."[7]

In the debate about aid to developing countries, peoples' participation and reliance on their own resources was emphasized. Under a certain influence from the churches in Eastern Europe, "a just, participatory, and sustainable society" became, in the 1970s, the descriptive slogan for the churches' contribution toward an international social, economic, and political world order. Threats of nuclear weapons and environmental degradation later changed this to "justice, peace, and the integrity of creation." The objective was a clearly Christian position against everything that threatens life. In 1990 four areas were chosen for the churches' action together: the cancellation of debt and development of an alternative world economic order; demilitarization and nonviolence; the environment and climate change; and opposition to racism and discrimination. Since the churches in developing countries found it necessary to make specifically local conditions their starting points, the WCC could not easily unite in principled opposition to globalization and to global institutions such as the International Monetary Fund and the World Bank. After the fall of the Berlin Wall, however, globalization became a main issue in international debate, and ecumenical positions became clearer.[8]

Globalization could be interpreted as a prolongation of Western colonialism. Poor countries were plundered of their natural resources and were too weak and dependent to offer resistance. "Globalization," therefore, became an expression that described the continued control of the developing countries by the Western powers. The free market economy which had been so successful in the wealthy countries should now be spread over all. The Western world's way of managing corporations and business became the norm. Many experienced this as neocolonialism or neo-imperialism. The impoverished countries were made into satellite states that in their dependence had no other function than to supply industrialized lands with cheap labor and goods.[9] The possibility of profiting from the advantages of globalization varied greatly, and the churches saw it as their duty to be in solidarity precisely with those who did not share in economic growth. The Reformed churches went so far as to characterize their position for economic justice as a matter of faith *(processus confessionis)*, and in this view they were given the support of the World Council of Churches.[10]

Simply put, globalization was described as a limitless deregulated market for goods and services. It intensified trans-border cooperation in a complex system of mutual dependence. It changed conditions for national states and for corporations and strongly influenced the traditional social life of hundreds of millions of people. It was a continuation of the twentieth-century internationalization of politics and corporate institutions, but it became something qualitatively different when the electronic revolution changed both communication — the handling and distribution of information by mass media — and its production. In less than twenty years the world was fundamentally changed. Global markets exploded, and daily transactions of capital began to exceed in value all national currency reserves together. Geographical distance no longer presented a problem, and time appeared as an immediate present moving into the future and quickly leaving the past behind. Local cultures and histories were overshadowed by global information and new values, marketing and advertising flooded people's homes, consumption and mobility increased steadily, and politics tended to become theater. There were fewer fixed points left to hold on to.

The Ecumenical Movement Opposes Globalization

A reaction was not long in coming. A militant anti-globalization movement, together with historically conscious ethnic groups and strengthened communities of faith, was much in favor of a different order that would offer continuity, identity, and meaning. Even though technology and globalization were here to stay, people wanted to attain by democratic means the possibility of influencing globalization so that it would be of benefit for all, developing ethical norms, limiting negative effects on the environment, and preserving individual cultures' own values.

The churches' critique contained elements of political rhetoric and clear anti-capitalism. Those who were accustomed to criticizing the

WCC for being irresponsibly leftist were given grist for their mill. Leading scholars, politicians, and theologians chose not to participate as before in ecumenical conversations, often finding them too idealistic, unrealistic, even utopian in tone and content. The resources of the ecumenical organizations were too meager to influence the international debate in any appreciable way, although these organizations still did make an impression on church opinion and were able to carry on a dialogue with global economic institutions. The churches' international structures were sluggish, and they had difficulty keeping up with the changes that were taking place all around them. In comparison with the network of anti-globalization movements in secular society, both the World Council of Churches and the Lutheran World Federation were heavy-footed organizations. Thus it became a matter of importance that the ecumenical movement develop organizational structures that were able to combine the local with the global, include greater diversity, react quickly and in a well-informed way, and make common cause for a better world with organizations outside the churches. For some the World Social Forum with its loose composition became a model for future ecumenism.[11]

The 1998 Harare assembly of the World Council of Churches affirmed that the visions of globalization and ecumenism could not be combined:

> Globalization is not simply an economic issue. It is a cultural, political, ethical, and ecological issue.... The vision behind globalization includes a competing vision to the Christian commitment to the oikoumene, the unity of humankind and the whole inhabited earth.... Although globalization is an inescapable fact of life, we should not subject ourselves to the vision behind it, but strengthen our alternative ways towards visible unity in diversity, towards an oikoumene of faith and solidarity.
>
> The logic of globalization needs to be challenged by an alternative way of life of community in diversity. Christians and churches should reflect on the challenge of globalization from a faith perspective and therefore resist the unilateral domination of economic and cultural globalization. The search for alternative options to the present economic system and the realization of effective political limitations and corrections to the process of globalization and its implications are urgently needed.[12]

Thus the WCC chose its chief directions for the turn of the millennium. Globalization was to occupy a considerable portion of its work, but the assembly emphasized that this was not primarily a matter of taking political positions; rather, spiritual values were at stake:

> [T]he challenge of globalization to the churches must be seen first and foremost as a theological and spiritual challenge. The love of God, expressed fully in Christ, reveals a vision of fullness of life for all; the emerging global economy projects a vision of limitless material gratification for those who can afford it. The churches are called to witness to and embody God's intention for the world in the face of growing globalization and the values which underlie it.[13]

When the Central Committee of the Council translated this into a program, called "Common Witness and Service in the Time of Globalization," it chose to concentrate on the churches' opportunities to promote social justice, equitable trade, and a financial system free from oppressive imposition of debt, corruption, and exorbitant profit. A report was presented immediately prior to the assembly held in Porto Alegre, Brazil, in 2006. It reviewed a lengthy list of negative effects of globalization in poor countries and held the International Monetary Fund, the World Trade Organization, and the World Bank responsible for the world's injustices. It asserted, however, that it would not be adequate simply to establish new ethical guidelines for their work; the structures and regulations that guide world trade must be altered in a thoroughgoing way.[14] This report was met with sharp criticism, not least from the Nordic churches, for one-sidedness and over-simplification. It was never presented to the assembly for adoption and was instead sent back for further revision.

Over time, neoliberal ideas were more nuanced. The world's economic order was relatively stabilized, though the stability would prove fragile when a global financial crisis hit hard in 2009. Globalization undoubtedly contributed to a bettering of living conditions for many hundreds of millions of people, although at the same time economic gaps widened both within and between countries. Climate change, caused by increasing discharge of greenhouse gases, brought about some international agreements and a certain adaptation of the production of energy and transportation. Working conditions in poverty-stricken countries improved somewhat. In comparison with previous assemblies, the resolution regarding globalization passed in 2006 at Porto Alegre was relatively modest. The task, however, was not done: continued theological reflection was required along with solid political, social, and economic analysis, and the churches were mandated to carry on dialogue with different partners in order to communicate their practical and positive suggestions and contributions.[15]

To Overcome Violence

The "Decade to Overcome Violence: Churches Seeking Reconciliation and Peace" was launched in 2001 as the most pressing element in the WCC program. The Council had in 1983 rejected the possession and use of nuclear weapons even as the churches in practice supported the right to both self-defense and justified rebellion — with violence if the circumstances required. Such violence, however, often degenerated into blatant terrorism, victimizing totally innocent people.

Thus, the question of the right to armed rebellion came to the fore. Toward the end of the 1980s, the voices for nonviolence had become stronger. At the same time, violence in homes and streets and above all sexual violence against women were receiving greater attention even as international negotiations for disarmament reached a new phase. During a heated debate about the Gulf War, Konrad Raiser, a German delegate to the 1991 assembly in Canberra and subsequently general secretary of the Council, proposed that a radical formulation should be included in the formal resolution:

> We call upon [the churches] to give up any theological or moral justification of the use of military power, be it in war or through other forms of oppressive security systems, and to become public advocates of a just peace.[16]

The proposal was rejected on the basis of its "pacifist nature." But it was agreed that the time had come to modify the traditional doctrine of "just war," which had guided the churches' position for centuries, and replace it with a teaching on "just peace." The right to use military violence should no longer be the issue, but rather the basic demand for justice must be fulfilled in order for there to be just and durable peace.

Should not nonviolence be the alternative proposal of the ecumenical movement? The Seoul conference in 1991 committed itself "to practice nonviolence in all our personal relationships, to work for the banning of war as a legally recognized means of resolving conflicts, and to press governments for the establishment of an international legal order of peacemaking."[17]

The German Mennonite Fernando Enns, inspired by this commitment and by the "Ecumenical Decade of the Churches in Solidarity with Women" (1988-1998), proposed a similar decade against world violence. This proposal was accepted, and the "Decade to Overcome Violence" was proclaimed for the period 2000-2010. This period coincided with the United Nations' "Decade for a Culture of Peace and Nonviolence for the Children of the World," which opened the way for cooperation between the two global institutions.

The number of armed conflicts between nations decreased after the end of the Cold War. Many countries undertook genuine disarmament which actually went farther than was provided for in previous agreements. South Africa attained its freedom, and Central America moved into a period of relative calm. But brutal conflicts of other kinds broke out in which renegade troops, warlords, and organized violent groups worked together in the promotion of terror and ethnic cleansing. Some religious groups were brought into this, groups unable to maintain their integrity. The first Gulf War, which was going on at the same time as the assembly in Canberra in 1991, demonstrated that the United States was prepared to exercise military violence throughout the world. The appalling tribal genocide in Rwanda, in which hundreds of thousands of Christians slaughtered each other, and the spread of ethnic cleansing in Bosnia and Herzegovina were about to break out. Churches stood far apart from each other in their views of war and peace, sanctions, and peacekeeping actions, but on one point they were all in agreement: there was an indissoluble bond between justice and peace. Time and time again it was repeated:

> Peace is not just the absence of war. Peace cannot be built on foundations of injustice. Peace requires a new international order based on justice for and within all the nations, and respect for the God-given humanity and dignity of every person. Peace is, as the Prophet Isaiah has taught us, the effect of righteousness. . . . The ecumenical approach to peace and justice is based on the belief

that without justice for all everywhere we shall never have peace anywhere.[18]

An ethical dilemma was, however, encountered by the churches insofar as "humanitarian intervention" for the defense of human rights and peace sometimes required violence. In conflict, victims often became perpetrators when they defended themselves. During ongoing battles it was nearly impossible to establish the peace-creating dialogue frequently desired on both sides. The "Decade to Overcome Violence" was dedicated to strengthening a culture of nonviolence. Together with others, the churches wished to transform conflict into a "just peace," utilizing interreligious and intercultural dialogue in the effort. This was an element in creating an alternate globalization.

For churches that proclaimed reconciliation in Christ, differing forms of peace work and conciliation were readily available. The churches were encouraged to increase their understanding of physical, psychological, and structural violence and to reject every effort to theologically legitimize the use of violence; rather, they were to condemn it in the name of God, build security, cooperation, and community, develop relations with other religions, protest against militarization, and work to stop traffic in small weapons. The program included everything from mediating conflicts between nations to checking youth violence in the streets. The churches were admonished to pay special attention to hidden violence against women and children. Where previously war had been looked upon as a necessary evil, many now dreamed of a world with a minimal use of force, where methods of nonviolence were actively pursued in all situations. The historically pacifist churches had a special contribution to make to a culture of peace imbued with an ethic of nonviolence.

Many doubted, however, that the churches could steer the human mentality and conscience in the direction of nonviolence. Lutherans and others who claimed to possess a realistic understanding of human nature argued that life is a constant struggle. Only those who are able to defend themselves will survive. Violence seems to be ingrained in humanity's biological and social nature, and legal, controlled violence is necessary to preserve law and order. Violence thus is seen as inescapable, but it must by all means be kept within boundaries.

The "Decade to Overcome Violence" was dedicated to inspiring the churches to make more active contributions to the prevention of violence and to find peaceful solutions to the world's problems, but they were also urged to review their own traditions and cleanse all prayers and symbols which referred to war in a positive light or gave legitimacy to violence. Churches should avoid all pictures of God that had traits of violence and interpretations of atonement as sacrifice. Above all, the churches were to do away with warlike metaphors, hierarchical structures of power, spiritualities which emphasized obedience and self-denial, and every form of mission reminiscent of "crusade." The churches, however, had been given similar admonitions during the "Ecumenical Decade of Churches in Solidarity with Women." This had awakened strong reactions among some church leaders, and attention had been diverted from the main elements of the program. To criticize the churches directly this way was to swim in dangerous waters, but it also added urgency to the concern.

On the whole, the "Decade to Overcome Violence" was positively received. Everywhere the responsibility of the religions for peace was affirmed. In an unprecedented way, nearly all churches in the world kept their distance from the Iraq War, with the pope and the ecumenical patriarch joining their voices with most Protestant churches. Since then many concrete programs of nonviolence have been developed involving women and men, children and adults, and including some of the foremost leaders of society. Through its nearly pacifist image, its positive anthropology, and its local implementation, the program for nonviolence made a positive impression. An "International Ecumenical Peace Convocation," where the emphasis was on "just peace," was held in Jamaica in May 2011, bringing the decade to a close.

A Vision of a Just World

The ecumenical movement's common vision has high aims — it speaks of nothing less than the transformation of the world. The *oikumene*, the whole inhabited earth, shall become an *oikos*, a household marked by openness, trust, love, and justice.[19] This is to be a place where all people and cultures mutually acknowledge each other and where Christians form a moral community. By the sharing of narratives, symbols, pictures, and metaphors, Christians can gain insight as to how they belong together and how all things are interconnected. Words such as "justice" and "peace" are intended to help people with comparable experiences find, support, encourage, and enable one another. Those who share in the great common narrative of Christianity concerning God and the world are to tell that narrative in such liturgical and moral forms that the transcendent ground of all historical reality becomes visible. Recovering time and space for an authentic life in a durable community is to be the goal of Christian aspiration. The ecumenical movement is a worldwide network of local communities of faith, rooted in differing social, cultural, and historical settings. In its struggle against globalization by powerful and unjust structures and in its option for nonviolence, the churches continue to build on centuries of experience, solidarity, and hope. They must open their doors to all who seek moral and spiritual guidance in a clearly threatened time.

Local congregations should be a sign of the greater Christian communion and a means for the renewal of humanity's world, but the long ecumenical journey has taught that humans alone cannot renew God's world. Thus the theme for the 2006 World Council assembly in Porto Alegre, Brazil, became "God, in Your Grace, Transform the World." This was a prayer which echoed both the Orthodox and Lutheran traditions, a prayer for the world and not for the church. It bore the insight that humans themselves cannot bring about the radical change of which the Bible speaks. It carried an eschatological hope of a necessary transformation which could only be a gift from God, and it also encompassed both a critical view of globalization and a desire to come to terms with violence.

CHAPTER 9

The Retreat of Three Traditions

*Ecumenism can no longer be toyed with as a mere possibility.
It has become the test case of faith.*
                                            ERNST LANGE

The World Council of Churches held its eighth assembly in Harare in 1998. Zimbabwe was on its way into a deep crisis. President Robert Mugabe, who in the 1970s led one of the liberation movements supported by the World Council and who as long as Nelson Mandela was imprisoned stood out as the strongest leader in Southern Africa, had unexpectedly become a despot who within a few months would bring his proud land to ruin.

The ecumenical movement also found itself in a precarious position, not because of its leadership, but rather because the Orthodox churches were threatening to bring their cooperation to a halt. This was a crisis that had festered for a long time. The Orthodox had always felt themselves to be strange birds in a movement that was dominated by Protestantism, permeated by liberal values, and governed by British parliamentary methods. Those who lived on the borders between East and West — for instance, intellectual immigrants in Paris, acclimatized Greeks and Russians in New York, and self-aware minorities in Finland and Lebanon — had the easiest time adjusting to the rules of the ecumenical game. It was much more difficult for the national Orthodox churches of Eastern Europe, who had barely been touched by the Renaissance or Enlightenment and who held fast to premodern spiritual traditions. How could they identify with the activism and functional ecclesiology of the Western churches? They had originally chosen to participate in ecumenical work primarily because it provided a possibility for them to come out of their political confinement. The World Council of Churches and the Conference of European Churches were their most important lifelines during the oppression and isolation of the Soviet era.

In accordance with the Toronto Statement of 1950, "The Church, the Churches, and the World Council of Churches," the Orthodox had received a guarantee that their ecclesiological integrity would not be compromised. The World Council was not to be a "superchurch" which could decide things for its members, and unity was not to be a matter for negotiation. Membership did not mean renouncing one's own understanding of the church or accepting another's view. There was to be a place in the WCC for churches who fully recognized each other as churches and also for those who could not do so.[1] In practice, the Toronto Statement, at least as the Orthodox read it, allowed for the same view of the church as Vatican II's *Lumen Gentium*. There is only one church which corresponds to the description "one, holy, catholic, and apostolic," but there are elements of that true church even in other Christian communities. The statement made it possible for the Orthodox to be members of the WCC and for Roman Catholics to have a close relation to it, but in fact it also locked the ecumenical movement into an unsolvable ecclesiological dilemma which time and again would become a matter of dispute.

In the 1960s contacts between the Eastern and Western churches had increased. Each developed confidence and genuine interest in the other. The meeting of Patriarch Athenagoras and Pope Paul VI in 1964 in Jerusalem and their subsequent decision to "remove from the memory and from the midst of the church the excommunication of 1054" aroused great expectations. The Anglican Communion was especially concerned, as it enjoyed longstanding relations with the Orthodox. Faith and Order in particular became the ecumenical forum of the Orthodox churches, although they also received considerable interchurch aid for social projects, especially in Greece. Yet the fundamental differences between Protestantism and Orthodoxy were great. The Orthodox Church claimed to be the one true church and rejected the notion that all confessions were of equal validity. To the Orthodox there was only one way to the unity of the church — that those in schism returned:

> The Orthodox Church . . . faithful to her ecclesiology, to the identity of her internal structure, and to the teaching of the undivided church, while participating in the WCC, does not accept the idea of the "equality of confessions" and cannot consider church unity as an interconfessional adjustment. . . . God calls every Christian to the unity of faith which is lived in the sacraments and the tradition, as experienced in the Orthodox Church.[2]

Harsh Criticism of Ecumenism from within the Russian Orthodox Church

When the Berlin Wall and the Communist regime in the Soviet Union fell, the Orthodox Church became more outspoken, and an extremely promising renewal of the church in Russia ensued. Churches were filled to overflowing. Orthodoxy again became an integral part of Russian identity even for persons who had not for a long time practiced the faith. Simultaneously, however, the Russian Orthodox Church, with Metropolitan Kyrill of Smolensk and Kalingrad, who was made patriarch of Moscow and All Russia in 2009, as its spokesperson became more and more critical of the ecumenical movement. The church felt itself disadvantaged and sought structures and decision-making processes that allowed it to act in terms of its own identity rather than submitting to "majority rule" in questions such as the ordination of women. The Orthodox criticism was sharpened by events at the World Council assembly of 1991 and was received sympathetically among conservative Protestants. In Russia, reactionary, nationalistic, and frequently anti-Semitic voices that were extremely critical of the Church's ecumenical involvement were heard within Orthodoxy; the very word *ecumenical* became a symbol for the evil that threatened the Church. Ecumenism was described as heresy in a concentrated form and an apocalyptic attempt to establish the anti-Christian global church forewarned in Revelation 13.

All non-Orthodox were viewed as schismatic. Monks and nuns sometimes went so far as to forbid all non-Orthodox from setting foot in Russian churches. The Moscow Patriarchate again asserted itself as "the third Rome" and gave its undivided support to Vladimir Putin's ambitions to restore Russia to the status of superpower. At the same time, the Russian Orthodox Church was silent in respect to violations of human rights, oppression of minorities, and even the murder of political dissidents. It openly questioned Western interpretations of human rights and adopted a far from unambiguous position toward democracy.[3] Women priests, nonsexist liturgical language, and homosexuality became major ecclesiological, liturgical, and ethical symbols establishing absolute lines of division between the Russian Orthodox Church and the liberal, secularized, and socially adapted churches of the Reformation.

When anti-Semites used the disparaging and invective word *zhidovstvo*, they were renouncing not only those who supported Judaism, but even ecumenically oriented Orthodox Christians. The majority of bishops in the Holy Synod wanted to leave both the WCC and the Conference of European Churches, but Patriarch Alexei and his closest associates saw to it that such proposals never came to a vote. The extremely reactionary synod of the Russian Orthodox Church in Exile, which was not dissimilar to Archbishop Lefebvre's schismatic Catholic Church, exaggerated the anti-ecumenical atmosphere. They wanted to restore the church of the czars and cut all relations with other Christians. All "renewal" was rejected. An invasion of sects from America, Europe, and Korea into Russia did not make matters better. Proselytism created such great uneasiness that the Russian Orthodox Church requested the state to limit freedom of religion. Simultaneously, relations with the Roman Catholic Church deteriorated.

Metropolitan Kyrill, who was determined that the Russian Orthodox Church should maintain its ecumenical relations, had to walk a tightrope. At home he was criticized for doing the bidding of the hated ecumenical movement; abroad he was criticized for endangering the entire ecumenical project.

New Forms of Decision-Making
Accommodate the Orthodox Churches

Toward the end of the 1990s it became evident that the ecumenical movement was on the road to collapse. The Orthodox churches in Georgia and Bulgaria, under pressure from fundamentalist monks and the threat of internal division, had already left the World Council when the Ecumenical Patriarch of Constantinople in 1998 called all of the Orthodox churches to a meeting to consider the crisis. It was agreed that the Orthodox presence at the assembly in Harare would be minimal and that the Orthodox would abstain from voting and not participate in interconfessional worship. They would demand that the WCC seriously set about to face the crisis. The assembly, as a consequence, formed a Special Commission on Orthodox Participation in the WCC to deal with the issue. While this ultimately saved the World Council, in actual practice the Russian Orthodox Church dictated the conditions for participation.

In 2000 the Russian bishops published "Basic Principles of the Russian Orthodox Church towards the Other Christian Confessions." This document appeared shortly after the Roman Catholic statement *Dominus Iesus* and had much the same content. Its text identified the Orthodox Church with the church founded by Jesus Christ himself, while other Christian communities were seen not as churches in the precise meaning of the word but at most as possessing some ecclesial marks. This view was not new, but during the "ecumenical spring" that followed Vatican II it had not been seriously taken up by either Orthodox or Catholics. Both the Roman Catholic and Orthodox churches had emphasized that they desired to continue responsible dialogue with other Christians. The Russian bishops underscored that the restoration of Christian unity was "a task with the highest priority for the Orthodox Church at every level," but they also asserted that "genuine unity is possible only in the bosom of the one, holy, catholic, and apostolic church," by which they meant themselves. They indicated other unacceptable models for unity — for example, those that spoke of the churches as different branches of the same tree, or those that assumed equality of denominations. Orthodox membership in the World Council of Churches was to be decided when the Special Commission had laid out its proposals.[4] The World Council was left with no choice but to proceed toward far-reaching changes in its working style.

The Special Commission proposed that all WCC decisions involving substantive matters be reached by consensus rather than by balloting. A sophisticated protocol for debate and decision-making was to be developed in order to shield the Orthodox from simply being voted down in respect to issues that were important to them. A permanent committee should make certain that Orthodox views were heard at all levels of the organization and that these new procedures were followed. Churches could have associate membership in the WCC if they were not able to take responsibility for all the positions of the Council. Finally, worship at ecumenical conferences should largely follow the traditions of the different confessions and not be "trans-confessional," as had often been the case since the beginning of the 1980s. These proposals were approved by the Central Committee of the World Council in 2002 and ratified at the Porto Alegre assembly of 2006.[5] The Holy Synod in Russia declared its satisfaction, and the Russian Orthodox Church retained its membership in the Council.

This new form of decision-making lessened the World Council's ability to take positions in regard to controversial issues and thus rendered debate tamer. Some Protestant member churches were not prepared to agree to this. The German Lutheran Margot Kässmann, who was then bishop of Hannover and who for many years had played a leading role in the Central Committee, left the meeting and gave up many assignments when the decision was reached. The Russian delegate Bishop Hilarion Alfeyev insisted that the question of his church's membership should remain open. He held that the continuing liberalization of doctrine and morals in many Protestant churches had damaged their relations with the traditional churches more severely than anything that had happened since the Reformation and that the gap was continuing to widen. Among churches that he saw as going badly astray was the Church of Sweden, with which the Holy Synod of the Russian Orthodox Church in 2005 broke direct relations due to its approval of the blessing of same-sex partnerships.

Relations between the Russian Orthodox Church and the Roman Catholic Church Are Tested

While its criticism of the Reformation churches was primarily on the level of ethical questions, the Russian Orthodox Church's conflict with the Roman Catholic Church was chiefly over jurisdictional matters with clear political dimensions. These matters were primarily in relation to the Greek Catholic Uniate Church in western Ukraine, issues which stretched back to 1597 and the Treaty of Brest-Litovsk, when the majority of Ukrainian Orthodox joined Rome. The Orthodox rite was followed in the Uniate Church, but legal allegiance was given to the Roman pontiff. It was a strong church until 1946, when it was banned by Stalin, who imprisoned and executed many of its members and transferred the church buildings to the Russian Orthodox Church. At the end of the 1980s the Ukrainian Orthodox revived their church, an element in the independence movement of the Ukrainian people. They demanded the return of their church buildings, and the ensuing schism with the Russian Church was violently chaotic. The story of attempts to mediate between Rome, Moscow, and Lvov is extremely complicated, but in the early 1990s a theological and political agreement was reached concerning the Uniate Church. The controversy, however, did not come to an end. Relations between the Vatican and the Moscow Patriarchate deteriorated until finally Cardinal Edward Cassidy, president of the Pontifical Council for Promoting Christian Unity, traveled to Moscow for discussions; however, Metropolitan Kyrill refused to speak with this representative of the Roman Curia.[6] Ecumenism often has elements of diplomacy, but it seldom degenerates to the demonstration of pure power as it did in this case.

The situation worsened when the Vatican appointed four "apostolic administrators" to Russia — that is, bishops who had responsibility for Roman Catholics living there. This was interpreted by the Russians as a link in an overall strategy of Russian "conquest" by Rome. Hateful statements were exchanged, meetings were canceled, the dreams of a visit to Russia by the Polish Pope John Paul II were crushed, and it took a number of years before the situation became stable and official theological dialogues between the Roman Catholic and Orthodox churches could be renewed. At the second meeting of this dialogue in Ravenna in 2007, however, the Russian delegation left in protest at the presence of participants from the Estonian Church. The Russians could not accept the fact that the Estonian-speaking part of this church, which had been under the jurisdiction of Moscow in Soviet times, would give its allegiance to the Ecumenical Patriarch in Constantinople. That the two patriarchates were on a collision course had clear political implications.

John Paul II: An Ecumenical Pope

The springtime in the Roman Catholic Church in the 1960s and the summer that followed eventually turned into fall and even winter. When the Decree on Ecumenism *(Unitatis Redintegratio)* was adopted by Vatican II in 1964, other churches assumed that this was only a first step. The closed Catholic Church was opening itself to a wider Christian fellowship when it acknowledged elements of "church" in other Christian communities. Those communities were not "church" in the

Roman Catholic sense, but they were God's means for the salvation of many, and they possessed insights which the Catholic Church could acknowledge. Now on the basis of this cautious recognition of Protestant denominations it was hoped that genuine mutual dialogue might be possible. In time this might lead to a relation between equals.

This way was shortest for the Orthodox churches, but mutual recognition might also have been within reach with the Anglican churches, with their rich liturgical life, and the Lutheran churches, with their careful concern for doctrine. In the present author's own church, the Church of Sweden, many in the early 1990s hoped on the basis of very good relations that their church might be acknowledged as a "sister church" to Rome. In 1993, at a celebration in Uppsala of four hundred years as a national Lutheran church, there was a great manifestation of the Church of Sweden as an ecumenical "bridge" church. Both Patriarch Bartholomew of Constantinople and Cardinal Edward Cassidy preached in the Uppsala Cathedral along with the Swedish archbishop. In his message the cardinal proposed a deepened dialogue between Rome and the Lutheran churches of Sweden and Finland. At the time, things looked more promising with the Swedish and Finnish churches, with their doctrinal tradition, their preservation of the office of the bishop, and their sacramental life, than even with the Anglicans. But the wind had already begun to shift. The 1998 art exhibit "Ecce Homo" in the Uppsala Cathedral, depicting Jesus among gay people, the ordination of women as bishops, and the blessing of same-sex partnerships, was too much for both Orthodox and Roman Catholics. The all too blue-eyed hopes in the Church of Sweden of the early 1990s for real ecumenical progress were dashed.

John Paul II, who was so conservative in political and ethical matters, had little ecumenical experience when he was elected pope. His subsequent appointment of conservative bishops, his silencing of theologians who did not follow the Curia's strict line, and his fixation on questions of sexual morality were ominous signs. He put into practice a very narrow interpretation of the decisions of Vatican II. Yet he became, more than any previous pontiff, the prime spokesperson for all of Christianity. With great generosity he received Christians of all kinds, and he encountered church leaders in many conversations. He was a master at symbolic acts, and his ecumenical gestures drew great attention. When the Swedish and Finnish archbishops in full episcopal vestments celebrated vespers with him at the high altar of St. Peter's Basilica, television viewers could scarcely conclude other than that the Roman Catholic Church had recognized the office of the Nordic bishops. When the pope together with the archbishop of Canterbury and an Orthodox archbishop knocked on the great door of St. Paul's Basilica at the opening of the Jubilee Year 2000, it was for many a sign of deepened fellowship between the churches. But it was his 1995 encyclical *Ut Unum Sint* ("That All May Be One") that ensured his name as an ecumenical pope.[7]

In this encyclical, John Paul II confirmed what Vatican II had decreed. The commitment to follow the path of the ecumenical venture is irrevocable (§3). Ecumenism "is not just some sort of 'appendix' which is added to the church's traditional activity" but is rather "an organic part of her life and work, and consequently must pervade all that she is and does." He laid weight on unity as God's will and as concrete fellowship in faith and sacramental life under the guidance of the Holy Spirit. Unity is a direct expression of Christ's reconciling work and for that reason is compellingly urgent. To believe in Christ, the pope wrote, means to will unity; to will unity is to will the church; to will the church is to will the communion of grace that mirrors the Father's eternal plan — it is the content of the prayer *ut unum sint* (John 17:11, 21). He spoke of how the richness of God is manifested in the different Christian fellowships: "If Christians, despite their divisions, can grow ever more united in common prayer around Christ, they will grow in the awareness of how little divides them in comparison to what unites them" (§22).

As did Vatican II, John Paul confirmed the presence and activity of Christ in Christian communities other than the Roman Catholic Church but at the same time noted that there is a difference: it is only in the Catholic Church that the apostolic church is realized in its fullness. The goal of ecumenism, therefore, is that the imperfect but real unity which already exists between churches be deepened and expanded to complete and visible unity in truth and love. For this to happen, common prayer, the conversion of partners, and the renewal of the church are as necessary as the pope's own conversion and prayer for forgiveness for all the wounds caused by the papacy throughout history.

The encyclical noted ecumenical progress in our time and singled out the early church as a model. Throughout the whole text there runs an admonition to constant and deepened dialogue. Unity is possible only when truth and love go hand in hand. To compromise truth would be in conflict with the essential nature of God and with the desire that resides deep within every person. Dialogue is a way toward self-realization and an exchange of mutual gifts which expresses the catholicity of the church. There is a legitimate Christian diversity, and faith can be expressed in different ways without a loss of unity. Genuine dialogue is a way both of humbly seeking the truth together and of valuing other modes of expressing faith while simultaneously testing one's own formulations.

Ut Unum Sint was a remarkable document, not only in its elaboration of the conclusions of Vatican II concerning the unity of the church, but also in the pope's invitation to other Christians to exchange ideas about the ministry of Peter, the papal office. Neither the Orthodox nor the Reformation churches were able to acknowledge that the pope's jurisdiction, *Servus servorum Dei* (the servant of the servants of God), should be the primary symbol of unity, for the papacy itself has become a hindrance to that very unity. The pope cited various biblical texts concerning the special task that Jesus gave to Peter and also concerning Peter's denial and restoration, and he lifted up Peter's death as a martyr, for John Paul II regarded martyrdom as a special sign of the church's deepest unity with Christ. He then formulated a kind of job description for a pope in the service of unity, and he invited other Christians to contemplate how the ministry of Peter could be formed so as best to serve the communion of the entire church.[8]

Unity requires that faith in all that God has revealed, as clothed in doctrine and sacramental life, be made visible in obedience. An ecclesiology with *koinonia*, communion, as its cornerstone makes possible a nuanced understanding of the presence of Christ in all churches. In spite of his open and generous language and his high estimate of ecumenical progress, the pope went no farther than Vatican II in his recognition of other churches. Yet *Ut Unum Sint* was received with great joy. Many churches took seriously his admonition, giving lengthy answers to the question of possible formations of the Petrine office.

Cardinal Ratzinger Draws the Boundaries

Just a few years later, in the midst of the Jubilee Year 2000, the declaration *Dominus Iesus* appeared. It came as a cold shower over the entire ecumenical movement. The president of the Vatican Congregation for the Doctrine of the Faith, Cardinal Joseph Ratzinger, stood behind the document, which, to be sure, was primarily addressed to his own church and was intended to clarify the boundaries for dialogue with other religions. But in sharp and explicit words it also took up the view of the Roman Catholic Church toward other communions:

> there exists a single church of Christ, which subsists in the Catholic Church, governed by the successor of Peter and by the bishops in communion with him. The churches which, while not existing in perfect communion with the Catholic Church, remain united to her by means of the closest bonds, that is, by apostolic succession and a valid Eucharist are true particular churches. Therefore, the church of Christ is present and operative also in these churches, even though they lack full communion with the Catholic Church, since they do not accept the Catholic doctrine of the primacy, which, according to the will of God, the bishop of Rome objectively has and exercises over the entire church.
>
> On the other hand, the ecclesial communities which have not preserved the valid episcopate and the genuine and integral substance of the eucharistic mystery, are not churches in the proper sense; however, those who are baptized in these communities are by baptism incorporated in Christ and thus are in a certain communion, albeit imperfect, with the church. Baptism in fact tends per se toward the full development of life in Christ, through the integral profession of faith, the Eucharist, and full communion in the church. (§17)[9]

This document boldly asserted that the Roman Catholic Church regards itself in reality as the one true church, but also that the Orthodox Churches, even though they do not acknowledge the papacy, should also be regarded as proper churches, while the Protestant communions, not possessing a valid episcopate and therefore not able validly to celebrate the Eucharist, were not to be regarded as proper although their baptism could be acknowledged.

In principle this was nothing new, even if the declaration went farther than Vatican II in the direction of Catholic exclusivity. It contained no indication that the Body of Christ is greater than the Roman Catholic Church or that one could be a part of the former without belonging to the latter. It gave rise to a deep concern that the

Catholic Church, after forty years of interconfessional dialogue, had not budged an inch in its view of other churches. Some commentators attempted to tone down the significance of the document, but old wounds were opened and many hopes for progress were lost. *Dominus Iesus* revealed an amazing lack of sensitivity, and the heated debate which followed its release made the situation worse. The air nearly went out of ecumenical conversation. The negative reaction was particularly strong in Germany.

It seemed as though a fundamentalism had taken over in Rome in regard to the reading of the texts of the Vatican Council. These texts were now regarded as final, definitive, and binding documents down to the last comma. They were neither to be developed nor to be given a more reasonable interpretation. The past feeling that unity was both possible and necessary was cooled down. The Curia simultaneously took control over radical Catholic proponents of unity and reassured conservatives who feared that ecumenism would lead to a "Protestantification" of their church. Thus Cardinal Ratzinger put in place a conservative and narrow reading of the conciliar texts. When he became Pope Benedict XVI in 2005, the "dictatorship of relativism" was set aside, and he could proceed calmly and peacefully to nurture relations with other churches that now knew where the boundaries were.

Concerned ecumenism, which took basic questions seriously, recovered slowly. Then, with the new pope's approval, *Dominus Iesus* seemed to appear again, in replay as it were. In July 2007 the Congregation for the Doctrine of the Faith released another Declaration which again attempted to clarify how the conclusions of Vatican II are to be understood.[10] It was again intended primarily to reassure the most conservative Catholics, and perhaps win back the schismatic followers of Archbishop Lefebvre. Yet the Curia did not seem to understand that it could no longer make statements *ad intra*. In the worlds of both the media and the ecumenical movement, everything said by the pope was *ad extra* and read by all of Christianity. Yet again it was clearly asserted that the Roman Catholic Church, gathered around the pope, was the true church. The Orthodox Churches, having preserved the sacraments, especially the Eucharist, apostolic succession, and the office of the priesthood, merited the designation "church" even if they did not share the "internal constitutive principles" of the Roman Catholic Church. The churches of the Reformation, in contrast, lack apostolic succession and a sacramental priesthood and cannot be called "churches" in the Catholic sense even if they include many elements of genuine faith and convey the gospel of salvation.

Protestants reacted negatively and vigorously. The ecumenically experienced bishop of Berlin, Wolfgang Huber, who spoke on behalf of the German Evangelical Churches, criticized the declaration's curt tone and was of the view that the Vatican had erected an "ecumenical blockade" when it claimed that the Protestant churches were not churches "in the proper sense." Such language did not further the cause of ecumenism. He agreed that they were not churches in the "Catholic" sense, but it is not the prerogative of the Congregation for the Doctrine of the Faith to decide who belongs to the church of Jesus Christ and who does not. Ecumenism presupposes that the partners acknowledge one another.[11] The WCC referred resignedly to a formulation of its member churches in 2005: "Every church is the Church catholic and not simply a part of it. Every church is the Church catholic but not the whole of it. Each church fulfills its catholicity when it lives in communion with the other churches."[12]

Cardinal Walter Kasper, who was president of the Pontifical Council for Promoting Christian Unity, sought earnestly and with great insight to make things right.[13] He pointed to the considerable ecumenical progress that had taken place through the years, and also to the fact that there was a mutual acknowledgment of baptism by the churches. Great honesty and clarity would only lead to the improvement of ongoing dialogue between the churches. The declaration did not reject the other churches, but clarified the Catholic view of the church which Protestants did not possess and did not desire to possess. For Protestants, however, the fact remained: if they did not make the Roman Catholic view of the church their own and recognize the primacy of the pope, they could not count on an ecumenical breakthrough.

Sharp Reactions from the German Protestant Churches

It was not surprising that reactions were strongest in the homeland of Benedict XVI, Germany, where the Catholic and Evangelical churches are of the same size and where they encounter each other in many contexts and where each church takes serious responsibility for society.[14] In 2002 the two churches celebrated the fact that they mutually recognize each other's baptism, which is the basic sacrament of unity. At the same time, however, one could observe that each church emphasized its own uniqueness and that their dialogue had taken on a new tone. Doubt had arisen as to whether the "consensus ecumenism" which had been pursued since Vatican II was really leading anywhere. The *Joint Declaration on the Doctrine of Justification* which had been signed in 1999 gave rise to opposition by a long list of professors of theology who felt that it swept fundamental and enduring differences under the rug.[15] The *Joint Declaration* did not, according to these theologians, take seriously into account the ecclesiological consequences of the dogmatic agreement. This debate became particularly sharp with John Paul II's general invitation to the Jubilee Year in Rome, which indicated that those who participated would receive an indulgence, something which Lutherans held to be out of conformity with the *Joint Declaration*. When *Dominus Iesus* was published soon afterwards and a statement also came from the Moscow Patriarchate, the scene was set for a confrontation. The churches approached each other on the basis of what they held to be the strength of their own traditions. Thus their differences became clearer, as did their mutual criticisms. When several of the German Evangelical *Landeskirchen* (regional churches), on the basis of both the doctrine of "the priesthood of all believers" and the shortage of clergy caused by the general economic downturn, opened the possibility for laity in their own congregations — *pro loco et tempore* — to preside at celebrations of the Holy Communion, sharp protests arose within the Roman Catholic Church. This decision was a departure from traditional churchly praxis and brought about a general chilling of relations not only with Catholic and Orthodox Churches but also with the Old Catholic and Anglican traditions.

The German Lutheran and Reformed churches were in agreement that the Reformation had brought to the whole church and especially to the culture of Northern Europe priceless values which must be kept alive. These churches proclaimed Jesus Christ as the definitive truth, life as a gift, and humans as free and responsible to shape the world. They sharpened their own ecclesial profiles against both the Roman Catholic Church and conservative "evangelical" movements and charismatic groups in order to make their message convincing in an increasingly competitive "religious market." They purposely expressed themselves differently than the Catholic Church in questions concerning marriage and family life, and they presented themselves as churches that fully accepted modernity and offered answers to its questions. All of this was a natural consequence of the fact that their position in German society had been weakened, but it was also a response to the critical attitudes in Rome and Moscow.

After centuries of disagreements and a common life in "united churches" enforced by civil authorities, the Lutheran and Reformed churches had, in 1973, reached — in Leuenberg — an agreement of full communion. Experiences during the Nazi era had brought these churches closer together. The Lutheran emphasis on the real presence of Christ in the eucharistic bread and wine was united with the Reformed view that this presence was bound to the whole worship service in all of its parts. The churches reached full communion on the basis of the well-known formula in the Seventh Article of the Augsburg Confession, *Confessio Augustana,* concerning the requirements for unity: "And it is enough for the true unity of the church to agree concerning the teaching of the gospel and the administration of the sacraments." These minimal conditions made it possible for more than a hundred church bodies to acknowledge each other's ministries and sacraments and to form the Communion of Protestant Churches in Europe.[16] This grouping has become a kind of Protestant Synod for all of Europe, with the responsibility of preserving the Reformation heritage that balances Orthodox and Roman Catholic influences, especially in relation to the European Union.

"Unity in Reconciled Diversity" and Profiled Ecumenism

The Leuenberg Agreement put into practice "unity in reconciled diversity," *Einheit in versöhnter Verschiedenheit,* the model of unity adopted by the Lutheran World Federation and the German churches. Churches remain different and live their own lives, but thanks to a shared basic view of the gospel they have "pulpit and altar fellowship." This model is rejected by the Roman Catholic Church and even by the churches, Nordic Lutheran and Anglican, within the fellowship of the Porvoo Common Statement. They claim that without a common sacramental theology and understanding of the ministry, unity in a deeper sense cannot be realized. If Rome requires a complete agreement in doctrine and sacramental life before there can be talk of unity, in the Porvoo Common Statement a shared understanding of doctrine and the administration of the sacraments is stipulated along with a common understanding of the episcopal office.[17] The Leuenberg Agreement chose first to declare church fellowship and then consciously to enter into a process to deepen that fellowship.

A debate concerning "profiled ecumenism" *(Ökumene der Profile)* arose within the Lutheran-Reformed fellowship. Wolfgang Huber was one of its chief spokespersons; his starting point has been that there is an enduring obligation to work together in seeking the visible unity of the church, but it must be recognized that there are such fundamental differences between the churches in respect to ecclesiology and ethics that full unity will not be possible within the foreseeable future. The churches, accordingly, are entering a time when their identities and fundamental commitments will be strengthened. "Identity," however, is an ambiguous concept. It could mean an anxious and defensive self-preoccupation which erects boundaries against others, but it could also mean confidence and openness in an awareness that self-understanding can be developed only in encounter with others. This debate about "profiles" began when the Protestant churches had lost much of their social relevance, the economy was weakened, and many congregations had difficulty finding their way. It appeared necessary to be more explicit in respect to confessional images so that people would know what the church really stood for. Churches endeavored to strengthen their "trademarks," to be as attractive as possible, which could lead them not only to explain but even to accept and excuse church divisions. Profiling made differences more visible, but did not in itself lead to an abandonment of ecumenical encounter. On the contrary, an explicit clarification of identities would reveal the actual conditions for ecumenical cooperation and give dialogue greater integrity. In spite of lasting differences, the churches must live together in mutual respect, continue their cooperation, and deepen their conversation.

Profiled ecumenism is characterized by the churches clarifying for themselves and for others what is indispensable in their faith and ministry. It does not intend to bring past controversies back to life, but rather to put into effect the truths that cannot and will not be renounced. A precise delineation of the differences between churches is thus the first step of profiled ecumenism. No considerations of church politics should prevent churches from — as far as possible — clarifying their positions for each other. The Evangelical churches in Germany speak readily of *Freiheit,* freedom, as their mission. The history of the postwar period and the fall of the Berlin Wall have made diversity, tolerance, relativism, and individual choice into central values. These are seen to correspond in a certain way to the gospel's promise of freedom. The churches proceeded from the Reformers' emphasis on the individual person's responsibility before God and from a respect for everyone's conscience; freedom is bound to the responsibility of all for justice and the environment.

The next step for profiled ecumenism is to find an ecumenically sustainable way of living together in spite of the lasting differences between the churches. The Leuenberg Agreement is often referred to as a model since it makes it possible to establish church fellowship without compromising the churches' uniqueness. The churches must respect diversity and not judge others by their own standards. A church must be able to preserve its own tradition without denying or limiting that of others. The churches are different in many respects, but that which they possess in common is greater than that which divides them. A church is strongest when it holds fast to keeping what is Evangelical Evangelical and what is Catholic Catholic.

The Traditional Churches Defend Their Integrity

The ecumenical developments that have taken place in Europe are not unique. The tendency to emphasize the particularity of one's church at the expense of what is common is also to be found in other parts of the Protestant world. When church leaders today speak of "realistic ecumenism," they should not be understood as being content with the status quo, no longer hoping for visible unity. But Protestant Christians do have a different understanding of the church and its ministry, of moral issues, and of decision-making processes than the Orthodox and Catholics. After many decades of convergence, these differences appear now to be increasing. The churches' readiness to listen to each other is waning, and their sense of mutual supervision *(episcopē)* is weakening. When the 500th anniversary of the Reformation is celebrated in 2017, it could become a demonstration of reconciliation and of the desire for unity, but it could also contribute to the cementing of church differences and to the deepening of old divisions. Tendencies that have been noticeable in the last few years point, unfortunately, to the latter.

The conditional ecclesiology described in the World Council of Churches' Toronto Statement of 1950 and in *Lumen Gentium* and *Unitatis*

Redintegratio of Vatican II has caught up with the ecumenical movement. During the euphoric 1960s the differences between the churches were held at a distance, but they can no longer be hidden. The three great traditions are in retreat and are engaged in defending their own particular interpretation of the common Christian tradition. In military contexts, "retreat" can mean a drawing back for reflection and regrouping. In Christian contexts the word "retreat" signifies seclusion, prayer, and self-examination. Both these meanings are applicable. The Orthodox, Catholic, and Reformation churches have retreated in order to see things a little more clearly, but there is a risk that they might develop such negative pictures of each other that they will hesitate to proceed on the ecumenical pilgrimage.

CHAPTER 10

A New Road Map

Being ecumenical means praying together, working together, suffering together, sharing together, witnessing together.

ARAM I

The World Council of Churches held its ninth assembly in Porto Alegre, Brazil, in 2006. It took place at the Roman Catholic university where the World Social Forum on many occasions had assembled hundreds of "people's movements" in protest against globalization. The assembly became a marketplace for analyses, experiences, and the formation of opinions. Local organizations erected stands all over the place in order to present themselves. Christians from all cultures met in debate about every matter of concern to them. In plenary sessions, three hundred delegates from member churches debated vigorously, and songs were sung from every corner of the globe. One could on one day hear a Pentecostal sermon, the next participate in Orthodox vespers, and on the third take part in Roman Catholic worship.

Uppsala '68, with its drama, hopes, and revolts, seemed far distant. Churches from the Southern Hemisphere were well represented, and there were many more women than in Uppsala. But truly influential church leaders, outstanding theologians, and well-known politicians were conspicuous by their absence. Resources had shrunk, the organization had contracted, and the WCC was now but one among many international organizations seeking attention. The expectations of the media were low, and its coverage of events was minimal. If everything that happened in Uppsala was broadcast over the world and if thousands of articles were published and many books were written about that event, the assembly that took place in Porto Alegre went nearly unnoticed. Significant lectures that might have drawn attention were nonexistent.[1]

No one was given the possibility of taking up arguments for their own sakes. The Roman Catholic observers were conspicuously silent, and the Orthodox, who were satisfied with the report of the Special Commission, laid low. Youth, who in 1968 had been so directed toward their goals of radicalizing the churches and who were driven by left-leaning extremists, were now content to demonstrate for seats on various decision-making bodies. The Fourth Church was barely noticed and liberation theology made no contribution. It was a disillusioned and stale assembly. One must read between the lines to discover that there were nevertheless important and forward-looking decisions made for the future of the whole ecumenical movement.

Marc Luyckx Ghisi, who had long served as an adviser to the European Union on questions about the future, led a few seminars which concluded that secular society now had seen its best days.[2] Modernity had not led to religious decline except in Europe. Religion and morality, he held, were being restored even to politics. But the meaning of life, ethics, and views of humanity are — like climate change, questions of intellectual property, and the destruction of biological diversity — more than political issues. They are deeply spiritual and moral matters. When politicians do not come forth with satisfying answers, people turn instead toward their religious leaders. Development and economic growth have certainly made life better for many and have diminished the number of destitute people in the world, but the price that is being paid by everyone is a life-threatening destruction of the environment and widening gaps between the rich and the poor. The inability of political leaders to create a better world is paralyzing. At Porto Alegre this concern was turned into prayer: "God, in your grace transform the world."

Church Divisions or Enriching Plurality?

That prayer, Luyckx pointed out, had already in a certain way been answered even though the churches had not noticed it. The world is in the process of transformation. A "transmodern" way of thinking is spreading. A creative mixture of rationalism, intuition, and tolerance is creating a different global culture. The very concept "transmodern" suggests that the best of modernity is being preserved, but without being enclosed within national or confessional walls. The transmodern person is open to spiritual guidance, but rejects the universal claims of religion. The truth remains at the center, but there are many approaches to it. Each person may walk the way offered by his or her own culture. A transmodern and pluralistic rather than a secular outlook has taken root above all among women and young adults who have broken with traditional views that "this is true and the other is false." Faith communities may be defending themselves against this development, but in the long run transmodern values will permeate all cultures since it is impossible completely to shut off external influences. The ecumenical organizations are, according to Luyckx, more open to global change than other international groups, and thus they potentially contribute to a more informed debate concerning religion and politics and to greater tolerance in intercultural relations. This is a mark of confidence in the fragile and questioned ecumenical structures.

In line with Luyckx's analysis, we can assert that the ecumenical movement, mirroring its times, must now face the fact that those times are rapidly changing. At the beginning, ecumenism's task was seen to be quite simple. It involved coming to terms with the churches' doctrinal and structural divisions. The theological problems were to be solved one after the other, and then the church leaders could draw the structural and pastoral consequences and unite the divided churches. Unity would come when the churches in dialogue with each other solved their dogmatic and ecclesiological conflicts.

This twentieth-century project, however, proved to be more complicated than first thought, and, worse, the quest itself lost momentum when it no longer had the support of modernity's impulse to unify and organize. The privatization of faith, the relativization of truth, and the corresponding weakening of church institutions have gone so far that people now take church divisions for granted and speak of them as an "enriching plurality" rather than as a scandal. The relationship between unity and diversity has become central to ecumenical discourse. Is it possible to hold unity as the norm without it leading to hierarchical structures, subordination, and conformity? Is the whole idea of unity a Western invention and a means of power for (male) church leaders? Should the concept of visible institutional unity be eliminated from the ecumenical vocabulary? Does it not too often undermine *koinonia,* which points toward dynamic and changing relationships? Such questions are justified. The demand for unity can be a kind of oppression. It is no coincidence that Faith and Order has its strongest support in the Roman Catholic, Anglican, Orthodox, and Lutheran churches, which are relatively unified in doctrine and hierarchical in structure. But if freedom and plurality are emphasized at the cost of unity, will not church division grow worse? Limits to diversity must be found if the most fundamental ecumenical task is not to be lost.[3]

Individuals do not always see the connection between their own faith and the questions dealt with in ecumenical dialogue, and they are often content with a more flexible notion of truth than the theologians and with a greater degree of tolerance for different forms of life than many church leaders. People have good reason to mistrust church ecumenics since so little seems to happen. For instance, not even those who live in "mixed marriages" can take communion together! Large churches are not willing to accommodate themselves to smaller churches. All defend their independence, seek validation for their own liturgical praxis and ethical teaching, and are unwilling to be the objects of criticism.

Churches tend to compare themselves with others, making their own tradition the standard, but they no longer regard confessional diversity as a scandal. That new communities grow like mushrooms from the earth and Christianity appears more split than ever is without doubt to mock Jesus, to repudiate Paul, to deny Peter, and to scorn the entire ecumenical endeavor. But fewer and fewer people think this way. To overcome divisions is not considered as crucial as it was in the past. Thus interest is weakened and serious ecumenism is at times branded as conservative and even reactionary. This is a paradox. For years the ecumenical movement was criticized for its radicalism, distancing it from the churches. Now it is often accused of paying too much attention to outdated values, institutional forms, and ancient Christian tradition.

Shared Experiences: A Presupposition for Unity

It is possible to choose a more inspiring starting point for ecumenical work than division. Unity is not only a task to be fulfilled through dialogue, witness, and service; first and foremost it is a gift to be received in faith. The twentieth century opened up new worlds of spirituality, beauty, and commitment in which Christians from widely differing traditions are able to meet. These Christians have recognized each other in the fundamental confession that Jesus is Lord, and they have experienced a fellowship which neutralizes confessional and cultural differences. The identity given them in baptism has drawn them toward each other. Such solidarity has often been strong enough to resist forces which might make them enemies. In the ecumenical encounter they have exercised mutual supervision *(episcopē)* that has helped them find the narrow Christian path through forests of ideologies, philosophies, and views of life. The universal church has become visible, and humanity has been given a face. The gift of unity, no matter how incomplete, has made worthwhile all efforts to grow and share a life of faith.

Deep experiences of solidarity give wings to visions. Many ecumenical conferences have been enriched by the personal testimonies of participants, resulting in joint participation in struggles for justice and providing courage to persevere in spite of difficulties. Shared testimonies point to a unity that is not governed by agreements but which is nevertheless genuine. If unity did not already exist behind all inherited theological and cultural traditions, it would be meaningless to seek after it. Ecumenical theology must always build common experience and praxis in order to have anything to say.[4] There is power in women's testimonies to each other, in the witness of those who suffer from AIDS, and in the fellowship of prayer within congregations. A concrete solidarity carries more weight than the differences which some theologians call "fundamental." Interconfessional dialogue is indispensable, but it must be complemented by shared experience if the fire of ecumenism is not to be extinguished.

Hope Must Live On

When the resolute optimism of the 1960s was overwhelmed by diversity of opinion and a plurality of proposed solutions, and when christological eschatology capitulated to apocalyptic descriptions of the future, the ecumenical movement lost its footing. During the 1990s the movement devoted itself to carving out a new vision and to developing relevant structures that might support ecumenism through modernity's crisis. Attention was focused more on the social and economic consequences of globalization than on the renewal of the traditional churches now weakened by inner conflicts and facing the dramatic rise of a new Christianity that has often been anti-ecumenical and even fundamentalist. There was not much discussion of what postmodernism might imply for spirituality, theology, and loyalty to institutional churches. Churches endeavored to safeguard their own continuity, to increase centralization, and to preserve as much as possible of their traditions. An *aggiornamento* to contextual values stood on occasion against a return to biblical sources, which resulted in divisive conflicts within and between churches. The most serious of these conflicts took place within the Anglican Communion, which for years has been on the verge of collapse over questions concerning homosexuality. The tension and balance between contextuality and catholicity, which is essential for the preservation of the churches' relevance and authenticity, has become more and more difficult to maintain.

At Uppsala in 1968 there was extensive discussion concerning the church's catholicity. When this has been pitted against a legitimate contextual plurality and combined with centralism, hierarchy, and authority, it has become problematic. In Uppsala there was also considerable hopefulness about the world's future. But dreams of a better world do not only inspire social and technological development; they may also justify dreadful violence against humanity, as in Pol Pot's Cambodia or Mao's China. Violence can bring utopian ideologies to an end. Pandemics like HIV/AIDS and environmental degradation cause the myths of control and unlimited growth to falter. Postmodernism broadens the present at the cost of both the past and the future. The feeling that one lives in a society at risk grows, and the realization of life's vulnerability is always present. Deep-rooted collective memories which create confidence are replaced by the temporary assurances of the information society. Hope is drained by an incomprehensible global culture with unclear pictures of the future. Realistically, many people cannot expect their future to be substantially better than their present.

A language and symbols of hope are indispensable elements in the cultural capital needed if humanity is to survive. Thus the return of religion ought not to be surprising. People have confidence in intimate social and religious communities which at their best unite spiritual traditions with openness to diversity and change. It is in local communities rather than in universal fellowships that Christian solidarity can be realized. When the world is globalized, the local congregation becomes increasingly the Christian's home, and at its best it provides an ecumenical horizon and commitment. *Hope* has been the modern ecumenical movement's distinctive mark. The movement's pioneers were dreamers who were challenged by the gospel. The movement's eschatological dimension has been as prominent as its universal compass. That which is impossible for humans is possible for God, through whom all things were made and in whom all things will be brought together. Thus, when the hope for the churches' visible unity began to dim, the movement's utopian idealism was called into question. Voices speaking for an ecumenical "realism" became louder. Uncertainty increased as to what ecumenism actually involves:

> Among churches and ecumenical organizations uncertainty, ambiguity, and even confusion prevail about what is meant by the "ecumenical movement." There is agreement that the term "ecumenical" embraces the quest for Christian unity, common witness in the worldwide task of mission and evangelism, and commitment to diakonia and to the promotion of justice and peace. But there is no authoritative definition of the term, and it is in fact used to characterize a wide range of activities, ideas and organizational arrangements.[5]

The Ecumenical Movement: An Alternative Movement?

It is difficult to integrate Jesus' prayer "that they may all be one" with God's plan that "everything in heaven and on earth" shall be consummated in Christ. There has been a persistent tension between ecumenists who give priority to spiritual and ecclesial communion and those who place the gospel's social dimension in the first rank of importance. No fixed descriptive or normative definition of ecumenism can overcome this tension, nor can any attempt to identify one special model of unity or organizational form be considered more ecumenical than any other. Ecumenism must include a host of subjects and perspectives. It must also encompass the dynamic tension between how the churches actually appear and the ideal of *koinonia* which is God's gift. It must also take in the entire breadth of the church's mission to renew humanity in accordance with the model of God's reign. Humanity's deep sense of belonging together, given in creation, and the church's constitutive unity in Christ are constantly threatened by powers which, in their own interest, press for another kind of unity than that which God wills:

> The emergence over the last decades of transnational and increasingly worldwide structures of communication, finance and economy has created a particular kind of global unity. It is evident that the cost of this has been growing fragmentation of societies and exclusion for more and more of the human family. In their own international relationships the churches are under pressure to adapt themselves to this system and to accept its values, which tend to overlook if not deny the spiritual dimension of human life. This therefore constitutes a serious threat to the integrity of the ecumenical movement, whose organizational forms represent a distinctly different model of relationships, based on solidarity and sharing, mutual accountability and empowerment. On the threshold of the twenty-first century, all existing ecumenical structures must reassess themselves in the light of the challenge to manifest a form and quality of global community characterized by inclusiveness and reconciliation.[6]

The ecumenical movement as a global fellowship has thus described itself as an "alternative movement" standing at the side of the losers in the process of globalization.[7] In 1968 at Uppsala, where it was emphasized that the world determines the churches' agenda, there was a strong conviction that Christians should contribute to justice and peace by participating in ordinary political and economic life. A theology of secularization, combined with the Lutheran insight that persons as Christians are called to serve their neighbors in daily life in the world, laid the groundwork for an ecumenism that does not need to refer constantly to the gospel in order to make its contribution to a more just society. The church is in the world to participate in the mission of God, but it is not of the world.

This secular ecumenism was called into question by people for whom the church as a community of the faithful is a God-given alternate social organization and a visible sign of the reign of God. In the 1970s a number of charismatic and socially radical movements arose that wanted to organize their communal life along the lines of primitive Christian communities. Their way of living together was to function as "salt and light" in society. Especially in the highly diverse family of Reformed churches, social activism was often united with committed communal lifestyles and a belief that ecclesiology and ethics belong indissolubly together. The churches should anticipate social and moral renewal, and their unity should be a sign for humanity's peace.

Since the time of the early church, the marks of the true church have been unity, holiness, catholicity, and apostolicity. To these four marks *(notae ecclesiae)* Martin Luther added three others, including the "holy possession of the sacred cross."[8] During the 1970s, when Lutheran churches were apprehensive about being radicalized, the Lutheran World Federation referred often to this point. A "true" church must share in the suffering of Christ and choose the side of those who are oppressed by injustice. The church's faithfulness to the gospel is through showing itself in solidarity with those who are without power and influence. The fact was, however, that many churches at that time had such compromising connections with the political powers that one could hardly call them prophetic, much less alternative movements. This was especially true of Lutheran state churches, but also of conservative Roman Catholics, and surely of American evangelical groups that were rapidly moving toward social acceptance and direct political involvement. The churches were, therefore, in spite of all rhetoric, cautious about taking controversial positions, and they were extremely reluctant to see the WCC go further than they did in that direction. Genuine mutual sharing of suffering was seldom seen to be a mark of the churches, especially in the wealthy world.

Even if the World Council were more than an organization for cooperation and deliberation, its member churches rarely appeared together as a moral fellowship. They did not present themselves as a critical or trustworthy alternative in the globalized world. The ecumenical movement as represented by the WCC was not more than a *fellowship*. It was certainly not a church, even if it possessed ecclesial characteristics.

After fifty years, had not the time come to reconsider the Toronto Statement of 1950 and give a more binding character to the churches' spiritual and moral solidarity? In the superficial and stratified climate of the globalized world, could not the WCC, with its roots in local congregations, its long history, and its considerable experience of living with diversity, become a symbol for an inclusive human fellowship that provides open space for all who together are willing to test the signs of the times and seek the guidance of God?[9] There were strong voices calling to upgrade the "fellowship" to more of an ecclesial communion, but the Orthodox refused to give any ecclesial character to the Council, and the Protestant member churches were not prepared to make ecumenical solidarity so binding that it impinged on their own freedom. Few were ready to pay the price for a deepened mutuality even for the sake of the world. Thus all efforts to formulate a renewed vision came only half-way. The WCC remained largely a toothless, disparate, and tension-filled organization.

Concentrating on the Traditional Areas

In these circumstances, the World Council of Churches found itself reduced from being a community with the unity of the church as its goal to an organization designed for practical cooperation. There was an obvious risk that the WCC would degenerate into an association of like-minded groups rather than being a responsible council of churches. This was what the Russian Orthodox Church wanted, but the Council was not willing to compromise its original calling. Thus there followed a kind of retrenchment and a narrowing down of programs. A number of global relief and service organizations combined to form Action of Churches Together (ACT), loosely related to the World Council and the Lutheran World Federation. Several ecumenical entities built alliances in order to disseminate news and to form agencies for advocacy — for example, in respect to the HIV/AIDS pandemic. The WCC was forced, not least for economic reasons, again to concentrate on its traditional program areas: interchurch relations, theology, mission, diaconic service, communication, international politics, and interfaith dialogue.

In these areas progress was made. The Roman Catholic Church, which had been a distant and somewhat unfavorably disposed observer, became the ecumenical movement's most influential and enduring actor. The churches of the North forged genuine partnerships with impoverished churches of the South. In the theological dialogue which resulted in *Baptism, Eucharist and Ministry* (1982), all the major Christian traditions, including the Roman Catholics, reached what had been an unthinkable consensus regarding central theological questions. The *Joint Declaration on the Doctrine of Justification* between the Roman Catholic Church and the Lutheran churches (1999) took the sting out of the Reformation's most controversial issue. A number of churches united, and many agreements regarding "full communion" were reached. The churches rejected racism and contributed to the fall of the apartheid regime in South Africa. Similarly, they worked both to repudiate sexism and to press for the inclusion of women at all levels.

When globalization threatened to steamroll cultural differences, the defense of diversity became a concern for the ecumenical movement. The ecumenical organizations contributed to the debate over the environment, criticized the prevailing global economic order, and made efforts for justice and peace. Constructive dialogue with other world religions was begun. In various ways the ecumenical movement contributed significantly to the moderation of Christian, Islamic, and other religious extremism. Above all, an "ecumenical culture" took form. In spite of the reality that global convergences, so characteristic of the post–World War II period, had been transformed into nearly their opposite and societies were threatened by a fragmentation that was also felt in the churches, ecumenists held fast to the conviction that the future must be shaped in community. The words of Kathleen Bliss at the 1948 Amsterdam assembly of the World Council of Churches were often cited: "We intend to stay together."[10] Few church leaders with self-respect distanced themselves from ecumenism. Among Christians in general there was an expectation that leaders would move further and faster than they did. They wanted friendship to be deepened into a love that recognized the otherness of the other.

The ecumenical movement in all of its breadth, with the WCC as a central point of reference, had for over sixty years renewed the world's churches and brought them ever closer to one another. The movement now faced a number of new challenges. It had to orient itself to the postmodern world, choose its stance in relation to the Fourth Church, restrain the exclusive claim of the large churches to catholicity and apostolicity, check the implosion of Protestantism, develop constructive relations with other religions, and find ways through the internal threats to the churches brought by complicated ethical issues. At the same time it had to fulfill its mission in a world that was each day becoming more complex and conflicted. Without mutual counsel and cooperation this was impossible. The churches risked losing themselves in temporary contextual adaptation if they did not listen to one another and deepen their roots in the apostolic tradition.

The ecumenical organizations continued to stir expectations, but foresight was limited and leadership was inadequate. They were tempted to retreat into organizational protectionism, tone down the Bible's uncompromising call for Christian unity, occupy themselves with popular and shortsighted projects, and continue to administer past achievements. Yet for the sake of credibility and in order to find new energy and life, the ecumenical movement had to include the Fourth Church, increase Orthodox participation, and deepen existing relations with the Roman Catholic Church. This work, which remains ongoing, required new ways of working that had to be acceptable to member churches. People who primarily want to see the Council as a prophetic and critical voice have not been interested in giving conservative churches greater influence, while those who above all seek the churches' visible unity are not content with a movement that includes less than all the baptized. For the latter, a Global Christian Forum has become one of the most promising initiatives in decades. The choice stands, as it often has, between a profile based on social ethics and one that calls for an inclusive ecclesiology.

A Wider Concept of Ecumenism?

Should the ecumenical movement include other faith communities than the Christian? Stanley Samartha, who led the WCC's program Dialogue with People of Living Faiths and Ideologies, as early as the 1970s spoke of widening ecumenism to include the world religions. Ecumenism, he argued, should not be limited to the churches and to healing their family quarrels and wounds, but should rather provide space for all people of faith.[11] S. Wesley Ariarajah has often returned to this point:

> At the global level, there is an increasing recognition that the world's problems are not Christian problems requiring Christian answers, but human problems that must be addressed together by all human beings. We know today that whether it is the issue of justice, peace, human rights, or the destruction of the environment, we need to work across boundaries of religions, nations, and cultures. There are calls for global movements and for a "global ethic" that would govern our life together.
>
> So the issue of "how ecumenical 'ecumenical' should be" is no longer a question of semantics or inclusion; it is a theological ques-

tion. It has to do with a reassessment of our understanding of God, of the scope of God's saving work, and of the agents of God's mission. Such reflections necessarily affect our present understandings of the mystery of the incarnation and the being and meaning of the church as the body of Christ.[12]

In a time when pluralism, which gives the same value to all religious groups, is winning adherents, there have been many discussions directed toward a wider view of ecumenism. Could a christologically centered ecumenism, with the visible unity of the church as its chief concern, find its place within a wider ecumenism that includes all faith communities? Interreligious relationships must not infringe on the fellowship that Christians have with each other through baptism or on their call to witness to Christ and to be his hands in the world. Yet interreligious relations certainly have a solid theological basis: all of humanity is created in God's image. Furthermore, the "ecumenical ecumenism" of interreligious dialogue aims not at unity but rather at mutual understanding. This makes it decisively different from the churches' dialogues with each other. The responsibility to preserve good relations and develop cooperation between world religions must not be confused with regaining the churches' visible and sacramental unity in Christ. If it is true that God has revealed himself in Christ and continues to act in the world through the Holy Spirit, the church has a unique narrative to share with all humanity. The Christian faith is inescapably christocentric and has an indispensable dimension of mission. Christians confess that "God was in Christ reconciling the world to himself" (2 Corinthians 5:19) and that he "emptied himself . . . and became obedient to the point of death" (Philippians 2:5-8). That confession must remain the foundation of the ecumenical movement.[13]

The Contours of a Renewed and United Ecumenical Movement

Another choice that must be made concerns the relationships between the many ecumenical organizations. In discussions about the reconfiguration of the movement it has been pointed out that, while there are many global, confessional, regional, and national actors that complement each other, the World Council of Churches nevertheless has a leading role in making their work together constructive. A reconfiguration is not limited to patching existing structures together but involves a dynamic development of relations and cooperative actions and the undertaking of shared tasks. Nothing is served by ironclad bureaucracies that only look out for themselves. The living ecumenism found in so many movements and voluntary organizations must be recognized. The WCC by virtue of its history, its far-reaching influence, and its name has the unique possibility of stimulating the initiatives of others. The crisis within the ecumenical movement, which has been evident since the fall of the Berlin Wall, requires new transparency, concentration, and coordination as goals are identified. The Orthodox churches have been given the space they have wanted. Closer relations with the Roman Catholic Church have been strengthened by the Joint Working Group. A similar group has been formed with the Pentecostal movement. The Global Christian Forum is moving to become a platform for nearly all of the world's Christians. After many years of confusion, it has become possible to see the contours of a renewed and united ecumenical movement.

All of this is to be found, albeit somewhat concealed, in the conclusions of the Porto Alegre assembly in 2006.[14] The decisions of the Special Commission include the provisions that new member churches shall not only confess their faith in the triune God, but shall do so in conformity with the Nicene Creed. They shall, moreover, baptize "in the Name of the Father, Son, and Holy Spirit," and must at least be moving toward the recognition of baptism by other church bodies. The WCC's Basis, which had been extremely open and usually understood in general Protestant terms, thus received a sharper ecclesiological interpretation. By also requiring that new member churches should have a certain number of communicant members and should give financial support to the Council, the risk of an increase in Protestant influence at the expense of the Orthodox has been minimized. The WCC, more than previously, has become the churches' own organization.

To make reference to the Nicene Creed and baptism in the Council's official documents was a significant step that had been discussed and debated over many years. "Through baptism, Christians are brought into union with Christ, with each other and with the Church of every time and place."[15] It is baptism and union with Christ that make it possible for persons to call each other Christians. Baptism is the funda-

A New Road Map

mental sacrament of the ecumenical movement. Most churches recognize each other's baptism, but they have not yet drawn the full ecumenical consequences of such recognition.[16] There are many indications that baptism in years to come will occupy a greater place in both ecumenical conversation and congregational worship and instruction.

The only theological statement that was adopted by the Porto Alegre assembly was "Called to Be One Church."[17] Together with an earlier text concerning the nature of the church and its mission,[18] it laid the groundwork for intensified and integrated work on ecclesiological questions. Many who have followed ecumenical developments during recent years and given attention to WCC texts on unity from New Delhi (1961), Nairobi (1975), and Canberra (1991) have expressed doubt concerning the Council's will and ability to carry such theological work further.[19] The Porto Alegre statement, however, gives a new possibility to integrate the different dimensions of ecumenism: the unity of the church and the unity of humanity; the renewal of spirituality, mission, and diaconia; work for justice, peace, and the integrity of creation; and mutual respect and cooperation between world religions. The WCC in comparison with 1968 has, to be sure, been greatly weakened, but it is far from exhausted. The fact that the Roman Catholic Church, in John Paul II's words, sees the quest for the visible unity of the church not as "something added on, but [standing] at the very heart of Christ's mission"[20] and thus has chosen to go the way of ecumenism will in the foreseeable future keep other churches on the same path.

The ecumenical movement was born out of the concerns for peace and international order after World War I. In Jamaica in 2011, a thousand delegates from churches in a hundred countries gathered to draw conclusions from ten years of work together in the "Decade to Overcome Violence." They were dedicated to peace in the community, peace with the earth, peace in the marketplace, and peace among the peoples. Their message to the churches and to the world is one of vibrant commitment and hope. The convocation was like a return to the roots of the ecumenical movement; it brought new energy. In spite of organizational and financial strain, the WCC is on the move again. Given the profoundly different culture of the new millennium and the fact that the churches are deeply affected by science and philosophy, media and politics, globalization and self-asserting nationalism and denominationalism, one could not but expect a twentieth-century organization of this kind to be in crisis. But the prayer of Jesus that they may all be one continues to bring new inspiration.

Even if the Orthodox churches are playing a waiting game, the Roman Catholic Church is hesitant, and the Reformation churches are plagued by inner conflicts, the ecumenical movement goes ahead. Conservative evangelical churches are taking greater responsibility in the struggle against poverty and environmental destruction. Charismatic movements are changing the face of global Christianity. And the World Council of Churches, the Christian World Communions, and the Pontifical Council for Promoting Christian Unity in Rome continue to provide content and structure for the ecumenical movement. Since 1968 the Roman Catholic Church, more than any other, has given substance to matters of ecclesiology. The Orthodox remain intent on preserving the heritage of the early church. The Reformation churches continue to proclaim the message of unconditional grace and the freedom and responsibility of the individual. And the evangelicals are giving life to the call to mission and are emphasizing the transformative power of faith.

If all of these do not participate and make their contributions, the ecumenical movement cannot claim to be "ecumenical" in that word's basic meaning. Even though the Reformation churches were instrumental in organizing the ecumenical movement, they no longer have the influence they once had. Globally, liberal Protestantism is now a "loser," at least for the time being, while independent evangelical and charismatic churches grow. Not least for demographic reasons, the Roman Catholic Church will continue to comprise half of world Christianity. All of the churches without exception need to share theology, liturgy, and spirituality with each other. Experience from "the underside" combined with qualified theological reflection and prayer by many will continue to renew the church.

Prayer is at the heart of all ecumenism. Without prayer, ecumenism degenerates to soulless bureaucracy, academic debate, and an empty diplomacy which has no meaning for ordinary believers. "Spiritual ecumenism" brings energy to the churches.[21] Christian unity is not the result of human effort and joint church cooperation. It is a gift of the Holy Spirit. It is presented to those who take part in common worship, pilgrimages, or retreats. Spiritual ecumenism is encouraged at influential monasteries such as Taizé in France, Bose in Italy, and Chevetogne in Belgium, and by movements such as Sant'Egidio, Focolare, and

Syndesmos. It is inspired by Sojourners and a number of American initiatives for social justice. It is made visible in public events such as the biannual *Kirchentag* in Germany. It draws its credibility from unpretentious service to drug addicts in Hong Kong, victims of HIV/AIDS in Africa, and developmentally disabled children in China. Unity in Christ is found not only in sacramental life but also in the witness of Christian martyrs in our time. Through baptism, all Christians have been united with Christ and have received the gift of unity to be demonstrated in daily life.

No one can make amends for past violence, division, and plundering of persons and of the environment. In order to live with the victims and ruins of the past, without repressing guilt and repeating the crimes, there needs to be a hope of resurrection. Without hope for the past, there can be no hope for the future. Everyone who is born will die, and everyone who is not yet born will one day be gone. But the Christian hope is rooted beyond history where everything is united in Christ. Christ makes whole that which has been shattered. In the resurrection the churches encounter those who have gone before, among them saints and martyrs, but also those who have been slaughtered in wars of religion, those who were sacrificed in inquisitions, and all children victimized by abusers. The dead await us.

Whoever believes in the resurrection of the dead receives strength to remember the departed and feel their presence. The Christian faith is a "culture of memory" sustained by hope for the resurrection. When Jesus shared his last meal with the disciples he said, "Do this in remembrance of me" (Luke 22:19). Therefore, for two thousand years the church has celebrated the Eucharist. That celebration is more than simply remembering what happened a long time ago. In the Eucharist that which happened in Jerusalem and God's promise for the future are both made present. Christ comes to his people not from the past but from the future. He bears the dead with him and reconciles death with life.

Whoever sees the future in the light of Christ's resurrection can be shielded from resignation and cynicism and be given the courage to believe in the world's and the church's future. It is "the memory of the future" that in the deepest sense upholds the ecumenical movement. The future was the theme at Uppsala in 1968: "Behold, I make all things new." This future has often been confused with human progress. The promise of "new heavens and a new earth where righteousness is at home" (2 Peter 3:13) has often been translated into slogans and politics. Now the future has returned to the churches and their humble ecumenical movement in simple eschatological realism as the churches pray together, "God, in your grace, transform the world."

Notes

Notes to Chapter 1

1. Quoted in Bengt Sundkler, *Nathan Söderblom: His Life and Work* (Lund: Gleerups, 1968), 358.

2. Cf. Brian Stanley, *The World Missionary Conference, Edinburgh 1910* (Grand Rapids: Eerdmans, 2009).

3. The basis was first formulated at the inaugural assembly in 1948. It was revised in 1961 to add a more Trinitarian confession. The WCC's function and purpose were revised in 1975. Cf. T. K. Thomas, "WCC, Basis of," in *Dictionary of the Ecumenical Movement*, 1238-39.

4. W. A. Visser 't Hooft, *The Pressure of Our Common Calling* (New York: Doubleday, 1959), 73.

5. Konrad Raiser in *Ecumenism in Transition: A Paradigm Shift in the Ecumenical Movement?* (Geneva: WCC Publications, 1991), 36-43, discusses the view of Visser 't Hooft concerning this "christocentric universalism" as the ecumenical paradigm.

6. The Council can be followed virtually day-by-day in John W. O'Malley, *What Happened at Vatican II* (Cambridge, MA: Belknap Press, 2008).

7. Cf. Jerome-Michael Vereb, C.P., *"Because He Was a German!" Cardinal Bea and the Origins of Roman Catholic Engagement in the Ecumenical Movement* (Grand Rapids: Eerdmans, 2006).

8. Austin Flannery, O.P., ed., *Vatican Council II*, vol. 1: *The Conciliar and Post Conciliar Documents*, rev. ed. (Collegeville: Liturgical Press, 1992), 350-426.

9. *Lumen Gentium* I, 8, in Flannery, *Vatican Council II*, 1:357.

10. *Lumen Gentium* II, 15, in Flannery, *Vatican Council II*, 1:366-67.

11. Flannery, *Vatican Council II*, 1:452-70.

12. *Unitatis Redintegratio* I, 3, in Flannery, *Vatican Council II*, 1:455.

13. Flannery, *Vatican Council II*, 1:903-1001.

14. Carl Henrik Grenholm, *Christian Social Ethics in a Revolutionary Age* (Stockholm:

Verbum, 1973). Cf. also Lukas Vischer, "The Vision of a Responsible Society after Fifty Years," *Ecumenical Review* 50, no. 4 (1998).

15. Cf. Risto Lehtonen, *Story of a Storm: The Ecumenical Student Movement in the Turmoil of Revolution, 1968-1973* (Grand Rapids: Eerdmans, 1998).

16. Paul Abrecht, "The Development of Ecumenical Thought and Action," in *History of the Ecumenical Movement*, 2, 233-59, esp. 250-57.

Notes to Chapter 2

1. *WCC, Uppsala, 1968*, 99.

2. Harvey Cox, *The Secular City: Secularization and Urbanization in Theological Perspective* (New York: Macmillan, 1965).

3. John A. T. Robinson, *Honest to God* (London: SCM Press, 1963).

4. *WCC, Uppsala, 1968*, xvii.

5. Olov Hartman, *On That Day*, trans. Brita Stendahl (Philadelphia: Fortress Press, 1968).

6. The philosopher Herbert Marcuse's most widely read book was *One Dimensional Man: Studies in the Ideology of Advanced Industrial Society* (Boston: Beacon Press, 1964). By "repressive tolerance" he meant the toleration by liberal society of critiques of society as long as they did not threaten an overthrow of society. Marshall McLuhan, the Canadian communication theorist, was best known for slogans such as "the global village" and "the medium is the message."

7. *WCC, Uppsala, 1968*, 129ff.

8. Trevor Beeson, *Discretion and Valour: Religious Conditions in Russia and Eastern Europe*, rev. ed. (Philadelphia: Fortress Press, 1982). The first edition of this book, published in 1974, was written at the behest of the British Council of Churches. Together with Michael Bourdeaux and Paul Oestreicher, Beeson was one of the persons most knowledgeable about church conditions behind the iron curtain.

9. Gerhard Besier, Armin Boyens, and Gerhard Lindemann, *Nationaler Protestantismus und ökumenische Bewegung. Kirchliches Handeln im Kalten Krieg (1945-1990)* (Berlin: Duncker and Humblot, 1999). This book contains detailed documentation but has an evident Western perspective. Cf. also Owen Chadwick, *The Christian Church in the Cold War* (New York: Penguin Books, 1992); Dianne Kirby, ed., *Religion and the Cold War* (Basingstoke: Palgrave, 2003); and Julius Filo, ed., *Christian World Community and the Cold War* (Bratislava: International Visegradfund, 2012).

10. Joachim Garstecki, ed., *Die Ökumene und der Widerstand gegen Diktaturen. Nationalsozialismus und Kommunismus als Herausforderung an die Kirchen* (Stuttgart: Kohlhammer, 2007). This book contains articles by, among others, Konrad Raiser, John Arnold, and Paul Oestreicher, together with a project overview by Katharina Kunter.

11. *WCC, Uppsala, 1968*, 12.

12. *WCC, Uppsala, 1968*, 103.

13. Cf. Dietrich Bonhoeffer, *Discipleship*, trans. Barbara Green and Reinhard Krauss, Dietrich Bonhoeffer Works 4 (Minneapolis: Fortress Press, 2001). The first German edition was published in 1937.

14. A. Th. Van Leeuwen, *Christianity in World History: The Meeting of the Faiths of East and*

West (London: Edinburgh House, 1964). For many years this book stimulated debates concerning mission.

15. Lesslie Newbigin, *One Body, One Gospel, One World: The Christian Mission Today* (New York: International Missionary Council, 1958); D. T. Niles, *Upon the Earth* (London: Lutterworth Press, 1962).

16. WCC, *Uppsala, 1968*, 29.

17. WCC, *Uppsala, 1968*, 26.

18. Lesslie Newbigin, *Unfinished Agenda: An Autobiography* (London: SPCK, 1985).

19. WCC, *Uppsala, 1968*, 45.

20. In his address to the assembly, the former general secretary Visser 't Hooft said, "A Christianity which has lost its vertical dimension has lost its salt and is not only insipid in itself, but useless for the world. But a Christianity which would use the vertical preoccupation as a means to escape from its responsibility for and in the common life of man is a denial of the incarnation, of God's love for the world manifested in Christ." Cf. his own commentary on this in W. A. Visser 't Hooft, *Memoirs* (Philadelphia: Westminster Press, 1973), 363. (An unchanged edition of this book was published in 1987 [Geneva: WCC Publications].)

21. WCC, *Uppsala, 1968*, 157.

22. Konrad Raiser, *Ecumenism in Transition: A Paradigm Shift in the Ecumenical Movement?* (Geneva: WCC Publications, 1991). This book, published just before its author became general secretary of the World Council of Churches, was much discussed and for a long period determined how changes in the ecumenical movement were interpreted.

Notes to Chapter 3

1. Jonas Jonson, *Vänner kallar jag er. En resa till Ekumene* (Örebro: Cordia, 2004), 116ff.

2. Baldwin Sjollema, "The Initial Challenge," in *A Long Struggle: The Involvement of the World Council of Churches in South Africa*, ed. Pauline Webb (Geneva: WCC Publications, 1994), 3-11.

3. Paul Abrecht, "The Development of Ecumenical Social Thought and Action," in *History of the Ecumenical Movement*, 2, 245.

4. Martin Conway, "Under Public Scrutiny," in *History of the Ecumenical Movement*, 3, 435-40.

5. Jens Holger Schjørring, Prasanna Kumari, and Norman A. Hjelm, eds., *From Federation to Communion: The History of the Lutheran World Federation* (Minneapolis: Fortress Press, 1997), 71-73, 227ff.

6. WCC, *Harare, 1998*, 228-29.

7. "Report of the Chairman of the Executive Committee," *The Ecumenical Review* 24, no. 4 (1972): 409.

8. Cited by Janice Love, "The Decade to Overcome Violence: Harvest from an Ecumenical Journey," *The Ecumenical Review* 53, no. 2 (2001): 137.

9. Elisabeth Raiser, "Inclusive Community," in *History of the Ecumenical Movement*, 3, 243-77.

10. Björn Ryman, "Ärkebiskop Olof Sundbys sista initiative: Liv och Fredkonferensen 1983," *Kyrkohistorisk Årsskrift* (Uppsala, 2004). A deeper analysis of this conference is Sara

Gehlin, *For Life and Peace: An Analysis of International Peacemaking through Ecumenical Cooperation at the Life and Peace Conference in Uppsala 1983* (Lund: Center for Theology and Religious Studies, 2007).

11. "The Message — Adopted by the Conference on April 23, 1983," Life and Peace Christian World Conference, Uppsala, Sweden, 20-24 April 1983 (Konferens "Liv och Fred," Uppsala 1983, Box F, 2:1, Royal Archives, Stockholm).

12. *WCC, Vancouver, 1983,* 137.

13. Donella H. Meadows et al., *The Limits to Growth: A Report on the Club of Rome's Project on the Predicament of Mankind* (New York: Universe Books, 1972). This report has had a circulation of at least thirty million copies and was revised in 2004. To a large degree it stimulated the debate on development and the environment. It has, to be sure, been criticized for its position that the earth's resources, especially oil, are not adequate because of the growth in population.

14. For an important survey of ecological thought in the World Council of Churches, cf. David G. Hallman, ed., *Ecotheology: Voices from South and North* (Geneva: WCC Publications, 1994). Also Larry L. Rasmussen, *Earth Community, Earth Ethics* (Geneva: WCC Publications, 1996).

15. World Council of Churches, *Faith and Science in an Unjust World: Report of the World Council of Churches' Conference on Faith, Science, and the Future,* 2 vols. (Philadelphia: Fortress Press, 1980).

16. Thomas Stransky, "SODEPAX," in *Dictionary of the Ecumenical Movement,* 1055-56.

17. *WCC, Canberra, 1991,* 63-64.

18. In the Preamble to the United Nations Universal Declaration on Human Rights this is explained by the assertion that human rights must legally be protected by the state as a matter of principle since "it is essential, if man is not to be compelled to have recourse, as a last resort, to rebellion against tyranny and oppression, that human rights should be protected by the rule of law."

19. This Commission, CCPD, was established in 1970 and worked parallel to SODEPAX. It took the position that poverty was caused by the incapability of political and economic organizations of dealing with the right of every human to a life of dignity. At the beginning of the 1970s the WCC went from speaking of "poverty" to speaking of "the poor" and "the oppressed" who must themselves change their situation. Cf. Julio de Santa Ana, *Towards a Church of the Poor* (Geneva: WCC Publications, 1979).

20. Paulo Freire, *Pedagogy of the Oppressed,* trans. M. B. Ramos (New York: Herder and Herder, 1972).

21. Cf. M. M. Thomas, *My Ecumenical Journey* (Trivandrum: Ecumenical Publishing Center, 1990), 390ff. Thomas shows how the CCIA under the leadership of the Argentinian Leopoldo Niilus began to relinquish its ideological neutrality.

22. D. Preman Niles, comp., *Between the Flood and the Rainbow: Interpreting the Conciliar Process of Mutual Commitment (Covenant) to Justice, Peace and the Integrity of Creation* (Geneva: WCC Publications, 1992). This book is a critical survey of the whole process that led to the 1990 world convocation on "Justice, Peace, and the Integrity of Creation" in Seoul.

23. The initiative for this conciliar process came from Germany where in 1985 Carl Friedrich von Weizäcker, the renowned physicist, proposed a "peace council," a proposal which resulted in the JPIC process and the 1989 conference in Basel, sponsored by the

Conference of European Churches and the Roman Catholic Council of European Bishops' Conferences, on "Peace, with Justice for the Whole Creation." Cf. Margot Kässman, "The Process Leading to Seoul and Canberra," in Niles, *Between the Flood and the Rainbow,* 8-16.

24. "Final Document: Entering into Covenant Solidarity for Justice, Peace and the Integrity of Creation" in Niles, *Between the Flood and the Rainbow,* 164-90.

25. Cf. Thomas F. Best and Martin Robra, eds., *Ecclesiology and Ethics: Ecumenical Ethical Engagement, Moral Formation, and the Nature of the Church* (Geneva: WCC Publications, 1997), and Lewis S. Mudge, *The Church as Moral Community: Ecclesiology and Ethics in Ecumenical Debate* (Geneva: WCC Publications, 1998).

26. Paul Abrecht, "Ecumenical Social Thought in the Post-Cold War Period," *The Ecumenial Review* 43, no. 3 (July 1991): 305ff.

27. Charles C. West, "Power," in *Dictionary of the Ecumenical Movement,* 923.

28. Julio de Santa Ana et al., *Beyond Idealism: A Way Ahead for Ecumenical Ethics* (Grand Rapids: Eerdmans, 2006), xix.

Notes to Chapter 4

1. Michael Kinnamon and Brian E. Cope, eds., *The Ecumenical Movement: An Anthology of Key Texts and Voices* (Grand Rapids: Eerdmans, 1997), 356.

2. "Message of Patriarch Pimen of Moscow and All Russia and the Holy Synod of the Russian Orthodox Church to the Central Committee of the WCC," in *The Orthodox Church in the Ecumenical Movement: Documents and Statements, 1902-1975,* ed. Constantin G. Patelos (Geneva: World Council of Churches, 1978), 47-52.

3. Cf. Ion Bria, *Go Forth in Peace: A Pastoral and Missionary Guidebook* (Geneva: WCC Publications, 1982), and *The Liturgy after the Liturgy: Mission and Witness from an Orthodox Perspective* (Geneva: WCC Publications, 1996).

4. Birgitta Larson and Emilio Castro, "From Missions to Mission," in *History of the Ecumenical Movement, 3,* 125-48.

5. *WCC, Uppsala, 1968,* 42.

6. *Hearing on AIDS: Central Committee, World Council of Churches* (Geneva, January 1987); "AIDS and the Church," Church and Society Documents I (Geneva: World Council of Churches, 1987), 2.

7. Ivan Illich, *Deschooling Society* (London: Calder and Boyars, 1971).

8. *WCC, Nairobi, 1975,* 86-97. This report, "Education for Liberation and Community," is an uncommonly well worked out statement which made a strong impression on churches throughout the world.

9. Austin Flannery, O.P., ed., *Vatican Council II: The Conciliar and Post Conciliar Documents,* vol. 1 (Collegeville: Liturgical Press, 1992), 738-49. Cf. also Declaration on Religious Liberty, *Dignitatis Humanae,* in the same book, 799-812.

10. *WCC, Uppsala, 1968,* 29.

11. *WCC, Nairobi, 1975,* 70ff.

12. Diana Eck, *Encountering God: A Spiritual Journey from Bozeman to Banaras* (Boston: Beacon Press, 1993). Eck has for many years had an important influence in the WCC.

13. *WCC, Canberra, 1991,* 37-47.

14. *WCC, Porto Alegre, 2006.*

15. Klas Lundström, *Gospel and Culture in the World Council of Churches and the Lausanne Movement* (Uppsala: Studia Missionalia Svecana CIII, 2006). This dissertation presents a penetrating analysis and a general overview of the theologies of mission characteristic of both the World Council of Churches and the Lausanne movement.

16. "While no single document can represent all Evangelicals, the covenant is widely acknowledged as a major milestone, reflecting the spirit and stance of the evangelical community in the late twentieth century." Robert T. Coote, "Lausanne Covenant," in *Dictionary of the Ecumenical Movement,* 673-74.

17. The best survey of the Edinburgh Conference and its implications is Brian Stanley, *The World Missionary Conference: Edinburgh 1910* (Grand Rapids: Eerdmans, 2009).

18. Emilio Castro, *A Passion for Unity: Essays on Ecumenical Hopes and Challenges* (Geneva: WCC Publications, 1992).

19. World Council of Churches Commission on World Mission and Evangelism, "Mission and Evangelism — an Ecumenical Affirmation," in *The Ecumenical Movement,* ed. Michael Kinnamon and Brian E. Cope, 372-83.

20. Samuel Kobia, *Called to the One Hope: A New Ecumenical Epoch* (Geneva: WCC Publications, 2006), 46.

Notes to Chapter 5

1. *WCC, Vancouver, 1983,* 44-45.

2. Anna Marie Aagard, *Ånd har krop. Teologiske essays* (Copenhagen: Anis, 2005), 15-49.

3. *Baptism, Eucharist and Ministry,* Faith and Order Paper 111 (Geneva: WCC Publications, 1982).

4. *Baptism, Eucharist and Ministry, 1982-1990: Report on the Process and Responses,* Faith and Order Paper 149 (Geneva: WCC Publications, 1990). *Churches Respond to BEM: Official Responses to the 'Baptism, Eucharist and Ministry' Text,* was published in six volumes by the WCC between 1986 and 1988 under the editorship of Max Thurian.

5. Constance F. Parvey, ed., *The Community of Women and Men in the Church: The Sheffield Report* (Philadelphia: Fortress Press, 1983).

6. *Church and World: The Unity of the Church and the Renewal of Human Community,* Faith and Order Paper 151 (Geneva: WCC Publications, 1990).

7. Gustavo Gutiérrez, *A Theology of Liberation: History, Politics, and Salvation,* trans. and ed. Sr. Caridad Inda and John Eagleson (Maryknoll: Orbis Books, 1973), 104.

8. *WCC, Vancouver, 1983,* 49.

9. Cf. Bengt Sundkler, *Church of South India: The Movement towards Union, 1900-1947* (London: Lutterworth Press, 1954).

10. Harding Meyer, *That All May Be One: Perceptions and Models of Ecumenicity,* trans. William G. Rusch (Grand Rapids: Eerdmans, 1999).

11. Cf. Ulrich Duchrow, *Conflict over the Ecumenical Movement: Confessing Christ Today in the Universal Church,* trans. David Lewis (Geneva: WCC Publications, 1981).

12. William G. Rusch and Daniel F. Martensen, eds., *The Leuenberg Agreement and Lutheran-Reformed Relationships: Evaluations by North American and European Theologians*

(Minneapolis: Augsburg, 1989). The full text of the Leuenberg Agreement is given on pp. 139-54.

13. Ola Tjørhom, ed., *Apostolicity and Unity: Essays on the Porvoo Common Statement* (Grand Rapids: Eerdmans, 2002).

14. WCC, *Uppsala, 1968*, 17.

15. Quoted in Michael Kinnamon and Brian E. Cope, eds., *The Ecumenical Movement: An Anthology of Key Texts and Voices* (Grand Rapids: Eerdmans, 1997), 110.

16. A remarkable and helpful survey of the dialogues in which the Roman Catholic Church has participated is found in Cardinal Walter Kasper, *Harvesting the Fruits: Basic Aspects of Christian Faith in Ecumenical Dialogue* (New York: Continuum, 2009). Cardinal Kasper was for a number of years president of the Vatican's Pontifical Council for Promoting Christian Unity. Attention in this book is paid to Roman Catholic dialogue with the Lutheran, Reformed, Anglican, and Methodist traditions.

17. Harding Meyer, "Christian World Communions," in *History of the Ecumenical Movement*, 103-22.

18. Jens Holger Schjørring, Prasanna Kumari, and Norman A. Hjelm, eds., *From Federation to Communion: The History of the Lutheran World Federation* (Minneapolis: Fortress Press, 1997).

19. The American Lutheran Franklin Clark Fry was president of the Lutheran World Federation from 1957 to 1963 and chair of the World Council of Churches Central Committee from 1954 to 1968.

20. WCC, *Harare, 1998*, 165.

21. Michael Root, "Ecumenical Theology," in *The Modern Theologians: An Introduction to Christian Theology Since 1918*, ed. David F. Ford (Oxford: Blackwell Publishing, 2005), 538-54. This is a remarkable summary of the main themes of the ecumenical dialogues, their difficulties, and their results.

22. The most current study of "ecumenical reception" is William G. Rusch, *Ecumenical Reception: Its Challenge and Opportunity* (Grand Rapids: Eerdmans, 2007).

23. The Lutheran World Federation and the Roman Catholic Church, *Joint Declaration on the Doctrine of Justification* (Grand Rapids: Eerdmans, 2000). Cf. also the websites of both the Lutheran World Federation and the Vatican.

24. William G. Rusch, ed., *Justification and the Future of the Ecumenical Movement: The Joint Declaration on the Doctrine of Justification* (Collegeville: Liturgical Press, 2003). This is an extremely informative book with contributions by, among others, George Lindbeck, Walter Kasper, Henry Chadwick, Michael Root, William Franklin, and Edward Idris Cassidy.

Notes to Chapter 6

1. W. A. Visser 't Hooft, *The Genesis and Formation of the World Council of Churches* (Geneva: WCC Publications, 1982). For short biographical sketches, cf. Ion Bria and Dagmar Heller, eds., *Ecumenical Pilgrims: Profiles of Pioneers in Christian Reconciliation* (Geneva: WCC Publications, 1995).

2. "Unto the Churches of Christ Everywhere: Encyclical of the Ecumenical Patriarch-

ate, 1920," in *The Ecumenical Movement: An Anthology of Key Texts and Voices*, ed. Michael Kinnamon and Brian E. Cope (Grand Rapids: Eerdmans, 1997), 10-14.

3. Bob Edgar, *Middle Church: Reclaiming the Moral Values of the Faithful Majority from the Religious Right* (New York: Simon and Schuster, 2006).

4. In 2011 the four largest churches in America were the Roman Catholic Church (68.5 million members), the Southern Baptist Convention (16.1 million), the United Methodist Church (7.75 million), and the Church of Jesus Christ of Latter-day Saints (6.1 million). Cf. Eileen Lindner, ed., *The Yearbook of American and Canadian Churches* (Nashville: Abingdon Press, 2011).

5. Cf. Robert D. Putnam and David E. Campbell, *American Grace: How Religion Divides and Unites Us* (New York: Simon and Schuster, 2010).

6. The WCC in 1970 had 373 staff members; in 2004 the number was 149, a decrease of 45 percent. At the same time the number of staff in the offices of member churches increased sharply.

7. An example of such a "movement" is the German *Kirchentag* ("Church Day"), which at the initiative of Reinhold von Thadden-Trieglatt since 1949 has involved, every other year, more than 100,000 participants. The *Kirchentag* is independent of the Evangelical Church of Germany (EKiD). In recent years the *Kirchentag* has worked closely with the comparable Roman Catholic movement in Germany.

8. Within the wide literature concerning the churches and the processes of European integration, I will refer to two items: Karel Blei, *On Being the Church across Frontiers* (Geneva: WCC Publications, 1992), and Jonas Jonson, "Svenska kyrkan I Europaprocessen," *Tro & Tanke* 7 (1994): 39-48.

9. The Synod of European Bishops, held in the fall of 1991, set loose among Protestants and Orthodox the fear of a "re-Catholicizing." Cf. Odilo Noti, ed., *Die Kirchen und Europa. Herausforgderungen — Perspektiven* (Lucerne: Edition Exodus, 1993), especially Odilo Noti, "Kirchenintegristische Eroberungsmentalität oder sozialetisch orientierte Ökumene," 31-56, and Richard Bäumlin, "Die Neu-evangelisierung Europas," 79-99.

10. Adrian Hastings, ed., *Modern Catholicism: Vatican II and After* (London: SPCK, 1991). A comprehensive study of the Council is John W. O'Malley, *What Happened at Vatican II* (Cambridge, MA, and London: The Belknap Press of Harvard University Press, 2008); this work has been followed up by James L. Heft, ed., with John O'Malley, *After Vatican II: Trajectories and Hermeneutics* (Grand Rapids: Eerdmans, 2012). Cf. also Massimo Faggioli, *Vatican II: The Battle for Meaning* (New York: Paulist Press, 2012).

11. Richard John Neuhaus, who died in 2009, was a 1990 convert from Lutheranism who became a Roman Catholic priest. In the same year his Institute on Religion and Public Life began the publication of *First Things*, a neoconservative journal of great influence. Neuhaus was at times an unofficial adviser on religious and ethical issues to President George W. Bush.

12. For statistics concerning the Roman Catholic Church, see *Annuario pontificio*, an annual publication of the Vatican. Cf. also "The Effect of the Council on World Catholicism," in Hastings, *Modern Catholicism*, 310-97.

13. A fine contribution to this discussion, written independently of the Sibiu meeting, is Cardinal Walter Kasper, *A Handbook of Spiritual Ecumenism* (Hyde Park: New City Press, 2007).

14. Cf. Jill Hawkey, *Mapping the Oikoumene: A Study of Current Ecumenical Structures and*

Relationships (Geneva: WCC Publications, 2004); *Reflections on Ecumenism in the 21st Century: A Working Document* (Geneva: WCC Publications, 2004); *Ecumenism in the 21st Century: Report of the Consultation Convened by the World Council of Churches, 30 November–3 December, 2004; A Working Document* (Geneva: WCC Publications, 2005).

15. Mercy Amba Oduyoye, "Africa," in *History of the Ecumenical Movement*, 3, 486. Cf. also Bengt Sundkler and Christopher Steed, *A History of the Church in Africa* (Cambridge: Cambridge University Press, 2000), 1018ff.

16. The "Inter-Faith Action for Peace in Africa," IFAPA, was founded in 2001 at the initiative of Ishmael Noko, then general secretary of the Lutheran World Federation. On subsequent occasions it has gathered leading African political and religious figures for deliberation.

17. The China Christian Council resumed what had been the membership of several church bodies in the World Council of Churches in 1991.

18. K. H. Ting, China's leading theologian and church leader, has often asserted that humans are sinners, but also that humans and particularly the poor are those who are *sinned against*. He has strongly warned against any idealization of the poor. K. H. Ting, *God Is Love* (Colorado Springs: Communications Ministries International, 2004), 509. An important study in this connection is Philip Wickeri, *Reconstructing Christianity in China: K. H. Ting and the Chinese Churches* (Maryknoll: Orbis Books, 2007).

19. Cf. K. C. Abraham and T. K. Thomas, "Asia," in *History of the Ecumenical Movement*, 3, 500.

20. *WCC, Canberra, 1991*, 37ff. For the immediate and negative reactions of Orthodox and evangelicals, cf. 281 and 285.

21. In the 1960s Professor Masao Takenaka of Japan at the request of the East Asia Christian Conference (later known as CCA) began to document Asian Christian art. Through books and exhibitions his work became well known. Cf. Takenaka, *Christian Art in Asia* (Tokyo: Kyo Bun Kwan and the Christian Conference of Asia, 1975). The Asian Institute for Liturgy and Music in Manila began in 1980 to educate church musicians in contextual music and liturgy under the direction of the composer and conductor Francisco Feliciano.

22. "Instruction on Certain Aspects of 'Theology of Liberation,'" issued by the Congregation for the Doctrine of the Faith on 6 August 1984, with the approval of Pope John Paul II. The chief point of this document is that one may not confuse the Kingdom of God, which is an eschatological promise, with the betterment of earthly conditions.

23. Dafne Sabanes Plou, "Latin America," in *History of the Ecumenical Movement*, 3, 565-89.

24. Melanie A. May, *Jerusalem Testament: Palestinian Christians Speak, 1988-2008* (Grand Rapids: Eerdmans, 2010). This is a most helpful compilation of ecumenical statements by Palestinian Christian leaders concerning the conflict in the Occupied Territories.

25. Harding Meyer, "Christian World Communions," in *History of the Ecumenical Movement*, 3, 103-22. To the annual meeting of these global confessional organizations come the leaders of the Anglican Communion, Baptist World Alliance, Disciples Ecumenical Consultative Council, Ecumenical Patriarchate, General Conference of Seventh-Day Adventists, International Old Catholics Bishops' Conference, Lutheran World Federation, Mennonite World Conference, Moravian Church Worldwide Unity Board, Moscow Patriarchate, Pentecostals, Pontifical Council for Promoting Christian

Unity (Roman Catholic Church), Reformed Ecumenical Council, Salvation Army, Friends World Committee for Consultation, World Alliance of Reformed Churches, World Convention of Churches of Christ, World Evangelical Fellowship, World Methodist Council. Cf. Huibert van Beek, *A Handbook of Churches and Councils: Profiles of Ecumenical Relationships* (Geneva: WCC Publications, 2006), 17.

26. WCC, Harare, 1998, 103-16.

27. WCC, Porto Alegre, 2006, 279ff.

28. Most notably, this crisis has torn the global Anglican Consultative Council since the Episcopal Church in the United States ordained an openly homosexual bishop. Cf. Stephan Bates, *A Church at War: Anglicans and Homosexuality* (London: I. B. Tauris, 2004); Ephraim Radner and Philip Turner, *The Fate of Communion: The Agony of Anglicanism and the Future of the Global Church* (Grand Rapids: Eerdmans, 2006); Miranda K. Hassett, *Anglican Communion in Crisis: How Episcopal Dissidents and Their African Allies Are Reshaping Anglicanism* (Princeton: Princeton University Press, 2007); and Oliver O'Donovan, *Church in Crisis: The Gay Controversy and the Anglican Communion* (Eugene: Cascade Books, 2008). At the beginning of the twenty-first century, the question of the churches' acknowledgment of same-sex relations became the most church-dividing issue of all.

Notes to Chapter 7

1. Cecil M. Robeck Jr., *The Azusa Street Mission and Revival: The Birth of the Global Pentecostal Movement* (Nashville: Thomas Nelson, 2006).

2. Harvey Cox, *Fire from Heaven: The Rise of Pentecostal Spirituality and the Reshaping of Religion in the Twenty-First Century* (Reading: Addison-Wesley Publishing, 1995), 81ff.

3. Peter Hocken, "Pentecostals," in *Dictionary of the Ecumenical Movement*, 900ff.

4. Walbert Buhlman, in *The Coming of the Third Church* (Maryknoll: Orbis Books, 1977), has used the expression "the Third Church," parallel to "the Third World." Samuel Kobia also uses that term in *Called to One Hope: A New Ecumenical Epoch* (Geneva: WCC Publications, 2006). The missiologist Andrew Walls describes the African churches as a distinct tradition comparable to Orthodoxy, Roman Catholicism, and Protestantism. I choose to speak of "the Fourth Church," since it is to be found not only in the Third World and it also is constituted as its own contemporary tradition.

5. For this whole presentation of the Pentecostal movement, the independent churches, and other faith movements I am indebted to Philip Jenkins, *The Next Christendom: The Coming of Global Christianity* (New York: Oxford University Press, 2002). He followed this pioneering and much-debated work with *The New Faces of Christianity: Believing the Bible in the Global South* (New York: Oxford University Press, 2006) and *God's Continent: Christianity, Islam, and Europe's Religious Crisis* (New York: Oxford University Press, 2007).

6. The person who began serious research concerning these movements was Bengt Sundkler in *Bantu Prophets in South Africa*, 2nd ed. (London: Oxford University Press, 1961) and also in *Zulu Zion and Some Swazi Zionists* (Oxford: Oxford University Press, 1976). He was also the primary author of a standard work on African church history; cf. Bengt Sundkler and Christopher Steed, *A History of the Church in Africa* (Cambridge and New York: Cambridge University Press, 2000).

7. These statistics are taken consistently from David Barrett, George Kurian, and Todd Johnson, *World Christian Encyclopedia,* 2nd ed. (New York: Oxford University Press, 2001). In respect to the Third World, this work's figures are tentative and inclined to overestimation.

8. Cf. Jenkins, *The Next Christendom,* 10ff.

9. Christian Smith, *American Evangelicalism: Embattled and Thriving* (Chicago: University of Chicago Press, 1998), 1ff.

10. Francis FitzGerald, "The Evangelical Surprise," *The New York Review of Books* 54, no. 7 (2007): 31-34; Walter Russell Mead, "God's Country," *Foreign Affairs* 85, no. 5 (2006): 24-43. A more recent description of American evangelical outlook, theology, and practice in relation to political expression is found in Marcia Pally, *The New Evangelicals: Expanding the Vision of the Common Good* (Grand Rapids: Eerdmans, 2011).

11. WCC Executive Committee, Minutes, 24-27 August 2004.

12. Peter Hocken, "Charismatic Movement," in *Dictionary of the Eumenical Movement,* 164-67. Cf. also K. M. George, "The Contemporary Search for Spirituality," in *History of the Ecumenical Movement, 3,* 217-41.

13. Arnold Bittlinger, ed., *The Church Is Charismatic: The World Council of Churches and the Charismatic Renewal* (Geneva: WCC Publications, 1981).

14. Walter Hollenweger, "Roman Catholics and Pentecostals in Dialogue," *The Ecumenical Review* 51, no. 2 (1999): 147-59. Cf. also Veli-Matti Kärkkäinen, *Spiritus Ubi Vult: Pneumatology in Roman Catholic–Pentecostal Dialogue (1979-1989)* (Helsinki: Luther-Agricola-Society, 1998).

15. Arthur P. Johnston, *The Battle for World Evangelism* (Wheaton: Tyndale House, 1978). Cited by Martin Conway, "Under Public Scrutiny," in *History of the Ecumenical Movement, 3,* 441.

16. "A Jubilee Call: A Letter to the WCC by Evangelical Participants at Harare," WCC, Harare, 1998, 266-71.

17. John Micklethwait and Adrian Wooldridge, *God Is Back: How the Global Revival of Faith Is Changing the World* (New York: Penguin Books, 2009).

18. Roger E. Olson, "Postconservative Evangelicals Greet the Postmodern Age," *The Christian Century,* 3 May 1995, 480-83. Some scholars are of the view that evangelicals in contrast to the "middle churches" fit into the postmodern world like a hand into a glove; cf. Carl Rashke, *The Next Reformation: Why Evangelicals Must Embrace Postmodernity* (Grand Rapids: Baker Academic, 2006) and *GloboChrist: The Great Commission Takes a Postmodern Turn* (Grand Rapids: Baker Academic, 2008).

19. A first-hand account of the genesis of Christian Churches Together is found in Wesley Granberg-Michaelson, *Unexpected Destinations: An Evangelical Pilgrimage to World Christianity* (Grand Rapids: Eerdmans, 2011), 249-63.

Notes to Chapter 8

1. University of British Columbia Human Security Center, *Human Security Brief* (Vancouver: University of British Columbia, 2006).

2. Grace Davie, *Europe: The Exceptional Case; Parameters of Faith in the Modern World* (London: Darton, Longman, and Todd, 2002).

3. Julio de Santa Ana et al., *Beyond Idealism: A Way Ahead for Ecumenical Social Ethics* (Grand Rapids: Eerdmans, 2006).

4. Hans Küng, *Global Responsibility: In Search of a New World Ethic*, trans. John Bowden (London: SCM Press, 1991).

5. Lewis S. Mudge, "Covenanting for a Renewing of Our Minds: A Way Together for the Abrahamic Faiths," in Santa Ana et al., *Beyond Idealism*, 163-208. See also Lewis S. Mudge, *The Gift of Responsibility: The Promise of Dialogue among Christians, Jews, and Muslims* (New York: Continuum, 2008).

6. J. H. Oldham, ed., *Foundations of Ecumenical Social Thought: The Oxford Conference Report; Report of the Conference on Church, Community and State at Oxford, July 12-25, 1937* (Philadelphia: Fortress Press, 1966), 46.

7. Rob van Drimmelen, "Transnational Corporations," in *Dictionary of the Ecumenical Movement*, 1148-49.

8. Konrad Raiser, *For a Culture of Life: Transforming Globalization and Violence* (Geneva: WCC Publications, 2002).

9. Julio de Santa Ana, ed., *Sustainability and Globalization* (Geneva: WCC Publications, 1998).

10. *Covenanting for Justice in the Economy and the Earth: The Accra Confession*, World Alliance of Reformed Churches, 24th General Council, Accra, Ghana, 2004.

11. Samuel Kobia, *Called to the One Hope: A New Ecumenical Epoch* (Geneva: WCC Publications, 2006), 33ff.

12. *WCC, Harare, 1998*, 183.

13. *WCC, Harare, 1998*, 146.

14. Justice, Peace, and Creation Team, *Alternative Globalization Addressing Peoples and Earth (AGAPE): A Background Document* (Geneva: WCC Publications, 2005).

15. *WCC, Porto Alegre, 2006*, 269.

16. *WCC, Canberra, 1991*, 203.

17. D. Preman Niles, comp., *Between the Flood and the Rainbow: Interpreting the Conciliar Process of Mutual Commitment (Covenant) to Justice, Peace, and the Integrity of Creation* (Geneva: WCC Publications, 1992), 173.

18. *WCC, Vancouver, 1983*, 132.

19. Raiser, *For a Culture of Life*, 160ff.

Notes to Chapter 9

1. Morris West, "Toronto Statement," in *Dictionary of the Ecumenical Movement*, 1137-39.

2. "The Orthodox Church and the Ecumenical Movement: Decisions of the Third Preconciliar Pan-Orthodox Conference (1986)," in *Orthodox Visions of Ecumenism: Statements, Messages and Reports on the Ecumenical Movement, 1902-1992*, ed. Gennadios Limouris (Geneva: WCC Publications, 1994), 113. Cf. also Anna Marie Aagaard and Peter Bouteneff, *Beyond the East-West Divide: The World Council of Churches and "the Orthodox Problem"* (Geneva: WCC Publications, 2001), 35ff.

3. Jonathan Luxmore, "Unholy Alliance," *The Tablet*, 16 June 2007, 4ff.

4. Hilarion Alfeyev, *Orthodox Witness Today* (Geneva: WCC Publications, 2006), 2-3.

5. Final Report of the Special Commission on Orthodox Participation in the WCC, approved by the WCC Central Committee, September 2002.
6. Alfeyev, *Orthodox Witness Today*, 28ff.
7. John Paul II, *Ut Unum Sint* (Washington, DC: Catholic News Service, 1995).
8. A remarkable ecumenical collection of essays on these themes is James F. Puglisi, ed., *How Can the Petrine Ministry Be a Service to the Unity of the Universal Church?* (Grand Rapids: Eerdmans, 2010).
9. The Congregation for the Doctrine of the Faith, *'Dominus Iesus': On the Unicity and Salvific Universality of Jesus Christ and the Church* (Washington, DC: Catholic News Service, 2000).
10. The Congregation for the Doctrine of the Faith, *Responses to Some Questions regarding Certain Aspects of the Doctrine on the Church* (Washington, DC: Catholic News Service, 2007).
11. Wolfgang Huber, *Reformatorischer Konsens und ökumenische Profile*, EKD Vorträge, 8 September 2007.
12. "Called to Be One Church," *WCC, Porto Alegre, 2006*, 257.
13. Close to his retirement as president of the Pontifical Council for Promoting Christian Unity, Cardinal Walter Kasper published an encouraging analysis of the ecumenical dialogues pursued by the Roman Catholic Church with Lutherans, Reformed, Anglicans, and Methodists, *Harvesting the Fruits: Basic Aspects of Christian Faith in Ecumenical Dialogue* (New York: Continuum, 2009).
14. In 2005, 64 percent of the German population identified themselves as Christian: 25,386,000 as Protestant, and 25,906,000 as Roman Catholic.
15. Cf. the Lutheran World Federation and the Roman Catholic Church, *Joint Declaration on the Doctrine of Justification* (Grand Rapids: Eerdmans, 2000), and the websites of both the Lutheran World Federation and the Vatican. For an English-language cautionary statement raising advance concerns about the Declaration, cf. The Faculty of Theology, Georgia Augusta University, Göttingen, *Outmoded Condemnations? Antitheses between the Council of Trent and the Reformation on Justification, the Sacrament, and the Ministry — Then and Now*, trans. Oliver K. Olson and Franz Posset (Fort Wayne: Luther Academy, 1992).
16. The Communion of Protestant Churches in Europe (CPCE) or Leuenberg Church Fellowship in 2007 had a total of 104 member churches, including the Waldensian Church, the Czech Brethren, and five church bodies in Latin America. For earlier American reflections, cf. William G. Rusch and Daniel F. Martensen, eds., *The Leuenberg Agreement and Lutheran-Reformed Relationships: Evaluations by North American and European Theologians* (Minneapolis: Augsburg, 1989).
17. Council for Christian Unity, *Together in Mission and Ministry: The Porvoo Common Statement, with Essays on Church and Ministry in Northern Europe* (London: Church Publishing House, 1993). Cf. also Ola Tjørhom, ed., *Apostolicity and Unity: Essays on the Porvoo Common Statement* (Grand Rapids: Eerdmans, 2002).

Notes to Chapter 10

1. The one exception was the address by Rowan Williams, archbishop of Canterbury, "Christian Identity and Religious Plurality," *WCC, Porto Alegre, 2006*, 179-86.

2. Marc Luyckx Ghisi, "WCC: Champion of Tolerance and Reenchantment," *WCC, Porto Alegre, 2006*.

3. An extremely clear discussion of unity and diversity is found in Michael Kinnamon, *The Vision of the Ecumenical Movement and How It Has Been Impoverished by Its Friends* (St. Louis: Chalice Press, 2003), especially chapter 4.

4. Anna Marie Aagaard, "Enlarge the Place of Your Tent; Let the Curtains of Your Habitations Be Stretched Out: On Church and Ecumenics Today" (unpublished).

5. *Towards a Common Understanding and Vision of the World Council of Churches: A Policy Statement* (Geneva: World Council of Churches, 1997), §2.2.

6. *Towards a Common Understanding*, §2.9.

7. Konrad Raiser, *For a Culture of Life: Transforming Globalization and Violence* (Geneva: WCC Publications, 2002), 49ff.

8. Martin Luther, "On the Councils and the Church," *Luther's Works* 41, trans. Eric W. Gritsch (Philadelphia: Fortress Press, 1966), 164.

9. Luther, "On the Councils and the Church," 166; cf. also Lewis S. Mudge, *The Church as Moral Community: Ecclesiology and Ethics in Ecumenical Debate* (Geneva: WCC Publications, 1998), 63ff.

10. Kathleen Bliss of the Church of England wrote these words in a preliminary draft of the Message of the Amsterdam Assembly. Ans J. Van der Bent, "Bliss, Kathleen," in *Dictionary of the Ecumenical Movement*, 123. Konrad Raiser in his General Secretary's Report at the Harare assembly in 1998 quoted these words. *WCC, Harare, 1998*, 83.

11. Stanley J. Samartha, *Courage for Dialogue: Ecumenical Issues in Inter-religious Relationships* (Geneva: WCC Publications, 1981), 34.

12. S. Wesley Ariarajah, "Wider Ecumenism: A Threat or a Promise?" *The Ecumenical Review* 50, no. 3 (July 1998): 327.

13. Kinnamon, *The Vision of the Ecumenical Movement*, 99ff.

14. *WCC, Porto Alegre, 2006*, 163-66.

15. *Baptism, Eucharist and Ministry* (Geneva: World Council of Churches, 1982), §6.

16. "Ecclesiological and Ecumenical Implications of a Common Baptism," *Joint Working Group between the Roman Catholic Church and the World Council of Churches, Eighth Report, 1999-2005* (Geneva: WCC Publications, 2005), 45-72.

17. *WCC, Porto Alegre, 2006*, 163-66.

18. *The Nature and Mission of the Church: A Stage on the Way to a Common Statement*, Faith and Order Paper 198 (Geneva: WCC Publications, 2005).

19. E.g., Institute for Ecumenical Research, Strasbourg, *Crisis and Challenge of the Ecumenical Movement: Integrity and Indivisibility* (Geneva: WCC Publications, 1994); Carl E. Braaten and Robert W. Jenson, eds., *In One Body through the Cross: The Princeton Proposal for Christian Unity* (Grand Rapids: Eerdmans, 2003); Carl E. Braaten and Robert W. Jenson, eds., *The Ecumenical Future: Background Papers for* In One Body through the Cross: The Princeton Proposal for Christian Unity (Grand Rapids: Eerdmans, 2004); J.-M. R. Tillard, *I Believe, Despite Everything: Reflections of an Ecumenist*, trans. William G. Rusch (Collegeville: Liturgical Press, 2003).

20. *Ut Unum Sint* (Washington, DC: Catholic News Service, 1995), §9.

21. Cf. Walter Kasper, *A Handbook of Spiritual Ecumenism* (Hyde Park: New City Press, 2007).

Selected Reading List

Aagaard, Anna Marie, and Peter Bouteneff. *Beyond the East-West Divide: The World Council of Churches and "the Orthodox Problem."* Geneva: WCC Publications, 2001.

Alfeyev, Hilarion. *The Mystery of Faith: An Introduction to the Teaching and Spirit of the Orthodox Church.* Crestwood: St. Vladimir's Seminary Press, 2011.

———. *Orthodox Witness Today.* Geneva: WCC Publications, 2006.

Ariarajah, S. Wesley. *Not without My Neighbor: Issues in Interfaith Relations.* Geneva: WCC Publications, 1999.

Beeson, Trevor. *Discretion and Valor: Religious Conditions in Russia and Eastern Europe.* Philadelphia: Fortress Press, 1982.

Benedict XVI. *Joseph Ratzinger in Communio.* Vol. 1, *The Unity of the Church.* Grand Rapids: Eerdmans, 2010.

Besier, Gerhard, Armin Boyens, and Gerhard Lindemann. *Nationaler Protestantismus und ökumenische Bewegung. Kirchliches Handeln im Kalten Krieg (1945-1990).* Berlin: Duncker and Humblot, 1999.

Best, Thomas F., and Martin Robra, eds. *Ecclesiology and Ethics: Ecumenical Ethical Engagement, Moral Formation, and the Nature of the Church.* Geneva: WCC Publications, 1997.

Bittlinger, Arnold, ed. *The Church Is Charismatic: The World Council of Churches and the Charismatic Renewal.* Geneva: WCC Publications, 1981.

Braaten, Carl E., and Robert W. Jenson, eds. *Church Unity and the Papal Office: An Ecumenical Dialogue on John Paul II's Encyclical* Ut Unum Sint. Grand Rapids: Eerdmans, 2001.

———. *The Ecumenical Future: Background Papers for* In One Body through the Cross. Grand Rapids: Eerdmans, 2004.

―――. *In One Body through the Cross: The Princeton Proposal for Christian Unity.* Grand Rapids: Eerdmans, 2003.

Bria, Ion. *The Liturgy after the Liturgy: Mission and Witness from an Orthodox Perspective.* Geneva: WCC Publications, 1996.

―――. *The Sense of Ecumenical Tradition: The Ecumenical Witness and Vision of the Orthodox.* Geneva: WCC Publications, 1991.

―――, and Dagmar Heller, eds. *Ecumenical Pilgrims: Profiles of Pioneers in Christian Reconciliation.* Geneva: WCC Publications, 1995.

Cassidy, Cardinal Edward Idris. *Ecumenism and Interreligious Dialogue:* Unitatis Redintegratio, Nostra Aetate. New York/Mahwah, NJ: Paulist Press, 2005.

Castro, Emilio. *A Passion for Unity: Essays on Ecumenical Hopes and Challenges.* Geneva: WCC Publications, 1992.

Chadwick, Owen. *The Christian Church in the Cold War.* London: Penguin Books, 1992.

Cox, Harvey. *Fire from Heaven: The Rise of Pentecostal Spirituality and the Reshaping of Religion in the Twenty-First Century.* Reading: Addison-Wesley, 1995.

Davie, Grace. *Europe: The Exceptional Case.* Parameters of Faith in the Modern World. London: Darton, Longman, and Todd, 2002.

de Santa Ana, Julio, ed. *Sustainability and Globalization.* Geneva: WCC Publications, 1998.

―――, et al. *Beyond Idealism: A Way Ahead for Ecumenical Social Ethics.* Grand Rapids: Eerdmans, 2006.

Duchrow, Ulrich. *Conflict over the Ecumenical Movement: Confessing Christ Today in the Universal Church.* Geneva: WCC Publications, 1981.

Edgar, Bob. *Middle Church: Reclaiming the Moral Values of the Faithful Majority from the Religious Right.* New York: Simon and Schuster, 2006.

Faggioli, Massimo. *Vatican II: The Battle for Meaning.* New York/Mahwah, NJ: Paulist Press, 2012.

Filo, Julius, ed., *Christian World Community and the Cold War.* Bratislava: International Visegradfund, 2011.

Flannery, Austin, ed. *Vatican Council II.* Vol. 1, *The Conciliar and Post Conciliar Documents.* Collegeville: Liturgical Press, 1975.

―――. *Vatican Council II.* Vol. 2, *More Post Conciliar Documents.* Collegeville: Liturgical Press, 1982.

Gaillardetz, Richard R., and Catherine E. Clifford. *Keys to the Council: Unlocking the Teaching of Vatican II.* Collegeville: Liturgical Press, 2011.

Garstecki, Joachim, ed. *Die Ökumene und der Widerstand gegen Diktaturen. National-sozialismus und Kommunismus als Herausforderung an die Kirchen.* Stuttgart: Kohlhammer, 2007.

Gassmann, Günther. *Documentary History of Faith and Order, 1963-1993.* Geneva: WCC Publications, 1983.

Selected Reading List

Heft, James L., ed., with John O'Malley. *After Vatican II: Trajectories and Hermeneutics.* Grand Rapids: Eerdmans, 2012.

Institute for Ecumenical Research, Strasbourg. *Crisis and Challenge of the Ecumenical Movement: Integrity and Indivisibility.* Geneva: WCC Publications, 1994.

Jenkins, Philip. *The Next Christendom: The Coming of Global Christianity.* New York: Oxford University Press, 2002.

Jonson, Jonas. *Vänner kallar jag er: En resa till Ekumene.* Örebro: Bokförlaget Cordia, 2004.

Kasper, Cardinal Walter. *A Handbook of Spiritual Ecumenism.* Hyde Park: New City Press, 2006.

———. *Harvesting the Fruits: Basic Aspects of Christian Faith in Ecumenical Dialogue.* New York: Continuum, 2009.

Kinnamon, Michael. *The Vision of the Ecumenical Movement and How It Has Been Impoverished by Its Friends.* St. Louis: Chalice Press, 2003.

———, and Brian E. Cope, eds. *The Ecumenical Movement: An Anthology of Key Texts and Voices.* Grand Rapids: Eerdmans, 1997.

Lange, Ernst. *And Yet It Moves: Dream and Reality of the Ecumenical Movement.* Translated by Edwin Robertson. Abridged by Konrad Raiser and Lukas Vischer. Geneva: WCC Publications, 1979.

Limouris, Gennadios, ed. *Orthodox Visions of Ecumenism: Statements, Messages and Reports on the Ecumenical Movement, 1902-1992.* Geneva: WCC Publications, 1992.

Lundström, Klas. *Gospel and Culture in the World Council of Churches and the Lausanne Movement.* Uppsala: Studia Missionalia Svecana CIII, 2006.

Lutheran World Federation and the Roman Catholic Church. *Joint Declaration on the Doctrine of Justification.* Grand Rapids: Eerdmans, 1999.

May, Melanie A. *Jerusalem Testament: Palestinian Christians Speak, 1988-2008.* Grand Rapids: Eerdmans, 2010.

Meyer, Harding. *That All May Be One: Perceptions and Models of Ecumenicity.* Translated by William G. Rusch. Grand Rapids: Eerdmans, 1999.

Mickelthwait, John, and Adrian Wooldridge. *God Is Back: How the Global Revival of Faith Is Changing the World.* New York: Penguin Books, 2009.

Mudge, Lewis S. *The Church as Moral Community: Ecclesiology and Ethics in Ecumenical Debate.* Geneva: WCC Publications, 1998.

Niles, Premin. *Resisting the Threats to Life: Covenanting for Justice, Peace, and the Integrity of Creation.* Geneva: WCC Publications, 1989.

———, ed. *Between the Flood and the Rainbow: Interpreting the Conciliar Process of Mutual Commitment (Covenant) to Justice, Peace and the Integrity of Creation.* Geneva: WCC Publications, 1992.

Norgren, William A. *Faith and Order in the U.S.A.* Grand Rapids: Eerdmans, 2011.

O'Malley, John W. *What Happened at Vatican II.* Cambridge, MA: Belknap Press, 2008.

Pally, Marcia. *The New Evangelicals: Expanding the Vision of the Common Good.* Grand Rapids: Eerdmans, 2011.

Paulos Mar Gregorios (Paul Verghese). *The Human Presence: An Orthodox View of Nature.* Geneva: WCC Publications, 1978.

Puglisi, James F., ed. *How Can the Petrine Ministry Be a Service to the Unity of the Universal Church?* Grand Rapids: Eerdmans, 2010.

Putnam, Robert D., and David E. Campbell. *American Grace: How Religion Divides and Unites Us.* New York: Simon and Schuster, 2010.

Quinn, John R. *The Reform of the Papacy: The Costly Call to Christian Unity.* New York: Crossroad, 1999.

Radano, John A., ed. *Celebrating a Century of Ecumenism: Exploring the Achievements of International Dialogue.* Grand Rapids: Eerdmans, 2012.

Radner, Ephraim, and Philip Turner. *The Fate of Communion: The Agony of Anglicanism and the Future of a Global Church.* Grand Rapids: Eerdmans, 2006.

Raiser, Konrad. *Ecumenism in Transition: A Paradigm Shift in the Ecumenical Movement?* Geneva: WCC Publications, 1991.

———. *For a Culture of Life: Transforming Globalization and Violence.* Geneva: WCC Publications, 2002.

Raschke, Carl. *The Next Reformation: Why Evangelicals Must Embrace Postmodernity.* Grand Rapids: Baker Academic, 2004.

Robeck, Cecil M., Jr. *The Azusa Street Mission and Revival: The Birth of the Global Pentecostal Movement.* Nashville: Nelson Reference and Electronic, 2006.

Rusch, William G. *Ecumenical Reception: Its Challenge and Opportunity.* Grand Rapids: Eerdmans, 2007.

———, ed. *Justification and the Future of the Ecumenical Movement: The Joint Declaration of Justification.* Collegeville: Liturgical Press, 2003.

———, and Daniel F. Martensen, eds. *The Leuenberg Agreement and Lutheran-Reformed Relationships: Evaluations by North American and European Theologians.* Minneapolis: Augsburg, 1989.

Sabev, Todor. *The Orthodox Churches in the World Council of Churches: Towards the Future.* Geneva: WCC Publications, 1996.

Schjørring, Jens Holger, Prasanna Kumari, and Norman A. Hjelm, eds. *From Federation to Communion: The History of the Lutheran World Federation.* Minneapolis: Fortress, 1997.

Shaull, Richard, and Waldo Cesar. *Pentecostalism and the Future of the Christian Churches: Promises, Limitations, Challenges.* Grand Rapids: Eerdmans, 2000.

Smith, Christian. *American Evangelicalism: Embattled and Thriving.* Chicago: University of Chicago Press, 1998.

Stanley, Brian. *The World Missionary Conference, Edinburgh 1910.* Grand Rapids: Eerdmans, 2009.

Selected Reading List

Takenaka, Masao. *Christian Art in Asia.* Tokyo: Kyo Bun Kwan, 1975.

Thurian, Max, ed. *Ecumenical Perspectives on* Baptism, Eucharist and Ministry. Faith and Order Paper No. 116. Geneva: WCC Publications, 1983.

Tjørhom, Ola. *Visible Church — Visible Unity: Ecumenical Ecclesiology and 'The Great Tradition of the Church.'* Collegeville: Liturgical Press, 2004.

———, ed. *Apostolicity and Unity: Essays on the Porvoo Common Statement.* Grand Rapids: Eerdmans, 2002.

Ucko, Hans. *Changing the Present, Dreaming the Future: A Critical Moment in Interreligious Dialogue.* Geneva: WCC Publications, 2006.

van Elderen, Marlin, and Martin Conway. *Introducing the World Council of Churches.* Geneva: WCC Publications, 2001.

Visser 't Hooft, W. A. *The Genesis and Formation of the World Council of Churches.* Geneva: WCC Publications, 1982.

Webb, Pauline, ed. *A Long Struggle: The Involvement of the World Council of Churches in South Africa.* Geneva: WCC Publications, 1994.

World Council of Churches. *Baptism, Eucharist and Ministry.* Faith and Order Paper No. 111. Geneva: WCC Publications, 1982.

Index of Names

Abrecht, Paul, 16, 45, 52
Adeboye, Enoch Adejare, 110
Adelaja, Sunday, 110
Alexei (metropolitan, later patriarch), 19, 138
Alfeye, Hilarion (bishop), 140
Alfrink, Bernardus (cardinal), 90
Alves, Rubem, 98
Aram I (catholicus), 153
Ariarajah, S. Wesley, 164-65
Athenagoras I (patriarch), 14, 82, 136

Baldwin, James, 23
Bam, Brigalia, 18
Barot, Madeleine, 18
Barth, Karl, 9
Bartholomew (patriarch), 138, 142
Bea, Augustin (cardinal), 12
Beeson, Trevor, 172n8
Benedict XVI (pope), 14, 89, 101, 146
Benedict of Nursia, 89
Bennett, Dennis, 114
Beyerhaus, Peter, 54
Biermann, Wolf, 59
Biko, Steve, 36
Birch, Charles, 43
Birgitta of Vadstena, 89
Blake, Eugene Carson, 18, 20, 37
Bliss, Kathleen, 18, 19, 163

Boff, Leonardo, 98
Bonhoeffer, Dietrich, 29
Bourdeaux, Michael, 172n8
Brent, Charles H. (bishop), 7
Brother Roger, 59
Buhlman, Walbert, 180n4
Burnett, Bill (archbishop), 116
Bush, George W., 178n11
Buthelezi, Manas, 36

Camara, Helder (dom), 58
Carey, George (archbishop), 143
Carroll, Lewis, 120
Carter, Jimmy, 117
Cassidy, Edward (cardinal), 142
Castro, Emilio, 18, 64
Catherine of Siena, 89
Ceaușescu, Nicolae, 25
Chandran, Russell, 60
Chipenda, José, 95
Cho, Paul Yonggi, 110
Chung Hyun Kyung, 62, 97
Congar, Yves, 10
Cooke, Leslie, 18
Coote, Robert T., 176n16
Costas, Orlando, 63
Cox, Harvey, 21, 106
Cyril, 89

Index of Names

Dahlén, Olle, 42
de Diétrich, Suzanne, 18
de Lubac, Henri, 10, 69
de Santa Ana, Julio, 27, 52
de Silva, Lynn A., 60
Dulles, John Foster, 26
du Plessis, David, 116

Eck, Diana, 175n12
Edgar, Bob, 86
Enns, Fernando, 131
Escobar, Samuel, 63
Escrivá, Josemaria, 90

Feliciano, Francisco, 179n21
Freire, Paolo, 47, 57
Fry, Franklin Clark, 177n19

Gatu, John, 55
Gehlin, Sara, 173-74n10
Goodall, Norman, 21-22
Graham, Billy, 63, 112
Gustav VI Adolf, 20
Gutiérrez, Gustavo, 75, 98

Habib, Gabriel, 100
Hammarskjøld, Dag, 1
Harris, William Wade, 107
Hartman, Olov, 22
Hollenweger, Walter, 116
Hromádka, Josef, 23, 26-27
Huber, Wolfgang, 147, 150

Ibiam, Francis Akanu, 19, 33
Iga, Bola, 33
Illich, Ivan, 57
Irenaeos (metropolitan), 58-59

Jenkins, Philip, 104, 180n5
John XXIII (pope), viii, 11-12, 25
John Paul I (pope), 25
John Paul II (pope), 82, 88-89, 90, 98, 100-101, 121, 123, 141, 142-44, 148, 167, 179n22
Johnston, Arthur P., 116-17
Josefson, Ruben (archbishop), 20, 21

Káldy, Zoltan (bishop), 26
Kasper, Walter (cardinal), 81, 147, 168, 177n16, 178n13, 183n13
Kässman, Margot (bishop), 140
Kaunda, Kenneth, 20
Khrushchev, Nikita, 25
Kimbangu, Simon, 107, 114
Kimpa Vita (Dona Beatrice), 107
King, Martin Luther, Jr., viii
Kinnamon, Michael, 183n3
Kobia, Samuel, 66, 84, 180n4
Koyama, Kosuke, 96
Küng, Hans, 124
Kyrill (metropolitan, later patriarch), 137, 138

Lange, Ernst, 135
Lefebvre, Marcel (archbishop), 89, 138
Lønning, Per (bishop), 60
Lossky, Nicolas, 18
Lundstrøm, Klas, 176n15
Luther, Martin, 81, 161
Luthuli, Albert, 36
Luyckx Ghisi, Marc, 154-55

Mandela, Nelson, 27, 36, 39-40, 135
Mao Zedong, viii, 17, 53, 96
Marcuse, Herbert, 22-23, 172n6
Mar Gregorius, Paulus, 18, 27, 43, 60
May, Melanie A., 179n24
McCarthy, Joseph, 113
McDonnell, Kilian, 116
McGavran, Donald, 63
McGovern, George, 37
McIntire, Carl, 113
McLuhan, Marshall, 23, 172n6
Mead, Margaret, 23
Methodius, 89
Míguez Bonino, José, 18, 98
Mondlane, Eduardo, 27
Mother Teresa, 58
Mott, John R., 7, 85
Mugabe, Robert, 27, 135
Myrdal, Gunnar, 23

Neuhaus, Richard John, 90, 178n11

Index of Names

Newbigin, Lesslie (bishop), 18, 31-32, 53
Niemøller, Martin, 19
Niilus, Leopoldo, 27, 174n21
Nikodim (metropolitan), 25
Niles, D. T., 18, 20-21, 31
Nissiotis, Nikos, 18
Nixon, Richard, 53
Nkonyane, Daniel, 107
Noko, Ishmael, 81, 179n16
Novak, Michael, 90
Nyerere, Julius, 27

Oduyoye, Mercy Amba, 18
Oestreicher, Paul, 172n8
Oldham, Joseph, 85

Padilla, René, 63
Paisley, Ian, 113
Palme, Olof, 29
Panikkar, Raimundo, 96
Parmer, Samuel, 23, 32-33
Paton, Alan, 36
Paul VI (pope), 14, 82, 89, 98, 100, 115, 136
Pierre (abbé), 58
Pimen (patriarch), 55
Pius X (pope), 10
Pius XI (pope), 10
Pius XII (pope), 10
Potter, Philip, 18, 20, 64, 116

Rahner, Karl, 10
Raiser, Konrad, 67, 130, 171n5, 173n22, 184n10
Ramsey, Michael (archbishop), 19
Rashke, Carl, 181n18
Ratzinger, Joseph (cardinal), 14, 89, 99, 145, 146. *See also* Benedict XVI (pope)
Robinson, John A. T. (bishop), 21
Romero, Oscar (archbishop), 99
Roncalli, Angelo (bishop), 11. *See also* John XXIII (pope)
Root, Michael, 177n21
Runcie, Robert (archbishop), 67
Rusch, William G., 177n22

Samartha, Stanley, 60, 96, 164
Seeger, Pete, 23
Seymour, William Joseph, 104
Shaull, Richard, 17
Silu, Bena, 114
Sjollema, Baldwin, 37
Søderblom, Nathan (archbishop), viii, 1, 2, 6-7, 85
Stanley, Brian, 176n17
Stein, Edith (Teresa Benedicta of the Cross), 90
Stott, John R., 31, 63
Strenopoulos, Germanos (Germanos of Thyatira), 85
Sundby, Olof (archbishop), 42
Sundkler, Bengt, 180n6

Takenaka, Masao, 18, 179n21
Tambo, Oliver, 37
Thomas, M. M., 18, 19, 40, 60, 96, 174n21
Ting, K. H., 27, 179n18
Toth, Károly, 26
Tutu, Desmond (archbishop), 18, 59, 95

van Drimmelen, Rob, 126
Van Leeuwen, A. Th., 172-73n14
Visser 't Hooft, Willem Adolf, 8-9, 18, 19-20, 28, 171n5, 173n20
von Thadden-Trieglatt, Reinhold, 178n7
von Weizäcker, Carl Friedrich, 174-75n23
Vorster, John, 38

Wallis, Jim, 117
Walls, Andrew, 180n4
Warren, Rick, 118
Weigel, George, 90
West, Charles, 52
Willebrands, Johannes, 12
Williams, Rowan (archbishop), 69, 183n1

Zizioulas, John, 69

www.ingramcontent.com/pod-product-compliance
Lightning Source LLC
Chambersburg PA
CBHW021810220426
43662CB00006B/250